Connecting Happiness and Success

Daily Happiness Tool

We have created an application that will provide you with daily happiness nudges. Go to MyHappiness.io on any device to login.

You can also find more tools and resources at ConnectingHappinessandSuccess.com

Foreword

I believe success begins with clarity.

In my book Strategic Acceleration, I establish the three-part foundation for succeeding at the speed of life: Clarity, Focus and Execution. Everything begins with a clear vision, and nothing excels without it. You may have laser-like focus, and your execution may be unparalleled, but if there is not clarity on where to apply those efforts, your efforts are wasted.

Another principle I've discovered over the past 30 years of working with some of the world's highest achievers is that those who live the most fulfilling lives are those who don't sacrifice happiness for success, but rather leverage their happiness to help fuel their success. They view happiness as a strategic asset, and they are deliberate about building a life that helps them do what uniquely makes them happy. They excel in the areas of clarity, focus and execution, and they apply them toward goals that make them happy.

Ray White is now providing clarity on the connection between happiness and success like no one ever has before. What you hold in your hands will not only give you a distinct advantage in your professional pursuits, but, more importantly, in that most elusive pursuit of all … the pursuit of happiness.

So many people go to great lengths to be successful, believing that from success comes happiness. Some cheat their health in exchange for wealth. Others shortchange relationships as they chase down promotions. In the name of "success," many miss life altogether, its lessons, its experiences and its simple pleasures.

In this book, Ray shows that happiness actually comes before success, not after it. He spells out how the two are eternally bound, and he walks you through a methodology that will change the way you think about success, and life.

Ray lives a life of clarity and conviction. The pages before you make this abundantly clear. His research, experiences, and approach are both unique and refreshing. From understanding the differences between pleasure and happiness, to identifying your unique and higher purpose, to defining success in a way that you have never attempted before, this book is a powerfully inspirational gift to anyone who reads it. As you read each page, commit to putting the principles and guidance to use. Let them catapult your results to another level.

Let this be the day that you make happiness a powerful priority.

Tony Jeary - The RESULTS Guy™
Coach to the World's Top CEOs and High Achievers

CONNECTING HAPPINESS AND SUCCESS

A Guide to Creating Success through Happiness

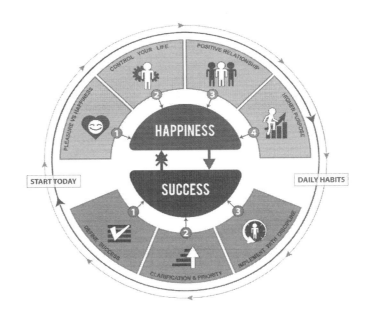

Ray White

Xilo Media

Dallas, Texas

Published in the United States by Xilo Media

Library of Congress Control Number: 2014940194

Xilo Media, Lewisville Texas

ISBN 978-0-692-21606-4

Printed in the United States of America

1 3 5 7 9 10 11 8 6 4 2

Edition 1.0

To my wonderful wife, Lindsey: My life is a reflection of your love and partnership.

To my fantastic kids, Andrew, Spencer, and Gabriele: There is nothing more powerful than our love for our children.

Acknowledgments

This book would not have been possible without hours of help from family, friends, and colleagues. Their help, support, and guidance, throughout the process enabled a dream to become a reality and helped me share a message without sacrificing my career and family life.

My wife and kids are at the heart of everything I do, and their encouragement and understanding has been key to ensuring a healthy balance between bringing a book to life and time with the family.

Ali Merchant has shown encouragement from the beginning and helped me refine the early classes and concepts. Jeff Rudluff and his company Online Performance Marketing helped test the theories and implement the marketing plans. Wayne Irwin has been a friend, editor, and confidant. Nicholas Ward provided help and insights at every step. John Weyand understood the message and my communication style and was able to turn a very rough manuscript into something that might be understood by the general public. Tammy Kling and Tony Jeary helped me take this book to the next level and multiply its success.

Thanks to everyone for their encouragement and support.

Contents

"A happy workforce makes for a more successful and productive team."

Richard Branson

Overview

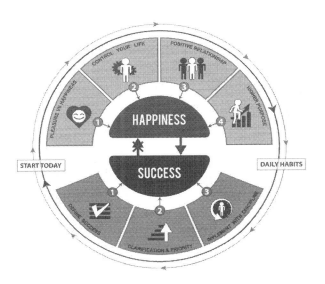

Chapter 1

On August 15th, 2013, Moritz Erhardt, an intern working for Bank of America in London, died from complications created by working three days straight without sleep. He was doing a "turnaround," which consists of an employee working all night, taking a cab home at 6 am, asking the cab to wait while he gets a quick shower and change of clothes, then hopping back in the cab to go back to work. He never got back in the cab. He was found dead in his shower. What happened?

Moritz's death is a dramatic and immediate example of how our culture encourages many people to blindly chase success while being oblivious to the negative impacts it has on their happiness, on their health, and in certain cases on their lives. For most people these things develop over decades. The signs are there, but they are much more subtle and obscure.

I have worked with dozens of people over the past decade who speak about, research, and live happiness and success. We have analyzed definitions of success collected from over 240 people and found that most contained the word "happiness," or at least concepts related to happiness. Most people connect success and happiness in their minds but have difficulty making the connection in their actions. Much like Moritz, only to a lesser degree, they pursue success single-mindedly, with the expectation that they will be happy once they achieve success; and that the more success they achieve, the happier they will be. Unfortunately that formula is backwards.

Success doesn't lead to happiness. Happiness leads to success.

Personally, I have been in business settings for over 35 years, and I have seen hundreds of examples of people working hard and unwittingly sacrificing happiness in pursuit of success, which they think will make them happy. It starts out innocently enough--not having time to go out with friends, not getting home in time for dinner with a spouse or kids, not having time to exercise or pursue a fulfilling hobby--but soon amounts to missing positive moments in life because they are busy trying to build a life that will be full of positive moments.

The drawback doesn't reveal itself until 5 or 10 years down the road, when a goal set early on has been achieved (a raise, a promotion, or a nice car); but for some reason, the satisfaction and fulfillment that were supposed to accompany the goal...don't. I have seen both men and women break down crying from the stress of wanting to give 100% in their work, yet feeling sad and unfulfilled because they were missing time with their new baby or significant other. Have you ever met someone who felt they'd missed their biggest opportunity? It's sad. Because missing important moments in your life leads to stress, and stress leads to unhappiness, disease, and a host of other challenges.

One example is a woman I worked with. Her name was Tina.

Tina was poised and confident, the kind of person that her peers wanted to emulate and every manager wanted to hire. She showed great leadership and had tremendous success early in her career. Five years, two promotions, and one baby later, she was sitting in a restaurant, tears streaming down her face from the stress of trying desperately to be successful in so many areas of her life while wondering what happened to the promise of happiness. She is one of hundreds of examples that played out in many different ways, but always had the same root cause. The long hours of hard work and dedication were never paid off with happiness, fulfillment, and satisfaction. They only led to more long hours and hard work in trying to reach the next goal, which itself was supposed to lead to happiness, fulfillment, and satisfaction.

Let me say it again: Success doesn't lead to happiness. Happiness leads to success.

This book is intended to teach you how to happily put in those long hours and dedication--how to be happy first, and then have that happiness lead you to even greater success. It is not a choice between happiness and success, or a choice between working hard and being happy. They are intertwined, and the actions you take to make yourself happier will also provide the energy, motivation, and positive habits that will lead to your success.

From early in my career I have been involved in researching success and leadership, and eventually happiness and the science behind happiness.

In the seminars I've led over the years on leadership and success, happiness is always a key discussion topic. People are no longer content to sacrifice everything to become successful at their job. They want to work and be happy at the same time.

The challenge is that people get caught up in an ambitious chase for success and unwittingly delay or even bypass their opportunities for happiness with the belief that happiness would come after the project was finished, after the next promotion, after the next big bump in salary, or after they land that next perfect job. Too often, it doesn't come as expected, and they end up forever looking over the horizon believing that happiness is just over the next hill. Those I have observed who did find happiness made simple, uncomplicated choices and changes in their lives. They found the secrets of happiness, and as a result, also became much more successful in the process.

How Happy and Successful Do You Feel?

Most people feel relatively happy and successful, and at the same time are looking to become even happier and more successful. It is natural to feel like there is more and to want to move to that next level. It is an instinct that helped our ancestors survive and prosper. The challenge is that many of us don't know what steps to take to become happier and more successful, or we don't know the correct steps. See if you identify with any of the examples below.

Have you ever woken up to the alarm and hit the snooze button too many times because you just didn't want to get out of bed and go to work? Have you ever had that feeling of dread in the pit of your stomach where you can't imagine going back into that office and facing that sadistic supervisor who seems to want to make your life miserable? What about that crazy manager in the other department who makes your life difficult just because she can?

Have you ever left the office at 8 or 9 pm with four more hours of work to do and three impossible deadlines for the next day? Have you ever felt so overwhelmed you wanted to cry or hide somewhere? These feelings can be especially confusing, given that six months ago you were on top of the world and everything was going great. Sometimes we feel as if we are on top of the mountain; at other times, down in a deep valley. What's going on?

Have you ever worked and worked and worked to get a promotion or raise you deserve, been really excited for about 30 days, and then wondered when the next raise or promotion would come? Have you ever gotten your life perfectly in line with your dreams, had everything on track, and then sat back and asked the question, "Why don't I feel happy? I should feel happy; what's wrong with me?"

Have you ever felt like what you did just didn't seem to matter and wasn't as important as what everyone else was doing? Have you felt like no matter how hard you tried you just couldn't make a difference? Does it ever seem like you are constantly banging your head against a wall and nothing ever changes?

These feelings are all natural and are indications that, armed with a little more information, you can take steps to become happier and more successful. As part of our culture, we learn to chase success as an end result rather than a daily habit. We are taught that the reward for success is happiness, and some day we will get to be happy if we just fight through and spend enough time being unhappy.

Happiness and success are connected. They are intertwined in our actions, but they are not a pinnacle we reach. They are daily habits and practices. They are small things we choose to do every day that eventually lead to milestones of success along a journey that lasts our entire lives. The antidote to the feelings described above is to choose positive actions every day that will help us feel contented and fulfilled, that will help us feel like we matter and can make a difference, and that will help us feel hopeful and excited to get up every morning.

Research also clearly indicates that happier people are healthier, have better relationships, and are more successful. Stress kills. So the antidote to stress, which is the cause for many health challenges, is happiness.

The good news is that there are steps you can take, and choices you can make, to be happier.

Where Things Get Off Track

> *"Happiness is not in our circumstances, but in ourselves. It is not something we see, like a rainbow, or feel, like the heat of a fire. Happiness is something we are"*
>
> *John B. Sheerin*

We want to be content, and we believe that getting that big house, promotion, or raise will be the thing that makes us feel fulfilled. Unfortunately, it is not achieving those goals that provides contentment. It is actually the <u>daily process</u> of working toward those goals that results in contentment, satisfaction, and fulfillment. It is not what we ultimately achieve, but what we achieve every day.

It doesn't work to try to be eventually happy or eventually successful. Life is better if we can find happiness and success every day in our daily adventures. Like John Sheerin mentioned above, happiness is something we are. The nice house will not bring contentment; it is simply a milestone on our daily journey to be happy and successful. The contentment comes from the satisfaction of knowing how much hard work and grit we put in on a daily basis to get the house. The roadblock to happiness and success is not in wanting to reach these milestones. It is that we are waiting for success and happiness rather than implementing it and experiencing it every day.

You can learn habits and techniques that will help you practice happiness every day. Let's start by looking at how many of us define happiness and success.

Analyzing Definitions of Success and Happiness

Happiness and success are connected. They are intertwined in our lives by similar thoughts, feelings, and aspirations.

I've compiled more than 240 definitions of success from leadership classes, coaching and mentoring sessions, and research. Based on the key words used in each definition, we categorized the definitions into one or more representative concepts. The results were clear: People use similar concepts to define happiness and success, and the two are interrelated. Happiness was mentioned in more than 25% of the definitions of success, and the top two concepts in the definitions of success were the same as the top two concepts in the definitions of happiness.

Concept	Success Rank	Happiness Rank
Contentment (contentment, satisfaction, and fulfillment)	1st (tied)	1st
Others (building positive relationships & creating a better world)	1st (tied)	2nd
Achievement (and accomplishing goals)	3rd	4th
Happiness	4th	N/A
Wealth (and financial stability)	8th	Not Mentioned
Success	N/A	7th

"Happiness is more than a mere pleasurable sensation. It is a deep sense of serenity and fulfillment."

Mathieu Ricard

The concept of contentment, which includes contentment, satisfaction, and fulfillment, was the top concept mentioned in the definitions of happiness, by a significant margin. It was also one of the most identified concepts in the definitions of success. Different people, in different environments and at different times, all came to similar conclusions when they defined success or happiness. Basically, they all agreed that feeling content, satisfied, and fulfilled in our lives is foundational to being successful and to being happy.

The next highest-ranked concept in the definitions of both success and happiness was others. Others includes building positive relationships with friends and family, contributing to the community, and helping make the world a better place. So most people place a high value on how we help others when they define happiness and success.

The concept of achievement, which includes achieving or accomplishing goals, was the third most mentioned concept in the definitions of success, and was the fourth most mentioned concept in the definitions of happiness. Achievement is part of success, but most people also believe we will be happier if we are achieving.

Interestingly, the concept of acquiring wealth or financial stability was a distant eighth for the definitions of success, only mentioned 6% of the time; and it was not mentioned at all in the definitions of happiness.

When we started this research, our assumptions were that most people would include the concept of acquiring wealth and financial stability in their definitions of success. What we found was that the concept of contentment was significantly more prevalent than the concept of wealth in their definitions. They indicated that money in the bank, a nice house, or a nice car, are all just means to help them feel contented, fulfilled, and satisfied.

How this Book is Organized

This book is divided into seven sections. The first four teach us how to be happier, and the last three focus on being more successful. We start with the research and science so we can understand what creates our challenges and how we can overcome them. We follow that with explanations of what to do and how to do it, and then we provide activities that will help you practically implement the recommendations and build the habits that will help you be happier and more successful.

1. **Pleasure vs. Happiness** - The first concept of the book is about understanding the difference between pleasure and happiness. Pleasure comes from external stimuli like food, pay raises, and playing Xbox. Happiness is an internal feeling of contentment, satisfaction, and fulfillment. We need both in our lives, but

pleasure has strings attached: too much pleasure can take away from happiness rather than add to it.

2. **Taking Control of Your Life** - The second concept covers taking control of your life. Science shows that you can choose to be happier and can implement actions that will make you happier. Understanding that you are not a victim of your circumstances, but rather that you are in control of how you feel and the choices you make, empowers you to take actions that will lead to happiness and success.

3. **Positive Relationships** - The third concept we cover is positive relationships. Other people are an enduring part of our lives, and our ability to build positive relationships with them, no matter what their faults and mistakes are, is a key to our happiness and success.

4. **Higher Purpose** - The fourth concept is finding a higher purpose. We want to matter and make a difference in the world. Identifying and living our higher purpose helps us focus our efforts on something bigger than ourselves.

5. **Defining Success** - The fifth concept we cover in the book is defining success, which leads off our discussion about how to become successful. You can't reach success if you have not clearly defined what it is.

6. **Clarify and Prioritize** - The sixth concept is clarifying and prioritizing. Once you have defined success you have to decide what takes priority. What are you going to do every day, and what are you going to stop doing?

7. **Implement with Discipline** - The seventh and final concept is implementing with discipline. Neither happiness nor success can be achieved without making choices daily that will move you forward on that path. Success and happiness are about what we do every day.

Our goal for this book is to help you understand how happiness and success are connected and provide specific actions you can take to become happier and more successful on a daily basis. Let's get started by learning the differences between happiness and pleasure.

1st Concept

Pleasure vs. Happiness

Chapter 2
Pleasure vs. Happiness

The first concept in connecting happiness and success is **understanding the difference between pleasure and happiness.** Are you chasing immediate pleasures like sex, decadent foods, couch time, and video time; or are you nurturing relationships, maintaining your health through diet and exercise, finding ways to improve yourself, and being thankful for what is working in your life? The pursuit of **pleasure** involves feeling good in the short term, and if overdone it can create a risk of negative long-term outcomes; in contrast, the pursuit of **happiness** consists of intentional activities and habits that promote long-term health and well-being.

Many people mistakenly chase pleasure, believing they are chasing happiness. They often end up unhappy and confused. They become victims of the Hedonic Treadmill: they experience pleasure and then the feeling fades; so they do more to experience more pleasure, but the feeling fades again. No matter what level they take their pleasure to, it only gives them short-term joy; and they eventually end up back at the same level of happiness where they started. By distinguishing between pleasure and happiness, we can help people find something that lasts, a happiness they can call on in good times and bad. We can help them get off the Hedonic Treadmill and create habits that can productively lead to the happiness they are searching for.

Something to note before we get too deep into this discussion: pleasure is not inherently bad. Pleasure is actually one part of happiness. The goal is not to avoid pleasure. As a matter of fact we should seek pleasure. The challenge is moderation. How much pleasure is too much and when is pleasure connecting us to happiness vs. disconnecting us from happiness? To answer these questions, we need to know the difference between pleasure and happiness.

Defining Happiness

Let's start by exploring what we are talking about when we say "happiness." Happiness means many different things to many different people. Our focus is on happiness as a higher-level pursuit or achievement. Several authors and philosophers have captured this concept:

Mathieu Ricard, a Buddhist Monk with a degree in Molecular Genetics, and author of the book Happiness says "Happiness is more than a mere pleasurable sensation. It is a deep sense of serenity and fulfillment. A state that pervades and underlies all emotional states and all the joys and sorrows that can come one's way."

Mahatma Gandhi said "Happiness is when what you think, what you say, and what you do are in harmony."

Gandhi also said "Man's happiness really lies in contentment."

Robert Ingersoll stated "Happiness is not a reward – it is a consequence."

Deepak Chopra said "Happiness is more than a mood. It's a long-lasting state that is more accurately called well-being."

Wayne Dyer, a self-development author and speaker, explains that "Happiness is something that you are and it comes from the way you think."

Margaret Lee Runbeck, another author, wrote "Happiness is not a station you arrive at, but a manner of traveling."

Over two thousand years ago, Aristotle proposed that "Happiness is the meaning and the purpose of life, the whole aim and end of human existence."

George Sheehan, a doctor and author, wrote "Happiness is different from pleasure. Happiness has something to do with struggling and enduring and accomplishing."

And finally, John B. Sheerin said "Happiness is not in our circumstances but in ourselves. It is not something we see, like a rainbow, or feel, like the heat of a fire. Happiness is something we are."

They all describe happiness as something that is within you, something that you create, rather than something that comes from external forces.

What is happiness?

1. Happiness is a feeling of contentment, satisfaction, and fulfillment.

2. Happiness is a sense of inner peace vs. external restlessness.

3. Happiness is an on-going state of well-being vs. a fleeting experience.

4. Happiness is a state of mind, rather than an event or activity.

5. Happiness includes bad as well good experiences.

6. Happiness is internal and not a victim of external experiences that we can't control.

7. Happiness is created, not received.

8. Happiness is within our control.

Defining Pleasure

So if happiness is an inner state of well-being that can be created, what is pleasure? To oversimplify, pleasure is an activity that makes you "feel good now." Pleasure is different from happiness in that, instead of being created within and by you, it comes from outside stimuli. You get pleasure from an event, activity, or occurrence that generates positive feelings. Eating a good meal, buying something nice, playing Xbox, or watching a movie can create pleasurable sensations. Because pleasure comes from outside stimuli, it is short-lived and limited to the timeframe during and immediately after the activity occurs. Pleasure is also different from happiness in that we quickly adapt to the level of pleasure an activity provides, and we need more and more of that activity to provide more pleasure.

Pleasure is subject to a phenomenon known as Hedonic Adaptation, or the Hedonic Treadmill. In other words, a person gets accustomed to the activity creating the pleasure; and in order to experience continued pleasure, the level of the activity has to be elevated. Video games are a great example of this phenomenon: there are always more levels to advance to, so the game is constantly changing and becoming more difficult. How fun would a game be if there were only one level, with one degree of difficulty? Personally, my kids gain a lot of pleasure from playing video games, but I've noticed they can't play the same game at the same level for an extended period of time.

The challenges of the game have to be constantly increased. They want more and more challenging levels; or they want to break their previous records; or, even better, they want to switch to more realistic game experiences.

Many of us believe that once we get that {fill in the blank: car, house, boyfriend, money}, that is all we'll need or want. We will not want anything else. Has that ever really happened for you? How long after you bought your new car were you ready to buy another one? How about that girl in high school— the one who, if she would just go out with you, all your dreams would come true? Did that work out? What about the beliefs that "if I can just graduate college, or if I can just get that first job, or if I can just get a promotion, or a raise, then I will be happy"? After those things happened, you were probably happy, even giddy for a while. But soon you returned to your normal level of happiness. This principle can also apply to more dangerous situations, such as drug addiction. The first time a person tries a particular drug, he only needs a little to get an intense reaction. But his body adapts quickly; and the next time he needs a little more, and the next time even more. His body continually adapts and needs more of the drug (or a more potent drug) to get the same feeling.

Over the centuries, our ancestors survived and prospered because of their amazing ability to adapt to changing circumstances. This is great when conditions are negative, such as in harsh climates or with limited food sources. They adapted so they would survive and not be miserable. They adjusted to the new normal and began looking for ways to flourish. The trait works similarly when conditions are good. Rather than being happy and comfortable with warm weather and plenty of food, they adapted to those comforts and looked to add more. Their brains were wired not to settle completely so they wouldn't become overly comfortable and stop trying to make things better. This trait we inherited pushes us to always get better, and to continue to evolve and move.

Unfortunately, it can also work against us now that we have all the comforts human beings could need. We are still trying to evolve, so we keep adapting, even to the great things in our life. When we encounter pleasure, chemicals in our brain are released that make us feel very good and make us want more. We instinctually look for ways to repeat and increase that level of pleasure. We are programmed to want more rather than to be grateful and satisfied with what we have. We find something pleasurable, and we adapt to it and want more. This is the basis of Hedonic Adaptation and the reason many of us run on the Hedonic Treadmill.

One of the most famous and surprising studies about Hedonic Adaptation was done in 1978. It showed that whether a person had won the lottery or became a paraplegic, as quickly as two months later, that person had returned to the level of happiness experienced prior to the event. It also showed that often, over the long term, the paraplegics actually became happier. The lottery winners quickly adapted to their new mansions instead of apartments, and champagne instead of beer. They had no way to move up after a series of initial improvements. The champagne was top of the line and the beer didn't taste as good anymore. Going back to a job paying $30,000 per year held no interest for someone who had won millions of dollars in the lottery.

The paraplegics, on the other hand, reached rock bottom. Every movement was new and appreciated. They had nowhere to go but up. Every day brought a new challenge, and overcoming each challenge brought joy and confidence that built on itself. The happiness came from overcoming lots of challenges and running into and overcoming roadblocks that they could face because of their experience in winning tiny battles in the past.

Winning tiny battles and overcoming obstacles builds self-confidence that can't be easily undone. If you appreciate and celebrate what you have accomplished, the next bigger challenge seems more doable. This creates a virtuous circle of success that builds on itself. Your ability to experience happiness over time becomes stronger. That is why older people and people who have experienced significant trauma in their lives tend to be happier. They have been through the trials and tribulations that strengthened their confidence, provided perspective, and gave them a reservoir of memories and successes to call on whenever life presents negative challenges.

One other reason lottery winners are not as happy as people might expect is related to activity in the brain created by earning a reward instead just being given the reward. Researchers at Emory University measured brain activity when subjects had to complete tasks to earn money vs. when they were just given envelopes of money with no effort required. The subjects who worked for their money showed significantly more activity in the pleasure centers of the brain, and these effects lasted much longer than those in the subjects who received money without expending any effort. It seems the Science of Happiness supports what grandfathers everywhere have believed and taught for years about money: "I get my money the old-fashioned way. I earn it."

Hedonic Adaptation also explains why the standard of living in the US has gone up 250% in the past 50 years, while the average level of happiness has not kept pace. We are adapting to the nicer houses, cars, and general consumerism faster than we can earn more money to buy bigger and even better stuff.

Pleasure, by definition, is something that is positive. If it is negative, we call it pain. Happiness, on the other hand, includes both positive and negative events. Happiness does not mean everything is always good and we are always wearing rose-colored glasses. Happiness is experiencing negative events and emotions and knowing that we can get through them and come out okay. It is also knowing how to get through those tough times, knowing how to use our minds and our memories to make the best of our current situations. People who have developed the skills for happiness are aware of something my mom has always said: "This too shall pass."

Another important point is that we can experience pleasure even when we are not happy. Again, drug use and alcoholism are clear examples. Addicts experience short-term pleasure when they indulge, even though they are often depressed, or at least unhappy. As soon as they sober up, a potential inability to deal with the present situation can cause them to jump back into chasing the quick pleasure again and again.

As an analogy, buying art is a pleasure. Putting it in your house and looking at it is pleasurable. Becoming an artist is more like happiness. You have to work at it. You can't buy it. It is not something you can get from outside of yourself. It can only happen if you spend the time and cultivate the skills necessary to become an artist. The small but important difference in becoming an artist and becoming happy is that talent may be a requisite to be a successful artist, while truly anyone can be successful at finding happiness if he or she is willing to put in the time and acquire the skills.

Let's do a quick review of the differences between pleasure and happiness:

Happiness	Pleasure
Internal	External
Ongoing	Present during the pleasurable activity
Builds on itself	Subject to Hedonic Adaptation
Lasting state	Temporary state
Way of thinking	Often an impact to the senses
No Limits	Too much can become addictive and disconnect you from happiness
Includes negative events	Defined as positive
Includes dealing with the pain	Attempt to avoid pain
Includes Pleasure	Can occur without happiness
Within our control	Dependent on external factors

Chapter 3

Real Life Examples of Pleasure vs. Happiness

"The chief cause of failure and unhappiness is trading what we want most for what we want at the moment." Unknown

To illustrate the differences between pursuing pleasure and pursuing happiness, let's take a look at the days of two young men I know, Dylan and Kyle.

Dylan opens his eyes from a rough night's sleep and decides to roll over and stay in bed. He doesn't have any pending commitments or any purpose for getting up. It's almost noon; and since he went to bed at 2 am, he has already gotten almost 10 hours of sleep. When he finally does crawl out of bed an hour later, it is because he is hungry and has to go to the bathroom. As he walks to the bathroom and then the kitchen, where dirty dishes are piled high, he has to weave through a maze of pizza boxes, candy wrappers, and empty soda cups. His apartment is a small one-bedroom in a low-income, high-crime part of town. (Actually, it's his girlfriend's apartment; she's just letting him stay there because he has overstayed his welcome with, or not followed the rules of, various family members and can no longer live with them.) Dylan's girlfriend Cindy has already left for work, so he grabs a piece of stale, cold pizza and sits down in front of the TV. After a few hours of thumbing through the five local channels he has reception for, he gives up and pulls out the Xbox. Dylan's girlfriend can't afford cable so he is stuck with whatever local channels are provided free of charge and his Xbox for entertainment. The Xbox is great. Cindy was surprised when it was delivered to their front door. He told her his mom sent it. He didn't want her to find out that he had maxed out her emergency credit card. He even had to use her cell phone to order it online, since they don't have Internet access for the apartment.

If he could afford Internet service, Dylan would log on and apply for jobs, though there are actually several challenges with applying for jobs. He had a slight brush with the law, and every application he fills out requires him to disclose it. He hasn't had a lot of success applying for jobs; it seems that he can't really make it past the first interview, if he gets called in for an interview at all.

He doesn't have a car or a driver's license, and there aren't a lot of jobs within walking distance. Lastly, he's not overly keen on doing some types of menial labor. It's just not what he enjoys. All of these excuses sounded reasonable when he first started looking for a job and before he had flunked out of college because he just didn't want to do the homework. But now, three years later, his friends and family don't seem to accept them as readily as they used to. They also mention, or even insist, that his hygiene and weight challenges may be a partial cause for his lack of interview success. He is still amazed how someone like himself, who can barely afford food, can still be 100 pounds overweight. He mostly drinks Cokes and eats pizza or hamburgers and fries.

These foods are relatively cheap and within walking distance. He knows he needs to exercise; but he really doesn't like to sweat, and he can't seem to find the right time or the energy. Even with all the caffeinated sodas he consumes, he still feels sluggish. Also, he doesn't understand the hygiene complaints. Since he doesn't work out, he doesn't sweat. He spends most of his time in the apartment, so he showers every two or three days, or when he feels he really needs to.

As he is starting his fifth game of Halo, the power goes out. Dylan does the calculations in his head and comes up with about three months. That's about how long he figures it's been since an electricity bill was paid. He wonders whether his grandma will pay the bill again. She said it was the last time three months ago. Maybe she will understand that this time is different.

This is an extreme example, but true. Names and events have been slightly altered or adjusted, but otherwise this represents how Dylan currently lives his life.

Let's look at another real example. Kyle gets up at 7 am when his alarm goes off for the second time. He wants to stay in bed, but he has things to accomplish. He has to get in 20 minutes on the treadmill and 15 minutes of weights before he leaves for work at 8 am. Kyle has put on a little extra weight since he finished college two years ago, and he's trying to reverse that trend. He's not thrilled with his job, and some days he really hates it; but he knows he has to build some experience and make some connections before he will be able to move into something else. He takes his lunch to work or goes home to eat when he can, because he needs to stay on a budget and a reasonable diet. He also works an extra job on Saturdays to save money for a cruise he is planning with his girlfriend. Kyle picks up the mess he made last night while watching TV and hanging out with his friends. He has roommates, and they don't appreciate living in a trashed house.

After a long day of work spent mostly on the phone with his customers, Kyle and a few friends go back to his house to have a few beers, play a little Xbox, and share the ups and downs of their days. Kyle is going to his girlfriend's for dinner that night, so he has to limit it to one beer and one hour of Halo. It's a good plan, since he seems to keep getting killed in Halo anyway.

Kyle and his girlfriend are eating in more than out so they can save money for the cruise, and because Kyle wants to make sure he never has to move back in with his parents. The three months after college were more than enough for him to learn that he is happier on his own, or at least with roommates. He still texts his parents on a regular basis and has dinner with them once every week or two.

Who would you choose to be, Dylan or Kyle? They are two different people with clearly different lives and motivations, but their extreme differences provide a great opportunity for comparison. They indulge in similar pleasures, but the degree to which those pleasures are constructive and support happiness vs. being destructive and disconnect from happiness is significant and makes a noteworthy impact on the quality of their lives.

Both were accepted to community colleges and had the opportunity to choose more enticing pleasures over homework. Dylan chose pleasure to an extreme, and as a result he failed out of college. Kyle chose those pleasures more sparingly and was able to complete college, although not as soon as he would have liked. Dylan enjoyed the pleasure of sleep, but practiced it to the detriment of exercise and job searches. Kyle got enough sleep but stopped enjoying that pleasure so he could move on to other additional happiness activities like exercise and contributing at a job. Neither was as pleasurable as staying in bed, but each was necessary for happiness.

Dylan was focused on getting as much pleasure from the Xbox as he could--so focused that he was willing to blow his budget, and more importantly the trust of his girlfriend, his best relationship, in order to indulge in that pleasure. By comparison, the pleasure of Xbox had a positive impact on Kyle's happiness. He played for a reasonable amount of time and was able to share the experience with close friends. By experiencing the pleasures with his friends, Kyle had a double positive impact on his happiness. He had the pleasure of playing, and the pleasure of spending enjoyable time with other human beings.

Experiencing pleasure is different for every individual. We all have different levels of sleep, Xbox, and financial responsibility that are right for us. Each one of us has to determine when the pleasure is contributing to our happiness, vs. when it is too much and is taking away from our happiness.

The table below provides some examples of pleasures, how they can connect to happiness, and how they can interfere with happiness.

Pleasure	Connection to Happiness	Disconnects from Happiness
Sleeping	When getting enough sleep improves your health and your mood	When staying in bed to avoid something that needs to be done
Playing Xbox	When playing and sharing with friends	When playing too long and/or by yourself
Drinking Alcohol	When in moderation and sharing good conversations with friends or family	When drinking too much, resulting in health, legal, and relationship risks
Eating	When eating a healthy diet and sharing with friends and family	When creating health risks because of over-indulgence or improper diet

Real Life Disastrous Consequences

Josh Brent, formerly a 24-year-old starting nose tackle for the Dallas Cowboys, was recently found guilty of intoxication manslaughter. This young man, with an extremely bright future, apparently chose to overindulge in his pleasures, which in this case appear to have included alcohol and driving. He wrecked his car, killing his passenger, a family friend and teammate (needless to say, another young man with a bright future). As a result, he is in jail, has retired from a job that millions aspire to have, and has probably derailed his happiness for the foreseeable future, not to mention the happiness of his lost teammate's family.

The pleasure of going out to have fun, drinking a few beers, and spending quality time with friends can connect you to happiness. But pleasure becomes disconnected from happiness when a choice is made to let those things go too far. Happiness includes having fun, but it also requires good choices and active consideration of future consequences.

2nd Concept

Take Control of Your Life

Chapter 4

Take Control of Your Life

In the previous chapters we established that happiness is internal and is a state of mind. That means it's something you can control. You can change your level of happiness. You can decide what your life will be.

Taking control of your life requires:

1. The desire to change and grow

2. A belief that you can actually make changes in your life

3. Identification of the areas to change or adjust

4. A choice to take the actions necessary to change your life rather than passively observing how the events in your life unfold

Sonja Lyubomirsky, in her book *The How of Happiness*, provided a summary of the research about what determines happiness. She illustrated it with a pie chart that showed 50% of happiness is determined by genetics. In other words, some people are born with more ability to be joyful and happy than others. It turns out that people have a set point, or a level of happiness that is natural to them. Another 10% of happiness is influenced by our external circumstances. Who we marry, how much money we have, what type of house we live in, etc. These are what most of us spend our time chasing and why we find it so difficult to capture happiness. They add to happiness, but only to a small degree and often only for a limited time.

That leaves 40% of happiness that can be determined by our thoughts and actions. This is what we can control. This 40% is how we think, feel, and act in the hundreds of little situations that we encounter every day. This 40% is our opportunity to increase our level of happiness. So even though we have a set genetic point and can't influence more than 10% of our happiness with money and other circumstances, we can control our thoughts and actions to raise our level of happiness above our set genetic point, if we so choose.

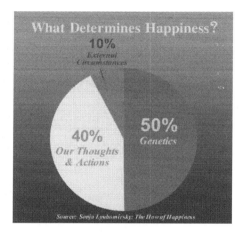

NOTE: Sonja Lyubomirsky points out that these numbers are based on a consolidation of many research studies--they are not exact and vary by person. The graph is intended to illustrate the concept that a high percentage of our happiness can be determined by controlling our thoughts and actions.

What are you choosing? Our state of mind has four times more impact on our happiness than do our circumstances. How are you influencing your state of mind? How are you categorizing your life? If you have to miss a meeting to stay home with a sick child, is it a catastrophe that makes you angry and unhappy, or are you grateful for the time with your son or daughter? Which feeling is your child seeing during your time together?

If your significant other gets you a gift on your birthday that you're not excited about, are you thinking about how bad the relationship is because they don't know what you want, or are you appreciating someone who remembered and was thoughtful enough to get you a gift? Do you become unhappy when, after reviewing your finances, you find out you can't buy that new house for another year? Or are you grateful that you have a job, can save money, and don't just have a home but can plan to upgrade your home? It all depends on your perspective.

Here are a few conclusions you can draw from the happiness research:

1. You choose happiness. It is not something you receive.

2. You have the power to influence your happiness.

3. Happiness starts today. If you are waiting until tomorrow to be happy, that day will never come.

4. Change how you think about happiness and the world and you will change your level of happiness.

Despite all of Americans' modern conveniences and growth in average income, we continue to have lower and lower happiness ratings and consistently increasing rates of depression. The things we think will make us happier are not, and our general knowledge of how we can control our own happiness seems to be fading away through the generations.

Lyubormirsky explains how happy people take control of their happiness:

> *If we observe genuinely happy people, we shall find that they do not just sit around being contented. They make things happen. They pursue new understandings, seek new achievements, and control their thoughts and feelings. In sum, our intentional, effortful activities have a powerful effect on how happy we are, over and above the effects of our set points and the circumstances in which we find ourselves. If an unhappy person wants to experience interest, enthusiasm, contentment, peace, and joy, he or she can make it happen by learning the habits of a happy person.*

In his book, *The Power of Habit*, Charles Duhigg came to similar conclusions: "If you believe you can change – if you make it a habit – the change becomes real." He relates a story about William James, who was an interesting 19th-century psychologist and philosopher trained as a physician. He taught the first psychology course in America. He decided, in a single day, to change his life. He was distraught by the success of his family members and his own complete lack of success. James's father was a wealthy and prominent theologian and his brother was a successful writer.

William had failed at being a painter, an adventurer, and a doctor. As a last resort, and in an effort to put off committing suicide, he decided to attempt a one-year experiment in free will. He would believe that he had the ability to change his life, then determine if that magnitude of change was possible. He knew and wrote that in order to change, he had to believe. "My first act of free will shall be to believe in free will," James said. Over the next 12 months, William James started creating habits and making changes. As a result, he got married, started teaching at Harvard, and began spending time with friends who would eventually become more famous than he. He spent time in discussions with Oliver Wendell Holmes, Jr. (who would eventually become a Supreme Court justice), Ralph Waldo Emerson, Mark Twain, and Sigmund Freud.

We can change our level of happiness by changing our thoughts and taking action on a daily basis. Going through the motions is not enough. You have to want to change and you have to believe you can change.

Ellen Langer did an interesting study on the ability of humans to change their thoughts and improve their lives. In 1979 she invited a group of senior men, in their 70s and 80s to a monastery in New Hampshire, where they would pretend to be 20 years younger. The real year was 1979, but they were going to pretend it was 1959 and live for a week as if they were younger, healthier version of themselves. Prior to the experiment, the participants were put through a series of tests to measure their weight, vision, flexibility, dexterity, intelligence, and health, as well as psychological function.

They also took photographs prior to the experiment that could be compared to photographs after the experiment. The monastery was set up like a resort so that everything the men would need for a week was within the 1959 environment. The men had badges that had their old pictures from 1959. They had regular discussions about politics and current events from 1959. They listened to music and watched movies from 1959. They discussed sporting events as if it were 1959. They even wrote their own bios as if it were 1959 to share with the other participants. They were instructed to talk and act as if it were really 1959. In this world, nothing after 1959 existed yet.

The results were astounding. Besides feeling younger and refreshed, their physical health based on objective measures actually improved. Their hearing improved, their eyesight improved, their grip improved, and their memory improved. Their arthritis diminished and they had more flexibility in their fingers. They had a separate group of people compare the before and after photos of the participants. In the photos taken after the experiment was completed, the participants looked younger than in the photos taken before the experiment.

By purposely changing their thoughts and actions, the participants were able to significantly change objective measures of their health and well-being. We can change our happiness and our lives by changing our thoughts and actions.

In a related experiment, Langer and her team worked with hotel maids. She divided them into two groups and measured their physical characteristics as well as their attitudes about health and well-being. The maids believed that they did not get any exercise and did not categorize the work they did as exercise. She explained to one group how the work they did was similar to exercises done in a gym. Pushing a vacuum cleaner or a cart, bending up and down, and making a bed all had physical benefits. Once they had educated the group about their work being much like exercise, they left them alone to go back to their normal lives. After a period of time they came back and interviewed them again. They asked the group if anything had changed. Had they started exercising or in any way changed their habits to improve their physical health? They had not. They also interviewed the maids' coworkers to confirm that nothing material in their lives had changed. So they had a group of maids whose only change was that they now believed the work they did was like exercise.

Once again, people's thoughts had resulted in changes to their physical condition. The maids who now believed their work was like exercise had lost weight, had reduced their waist-to-hip ratio, had reduced their BMI (Body Mass Index), and had lowered their blood pressure. How they thought about their work changed the physical characteristics of their lives. What about you?

When you think about changing your life it can seem big and overwhelming. In later chapters we will include a roadmap about how to make small, incremental changes. For now, it is important to note that most people don't change their lives in a day, and they don't change everything at once. They find a single small change they can turn into a habit. Then they add additional incremental changes, one at a time, until they have created the life they want to live. Take baby steps, focus on one thing. Find a small area where you can be successful, implement it, and then build on that success.

It Starts at an Early Age

The thoughts that help us learn to be happy come under attack at a young age. The Marketing Store Worldwide creates an index that measures kids' happiness around the globe. Their studies show that kids' belief that the world is "a good place" falls by more than 30% from the time they are 6 to the time they are 12. As our children start learning about the world from parents, teachers, their friends, and the media, they find that the world is not as full of cotton candy and balloons as they had once thought. They get introduced to the realities of life and death, relationships, financial challenges, crime, and other general impediments to constant happiness.

They learn to start thinking about the things that go badly instead of assuming everything will always be good. Unfortunately, along with those lessons they learn to give up instead of to persevere, to expect perfection instead of accepting good effort, and to try to control the world around them rather than risk being vulnerable and hurt.

We can increase our level of happiness by controlling our thoughts and actions. But starting in our early years, we build habits to protect ourselves from the world, which we see as scary and intimidating. At times we also forget what thoughts and actions enabled us to be happy in the first place. We learn early on not to control our thoughts and actions related to happiness, but instead to experience and suffer through what is making us unhappy.

Take Control of Your Life

Chapter 5

Autonomy

One of the first ways we can take control of our thoughts and actions is by cultivating Autonomy.

> *"Autonomy - the feeling that your life, its activities and habits, are self-chosen and self-endorsed"* Journal of Personality and Social Psychology

> *"Having a strong sense of controlling one's life is a more dependable predictor of positive feelings of well-being than any of the objective conditions of life we have considered..."* Angus Campbell

Research has shown that autonomy has a greater effect on happiness than does money, and that providing autonomy reduces negative psychological symptoms. Three studies that included more than 420,000 people across 63 countries and spanned more than 40 years found that money has an indirect positive effect on happiness, only in that it increases autonomy, and more autonomy has a direct positive effect on happiness. If autonomy decreases or stays the same, money does not increase happiness.

The research also showed that the 15% of Americans who felt in control of their lives also had extraordinarily positive feelings of happiness.

Autonomy at its core is the freedom to make choices. If you have a choice, you are in control. To cultivate a feeling of autonomy, then, requires you to focus on the choices you have instead of the choices you don't have. What is within your control vs. what is not within your control?

In the 1970s, Ellen Langer and Judith Rodin did a study with seniors in a Senior Care Center. One floor was given autonomy--the seniors on that floor could choose when and where they received visitors and what movies they'd watch. They were also each given a houseplant, which they could place anywhere and care for in any manner they chose. Seniors on the floor below were given plants, but weren't allowed to make any of the other choices, including how to care for the plants. Unsurprisingly, the seniors with choices were overall happier and healthier. What is surprising and very interesting is that the group with autonomy lived 50% longer, on average. Feeling like you have control over your life, like you get to make decisions that will have an impact on your life, can help you be healthier, feel happier, and possibly even live longer.

Studies with students have found that they get higher grades, more rigorously pursue their preferred careers, and are happier if they feel they are in control of their own lives. Workers are also happier at work and at home, are less stressed out, and stay in their jobs longer when they feel they have autonomy.

Think about times you were unhappy recently. There is a good probability that you were lacking the autonomy to make the decisions you wanted to make. If someone broke up with you romantically, you may feel like you had no choice in the matter. Or if you did have a choice, you may feel like you were forced by your partner's behavior to make a certain choice. Either way, you lacked the autonomy to create the situation you would have preferred to live in. Relationships are complicated for most people because we often cede our autonomy to other people. We can't control how they feel, how they react, or how they behave. We can attempt to influence how they feel and what choices they will make, but we can't control them. It can be frustrating not to have control over something so significant--how your partner interacts with you and affects your life. With relationships, focusing on what we can control and the decisions we can make can help us reclaim some of those feelings of autonomy. Feelings of autonomy arise out of clearly differentiating between what we can control and what the other people in the relationships control. We change what we can, and accept what we cannot change.

Outside of personal relationships, autonomy also plays a big role in our jobs and careers. In most cases, losing a job feels much worse than quitting a job. If you are unhappy with your job, it's probably related to being required to do things you would choose not to do if you had the autonomy to make those decisions. Research with pre-school children studied the "Sawyer Effect." The Sawyer Effect is based on a scene in Mark Twain's *Tom Sawyer*, in which young Tom cleverly made the chore of painting a fence sound so interesting that his friends volunteered to paint the fence for him. The study found that pre-school children who were offered a reward for drawing actually liked drawing and painting less when they were presented with future opportunities to do so. Getting the reward turned their intrinsic motivation into an extrinsic motivation. It took away their feeling of autonomy, because they were no longer choosing to paint for fun. By being rewarded they were no longer controlling their choices, and their motivation declined. We are more motivated by an ability to choose then by extrinsic rewards. In our jobs we want to focus on the outcomes or results rather than being told how to do something. Most of us want to understand why we are doing something and how it fits into the big picture, rather than simply being given a task with no additional information. We want our leaders to provide a vision of where to go, but we want to decide how we will get there.

In his book *Drive*, Daniel Pink cites Deci and Ryan's work on Self-Determination Theory, the concept that people are motivated by internal rewards as much as external rewards. He summarizes: "Human beings have an innate inner drive to be autonomous, self-determined, and connected to one another... People oriented toward autonomy and intrinsic motivation have higher self-esteem, better interpersonal relationships, and greater general well-being." Other studies have shown that autonomy results in more persistence at a task, which leads to higher grades, higher levels of productivity, and less burnout. In a 2007 study of two American Law schools, well-being deteriorated when autonomy was limited. Being unable to choose their courses, project topics, and relationships with professors had a negative impact on law students.

The link between autonomy and motivation is not a Western or a work-related phenomenon. The research has been confirmed all over the world and at varying income levels. No matter where you are from or how much you make, there is a desire to be autonomous. Increased autonomy leads to happier people.

Now that we understand how autonomy connects to happiness, here are a few activities to help you gain a feeling of autonomy.

Activity

1. Build an autonomy list – What things in your life do you get to choose?

    a. People you spend time with

    b. Activities

    c. How you do things

    d. What you eat

    e. What you wear

2. Most electronic calendars allow you to highlight your appointments in a chosen color. Review this month on your calendar and put blocks of red for times when you don't have autonomy or control over your calendar and blocks of green for when you do have autonomy. You can also print out one month of your calendar and do this with colored highlighters.

    Review the amount of Red and Green. Do you have more or less autonomy than you thought you had?

    Are there any areas you can move from red (no autonomy) to green (autonomy)?

3. Choose what gets done

    a) Pick three small things you can accomplish today. This is your list and can include things your boss needs done, things your spouse or family need done, or just things on your list. The most important aspect is that you choose them.

    b) Make sure those three things get done.

    c) Each day pick three more things that you can control and accomplish.

Accomplishment of even the smallest things will help you feel in control and happier about yourself.

Take Control of Your Life

Chapter 6
Taking Control

The Negative Effects of Not Having Control

In the late 1960s several famous studies showed how removing control can actually lead to depression. Martin Seligman, considered by many to be the father of the Positive Psychology movement, conducted experiments with dogs who were shocked and then given the opportunity to stop the shock. One group of dogs could push a lever and the shocks would stop, while another group of dogs saw no clear connection between their actions and the shocks starting or stopping. The research found that the dogs that could control the shocks recovered from the experience while the dogs without control over the shocks experienced "learned helplessness." In a later part of the experiment, when the helpless dogs were given the opportunity to control the shocks, they would do nothing. They would sit and endure the shocks, slipping into something similar to a depressed state. Similar experiments were done with mice and other animals with similar results. Animals that could control the outcome recovered, while animals that felt they couldn't control the outcome became helpless, even when the opportunity for control was returned to them.

Related studies were done with babies given the ability to move a mobile by moving their head on a pillow, and separately with adults who were exposed to distracting noise, with only some given the ability to turn it off. The results were similar. The babies and adults without control learned "helplessness." They would not attempt to control their environments, even when they were later given the opportunity.

On the positive side, the adults who could turn off the noise showed performance improvement on subsequent tests. So while not being able to control the noise created helplessness, having the autonomy to control the noise increased performance over a control group not exposed to the noise. Not having autonomy hurts us and can teach us a habit of helplessness, while having autonomy makes us better and happier.

Lisa was a young supervisor who was great at her job before she got promoted. She could do an amazing amount of work and knew the ins and outs of every system. When we promoted her, she was so confident in her methodologies that Tim, her direct report, was not allowed to change how things were done. Tim, who was bright, was bursting with new ideas; but no matter what recommendations he made, Lisa shot them down. Her message was "my way works and is efficient, so we don't need to make changes." Instead of growing, taking on new projects, and getting promoted, Tim stagnated. He went from motivated to bored. As Tim stopped trying to solve problems, Lisa became busier and busier trying to solve them for him. Tim learned to be helpless and fairly useless working for Lisa. Eventually we had to move Tim to another team, where he blossomed. He once again became engaged and excited. Instead of feeling helpless, he started to feel like he mattered and could make a difference. Feeling like we have some control over how we do our work will help us feel happier, more productive, and more successful.

Taking Control

> "You cannot control what happens in your life, but you can always control what you will feel and do about what happens to you." Viktor Frankl

One way to think about taking control of your life is to examine the consequences of someone else being responsible for your happiness. If you believe that you cannot be happy unless your spouse, children, parents, boss, or friends take certain actions, you become a victim of their decisions. They have control of your happiness and they may or may not behave in a way that will make you happy. Even if they do the things that will make you happy, how often is that going to happen? All the time, every day? If your happiness is dependent on other people, and the chances of all those people behaving in sync with your happiness all the time is low, what are your chances of being happy? If you want to be happier, take control of your life by deciding to be happy, and then appreciate when other people are in rhythm with your happiness. Be happier by forgiving or overlooking when they are behaving in a manner that does not make you happy.

Depending on other people to make you happy gives them control over you. If they get to decide when you are happy and when you are not, they can also influence other aspects of your life. What would you be willing to do for this other person if you believed they would do the things that would make you happy?

> *"Happiness comes from within. It is not dependent on external things or on other people. You become vulnerable and can be easily hurt when your feelings of security and happiness depend on the behavior and actions of other people. Never give your power to anyone else." Brian Weiss, MD*

So what about the emotional impacts of their actions? What about when they make you sad, frustrated, or angry? Remember, being happy does not mean you do not experience negative emotions. It means you don't let those emotions ruin your day or control your life. Feel the emotions. Embrace those negative experiences, and then choose to move forward and find something to be happy about. You can feel negative emotions without having to act on them. Many of us believe that if we are angry, we have to yell or scream. Releasing those emotions is just a part of having those emotions, but the two are separate. You can feel an emotion, and then you can choose how to act on it. Stephen Covey, in his book, *The 8th Habit*, calls it the millisecond between action and reaction. If someone cuts you off in traffic, is rude to you, or consciously disappoints you, certain feelings are automatically triggered. There is a small window of time, between the feelings being triggered and your physical reaction, when you get to own your life and decide how you will react. You get to decide whether those emotions will take control and result in a reaction you might regret or that could hurt someone else, or instead, a reaction that is in control and helps you experience and then move on from those feelings. It is not about controlling what you feel; it is about controlling how you react to what you feel.

We Control Our Lives

If someone walks up to you and slaps you, are you physically forced to slap them back or could you choose to walk away? This is central to the "Take control of your life" discussion. Although you might feel hurt, intimidated, angry, or a host of other emotions, you get to choose your response. You get to choose the action you take. This applies to any event in your life. Except under extreme circumstances, you are not forced by any natural law to react a certain way to an external event. You will feel emotions and they will influence what choices you think you have; but in the end, your action is still your choice.

In the millisecond between action and reaction, you control your life. When something happens to you, you have the option to choose what your reaction will be. Positive reactions will make your life and the lives of those around you happier, while negative reactions can have a negative influence on your happiness and the happiness of those around you.

Split-second reactions occur in many situations that are related to habits. Things like positive thinking and reacting with anger or frustration occur immediately after the stimulus occurs. But some of our actions are more long-term and thought out. I know a young lady whose parents are addicted to drugs. They are unable to support her financially, and she recognizes that their habits are a bad influence on her. She has been able to work and save her own money and is about to graduate college with an excellent grade point average. She has two great job offers and will do well in her career and life. Her parents often call her and attempt to pull her back into their negative environment, where they drain her financially or emotionally. She courteously says hello, explains her position, which is usually "Sorry, I can't help," and then she moves on with her life. The action is contact with her parents and her reaction is not to be pulled back into that negative environment, but at the same time, not to be bitter and angry about what her parents do not provide. In the moment between action and reaction she decides what her life will be like.

One of the reasons we often react to people and situations in a negative way is that we are focused on the challenges created by our own circumstances rather than evaluating and considering the circumstances of those around us. Stephen Covey tells a story of a passenger on a train who notices a man is letting his kids run wild all over the train. The father makes no attempt to control or discipline his kids. The passenger first ponders, then worries, and is eventually upset by this obvious lack of concern for any of the other passengers. The action is the kids being unruly and disruptive in the train. The passenger's reaction is to stew on the negative emotions this creates and to eventually snap at the father with the built-up anger and frustration. When the passenger yells at the father to control his children, the father sadly explains his situation. They have just come from the hospital where the children's mother, his wife, has died. The kids don't know how to react, and the father is distraught with grief and just doesn't know what to do. After hearing this information, the other passenger was devastated by his own lack of empathy. The challenge was, he had already reacted in a negative way to the stimulus. We are not privy to the private lives and thoughts of most of the people we interact with. We don't know what's behind their actions and behaviors. One way we can become better at controlling ourselves in that millisecond between action and reaction is to pause and remind ourselves that we don't know what is going on inside their heads or in their lives. If we assume there is a reason, bad or good, for them acting the way they are, we can often find more patience and charity in our reaction. It is not about us being right or wrong about our assumptions of their motivations. If we react more positively, no matter what the reasons, we will be happier and we provide them the opportunity to be happier.

Taking It to Another Level

Another story Covey tells is about a large, angry person creating havoc on a train. A 6'5", 280-pound man was yelling at and threatening people. Everyone was scared and cowering, and no one knew what to do. Then a small, older gentleman, showing no fear, walked right up to the angry man. He said something along the lines of "Whatever has happened to you must be horrible." The large angry man paused for a moment to contemplate the smaller man. The angry man then hung his head and his shoulders and said "Yes." The older, smaller man suggested they sit down and talk about it. Before the end of the train ride the older, smaller man had the large angry man curled up on the seat, crying and telling him the stories of his sadness and misfortune. The older man was able to control what were normal reactions for everyone involved: fear and flight. Everyone was avoiding the angry man, who clearly was a danger to their safety and possibly their lives. The small, older man had the compassion and empathy to understand that, for everyone, anger and yelling are reactions to something we're upset about. He chose a reaction to the stimulus that was courageous and helpful. I don't recommend that anyone risk their health or lives to show empathy, but the older man's actions are to be aspired to when we're working on owning the choices we have between the action and our reaction.

In a previous chapter we discussed Dylan and Kyle, two young men with similar circumstances who are taking very different paths. In working with Dylan, we offered to help him construct a job search. We gave him ideas on what types of companies to consider, where to look, and what his next steps should be. So the action was help from someone else with a job search. Dylan's chosen reaction was based on feelings of being pressured and feeling like his choices were being limited. As a result, he ignored all the advice he got, and three years later is still without a job. He continues to limit his opportunities for happiness. Meanwhile, we had similar discussions with Kyle about his job search. Kyle chose to take similar feelings of pressure and limitation and explore them. He asked questions about how to create the circumstances he was looking for; this led to additional deeper discussions about goal-setting and careers to help guide the job search discussions. Kyle was eventually able to create his own job search plan, and later found a job that works for him as a place to start. Both young men had similar circumstances in their lives, which led to similar feelings of pressure and limitation. Each chose to react differently, with one reducing his opportunities for happiness and success, and the other expanding his opportunities for happiness and success.

Are We Victims of Our Emotions?

Emotions are caused by chemicals released in the brain. Chemically, most will dissipate after about six seconds. But if we dwell in our thoughts on those emotions, we can make them last much longer. We can prolong and increase the amount of chemicals released and the intensity of the emotions by ruminating on how angry we are. So even though an external event can cause a feeling or emotion, that feeling will only last more than six seconds if we think about it and simmer in it with the stew of connected and related thoughts. If we are angry, we can focus on and think about why we are angry and increase our anger. Or, we can focus on and think about something else and let the chemicals that caused that feeling of anger dissipate. After six seconds, what we think controls how we feel.

This is a difficult concept to accept. Most of us feel that we have the right and the responsibility to get angry if someone wrongs us. That belief, however, is more closely associated to habit than to conscious thought. We react based on how we learned to respond when we saw other people react in similar circumstances. By taking a millisecond to stop and choose our reaction, we can improve our relationships, become calmer and more focused, and become happier.

Living with events and people in our lives that we can't control is scary. But becoming the victim of all the twists and turns in life is a form of the "learned helplessness" illustrated in the studies discussed earlier. We can choose how we respond. We can find autonomy and control over our lives by choosing our responses. It is empowering and gives us the confidence to face almost any situation if we know that we can experience the feelings, then choose our reaction. The events in our life are many and varied, but how we respond is completely within our control. Happiness is a choice. We can be victims of our circumstances and old habits, or we can create our lives to be whatever we want them to be. We can choose to be people who, no matter what is going on around them, are calm and deliberate in their reactions.

It is important to distinguish between suppressing your feelings and acknowledging your feelings and choosing a different reaction. Rather than pretending you don't feel anger, we are suggesting you accept that you feel angry and know that it is ok to feel it. But feeling the anger does not mean you have to act on it in a negative way. You have control and can decide how you will react. If we suppress our feelings for long periods of time, we run the risk of bursting out with a seemingly "out of character" reaction to what seems to everyone else to be a small challenge. We act irresponsibly or in a way we would prefer not to because of stress-related chemicals that have built up over time. Some event becomes the "last straw" in a long line of emotional reactions during that time period.

Stress creates cortisol in your body, which builds up over time, much like natural gas might collect in a house before an explosion. Once the cortisol has built up, it only takes one spark to ignite it and set off what would appear to be an unexplainable torrent of emotions. It is the fabled "straw that broke the camel's back." Your brain actually reacts to the cortisol by shifting into a fight-or-flight mode instead of remaining in a clear thinking mode.

Take the Moment to Choose

"Because how we spend our days is, of course, how we spend our lives." - Annie Dillard

Our lives are made up of years. Our years are made up of days and our days are made up of moments. How we spend the collection of those moments will determine how we spend our lives. We can control how we spend many of those moments by choosing how we react to the events in our lives. In the millisecond between action and reaction, we control our lives.

Between stimulus and response there is a space.

In that space lies our freedom and power to choose our response.

In those choices lie our growth and our happiness.

Stephen Covey, The 8th Habit

What You Can Control vs. What You Can't Control

The world is full of things we can't control. Something like the weather seems obvious. Yet how often are we unhappy because the rain ruins our plans?

It may be less obvious that we can't control the actions of another person, even someone close to us. Our ability to influence them makes us believe we can control their actions, but eventually we are disappointed when they make decisions and take actions different from what we would have preferred.

When we start listing the things we can control and the things we can't, the things we can control are centered on us and our actions while the things we can't control are external to us--people, nature, and the stock market, to name a few.

Start with the list of things you can control. Now list the decisions you are making. For example, you can control what you wear in the morning, what you eat, and how you get to work. You can even control which job you have. This is important; if you say "I have to work, I don't have a choice," you are still making a choice. You could choose at any moment to be homeless and hungry. It may not feel like a good choice, but it is still a choice you're making that many others have made differently. Recognizing your power to choose is important to feeling autonomy. Your choice may be to work at a place you don't like or risk not having enough money to live where you want to live or eat what you want to eat, but all of those are choices you are making. Appreciating the opportunity to make those choices is an important part of improving your happiness.

What Can you Control? What is your Choice?	What Can't You Control?
1. Who you hang out with	1. How they behave or react
2. Where you work	2. How nice your co-workers are
3. What time you wake up	3. Physically, your body requires sleep
4. What clothes you wear	4. What people think about the clothes you wear
5. Whether or not you brush your teeth	5. The bad breath or cavities that result from not brushing your teeth
6. Where you live	6. How much it costs
7. What time you leave for work	7. Whether or not there is construction or an accident that creates heavy traffic
8. What you read	8. What someone else writes
9. Whether you take action based on what you have read	9. Other people's reaction to those actions
Add Your Own	Add Your Own
10.	10.
11.	11.

Activities to help you "Take Control of Your Life"

1. Finish the list above with things you can and can't control. Think through what you do each day. How many choices are you actually making that you never thought about?
2. Go back through your list and put a check next to the areas where you can practice autonomy, where you can choose the course you are going to take rather than being a victim of your circumstances.
3. Start a new list. What areas of your life are you most unhappy about?
4. Write down what you can control in those areas of your life.
5. Write down what choice you are going to make to change it.

I AM UNHAPPY ABOUT...	I CAN CONTROL...	MY CHOICE IS TO...
1. My weight	1. What I eat and whether or not I exercise	1. Look at each bite before I put it in my mouth and walk for 20 minutes every day

6. Here are some quick activities to help us pause and work through our emotions rather than ruminating and prolonging the negative effects. It is important to note that these only work if you really want to reduce your negative feelings or negative actions.

   a. Pause. Breathe. Now count backward from 10 to 1. If that emotion is still strong and not fading, start at 100 and count backward. Focusing on counting backward will take your mind off the negative emotions.

   b. Sing your happy song. What is a song or a lyric that makes you feel better about yourself and the world? One of my favorites is, "In every life we have some trouble, when you worry you make it double. Don't worry, be happy," by Bobby McFerrin.

   c. Who is your favorite person in the world? What would they tell you about this situation?

   d. Go to your happy place. What is a memory of a real or imagined place that is just wonderful? Imagine in detail what it is like there. What is the temperature, what is around you, what are you doing?

   e. Breathe deeply. Count 10 breaths. Then start again and count 5 breaths.

   f. What is your happy thought? It could be a memory, or a goal, or just something that calms you down when you think about it. I like to think of seeing my family or sitting down and petting my dog.

Take Control of Your Life

Chapter 7
Being the Catalyst

Steering and Pedaling vs. Along for the Ride
Are you happening to life or is life happening to you?

Are you steering and pedaling down the road to happiness, or are you just along for the ride? Taking control of your life means playing an active role in deciding how your life unfolds. You can't control everything, but you can admit that not making decisions is a choice that has consequences in your life. If you get up every morning and say "I hate my job!", but take no action to change or improve your job, you're acting like a victim. It's an easy trap that many of us fall into; but if you act helpless, you create a life where you are the victim of your circumstances. It takes creativity, hard work, and energy to change your circumstances. But the rewards are significant, and they include happiness.

Let's continue with a discussion about occupations, which many people would name as a source of their unhappiness. There are many things that have led to your current job, including your education, experience, location, skills, connections, and level of effort. All of these things can be changed and improved. It won't be easy and it won't happen overnight; but there are thousands of stories about people who worked two jobs to save for a better house, or who went to school at night while working a full-time job, or who worked at one job to make money and worked at a second job to learn a skill.

A young woman I know, a few years out of college and into the work force in a stable government job, was employed for her writing skills. She'd graduated with a degree in Ancient Mediterranean Civilizations, a field with a relatively narrow real-world application. She had complaints about her job and its direction, as everyone does, until she made the decision to change her situation. She decided to become a doctor, which would mean starting from scratch on that career path: undergraduate science classes, volunteer work, standardized tests, everything. Nearly ten years later, she's graduated from one of the top three medical schools in the United States and will complete her residency in a matter of months. During the middle part of these years, by the way, she became a mother to two children. Needless to say, her choice and subsequent actions to change her life have been incredibly fulfilling, despite the huge amount of effort required.

Change, however, doesn't have to be this drastic: you have the ability to change how you think about your job. What attitudes are you taking into your job? If you hate your job, everyone knows it without your saying anything. The way you walk, talk, interact, and carry yourself are all indicators of your satisfaction on the job. Changing how you think about your job or how you talk about your job will change your attitude, which may improve the attitudes of those who interact with you. Are you accidentally putting out signals that you are grumpy and hate your life, or are you putting out signals that you want to improve your life?

You can also take action to change the job itself. Bring a plant to work. Find a friend you can talk to at work. Pick some part of your situation and start to improve it.

Is there someone who is ruining your day each time you go to work? Let's say there's one person in particular that you dread seeing because of his behavior. Ask yourself why he behaves that way. Are you the only one who feels conflict with him? Does it have more to do with you than with him? Does he know he has that kind of an impact on you? Spend some real effort attempting to get to know him. He is human like the rest of us and has fears and emotions. He is trying to get through life, just like we are. What makes him tick? What makes him happy? What is so negative in his current life or his past that he feels forced to behave this way?

Find something positive that comes out of your job each day. Who is helped by your work? Whose life is touched by what you do? If you are a roofer, can you find satisfaction in helping people stay safe and dry? If you have a monotonous desk job, are you helping people get approvals or get information that will help them in some way? What is work enabling you to do? Does it keep you from being homeless? Does it allow you to live where you want to live? Does it pay the bills while you figure out what you want to do with the next part of your life?

If you don't know what actions to take to change your life, ask a friend or family member. Write down your goals or your dreams. Build a plan as if there were no obstacles and you could create exactly the life you wanted, and then identify and overcome one obstacle at a time. Take one small step, and you will immediately start to feel more control over your life. Then take another and another until you can take one tiny step every day. Do something as small as deciding what time you will go to bed or what time you will get up. Decide what you will eat for breakfast every morning.

Decide what you will wear to work. If you wear a uniform, decide on some small token to wear underneath the uniform. Wear a band around your wrist or ankle. Wear a different color of underwear. Put a good luck charm in your pocket. I have two small medallions. One says patience and the other says wisdom. Depending on what I feel I am most in need of, usually patience, I choose one to put into my pocket for the day. I often reach into my pocket and rub the medallion to help me remember to be patient or to call on wisdom rather than rash reaction. Deciding which medallion and phrase to carry with me and focus on is my opportunity to choose. Choosing to be patient or trying to act with wisdom are things I can control.

Owning our Successes and Failures - Accomplishment

We have all felt that feeling of accomplishment, when the boss or customer liked something we put a lot of effort into at work or the teacher gave us an A on the paper or test at school. Part of taking control of our lives is recognizing those accomplishments ourselves and not depending on others for that feedback. It is great to hear feedback from other people. It keeps us grounded in reality and provides a boost for our ego. But many of the things we have to work on are internal and personal. We need to be able to appreciate ourselves and give ourselves that positive boost.

Also, we can't control who will or won't recognize or appreciate our efforts. We will become much more confident if we are proud of things we give 100% effort on, and then add feedback from other people as a bonus. It also makes it much easier and much more productive to hear feedback if we are not dependent on others for that feeling of accomplishment. If we know we put 100% effort into something and we already feel good about it, then when someone criticizes that work, we can listen to the feedback with less defensiveness and use that feedback to identify ways to improve or take our efforts to another level.

Accomplishments help us build happiness and confidence. Setting a goal and achieving it makes us feel good about our past and gives us confidence that in the future we can accomplish something else. It's like making deposits in a bank. When you are young, you only have a few memories or accomplishments to withdraw and invest in your confidence; but over time you build up a collection of all shapes and sizes, and you can access all kinds of examples that will give you confidence you can use for the next challenge.

Owning Small Successes

One challenge to owning our successes is not recognizing the small accomplishments. We think that accomplishing something everyone else can do, or something no one knows about is not really an accomplishment. But that's like taking money out of or not putting money into our confidence bank. Getting up and going to work every day is an accomplishment. We think of it as something we're just supposed to do, or something everyone does. But there are many people who can't keep jobs because they just can't drag themselves out of bed and make it to work. In many cases your boss and other people are not going to notice this accomplishment. But if you recognize yourself for this one effort, it will add a little to your confidence bank for the next accomplishment. Lots of little accomplishments add up to big accomplishments.

We should also track and savor our accomplishments. Don't let the day get away without stopping and appreciating what you have accomplished. We get so busy and have so much going on that we don't stop to appreciate what we really accomplish and how we're improving our lives a little each day. By taking a few moments to stop, think about, and appreciate these accomplishments, we build our confidence and make it easier to take on the next challenge. We can build a belief in ourselves just based on what we do every day without waiting for a heroic or extraordinary accomplishment. People don't graduate from college in one day. They put in years of attending classes, doing homework, and practicing discipline on a daily basis. People don't get promotions because of something they did one day. Promotions come from showing up every day and putting in the extra effort to make sure lots of small things are accomplished over and over again.

One Small Step Leads to Another

Large successes give us confidence to move forward, but we rarely start with large successes. Most big successes are a result of many small wins spread out over a long period of time.

As mentioned above, we don't just graduate from college in one day. Our preparation starts in high school, when we do our homework and keep our grades up. We attend class on a regular basis, and we study enough to score well on college entrance exams. Then we have to apply and be accepted into the college we will attend. Finally we have to find funding, attend classes, study, and overcome peer pressure and other obstacles to getting our work done.

We have to be disciplined and perform consistently for four, five, or more years. Getting decent grades in high school helps us be more confident about getting good grades in college. Attending class and doing our homework makes us more confident we can pass a test. Getting passing grades on the tests helps us believe we can pass the class. Passing a few classes and completing our first semester gives us confidence we can complete a full year and eventually graduate. Look for small wins to add to your confidence, and then build on those small wins to accomplish the next bigger task. Accomplishing small things today will give you the confidence to accomplish the big things in your future.

Being Perfect vs. Good Enough

Our accomplishments and small successes get lost in the list of things that did not go right. Many people miss out on celebrating the small successes because they are waiting for everything to go perfectly. As long as they know the results could have been better, it is not yet a success or accomplishment in their eyes. The challenge is, that time may never come--which means very little celebration, which severely limits your opportunity for positive feelings and increasing happiness. Focus on making the effort good enough vs. perfecting the results. We can control how much effort we put forth, but we can't always control the results. Often there are other factors that come into play. Since we are human, being perfect is impossible.

Perfectionism creates expectations that are always over the horizon-- expectations we think we are moving toward, but always seem just out of reach. Good enough enables us to forgive ourselves for our mistakes and shortcomings and celebrate the things that did go right. It gives us something to build on. Good enough provides us a positive feeling that we are making progress and lets us believe that we can accomplish even more. We can increase our happiness if we take the time to stop and think about our accomplishments and successes. If we try to be perfect, we may spend that time thinking about the details that did not go right, rather than the tiny successes we can build on.

Celebrating small successes and creating positive habits are connected. In order to create and sustain a habit, your mind needs some kind of reward for activating the proper behavior. A quick activity that represents your small "victory lap" or "victory dance" reinforces the positive behavior and makes you feel happier and able to take on another challenge. One method I use is the quick and inconspicuous thumbs up. I run several times a week to try to stay healthy. Every time I finish a mile, I give myself a "thumbs up." It is a small celebration that represents a small accomplishment. It is my small way to reinforce a good habit of running.

One of our teammates wanted to create a habit of arriving at meetings two minutes early. He was always busy with constant back-to-back meetings all day long. Every meeting would run a few minutes over; and then the after-meeting discussions and normal life events, like eating and going to the bathroom, would result in his being late for the next meeting, which would cause it to run a little longer and would result in his being late for the meeting after that. We put some ground rules in place to break the cycle, like scheduling 45-minute meetings and leaving 15 minutes for the follow-up activities. We also created a tiny "victory lap." Every time he was on time for a meeting, he would send an email proclaiming his small success. This provided a form of accountability, but it also provided the reward in his mind that would make him want to make it to the next meeting on time. He got a small celebration for each small success.

Create your own small "victory dance" or celebration. A literal two-step dance, a victory song, or some other small acknowledgement that you are making progress and succeeding will help you create positive habits and give your mind reasons to be happier.

Activity:

1. Create your own small "victory dance" or celebration.

2. Make a list of your accomplishments for the past week.

3. Give yourself a small "thumbs up" or celebration for each item you accomplished this week.

My personal celebration/"victory dance" is: _____

Accomplishments	I Celebrated?
	Yes No
	Yes No
	Yes No

Ongoing Activity

1. Buy a journal or identify an area on your smartphone or tablet to take notes on a daily basis.

2. At the end of every day, write down the accomplishments you are proud of. Make sure you have at least three every day.

3. Write down the strengths that are exhibited by these accomplishments.

4. Do your small celebration.

or

5. Build a PowerPoint file, Pinterest board, or scrapbook with pictures of your accomplishments.

Owning Failures

Much like we should own our accomplishments, we should also own our failures. We should hold ourselves accountable for the events and results in our lives we can control. Failing a test, not completing a project on time at work, or not putting in the time and effort needed to complete a task are things we can hold ourselves accountable for. It is easy for us to say the test was too hard, work was too busy, or the distractions in our lives were too crazy. But blaming circumstances or other people gives control of our lives to someone else or something else. We should be accountable for what we could have done--started earlier, planned better, studied more. If we don't own our failures, we can't take credit for our successes. If when something goes well it was us, and when something fails it was someone or something else, then we don't know when that someone or something else will interfere and cause us to fail; so we don't have control over our successes and our lives.

There are always contributing external factors to successes and failures. The key to building confidence and happiness is to give 100% effort to overcome and work around those factors. If it's hard to get to work on time every morning because a roommate likes to stay up late, you can politely inform your roommate of your need to get some sleep, you can buy earplugs, or you can get a new roommate.

If you're too busy to complete a task, you can break it into smaller chunks or schedule a time when you will complete it. If you have to take a test or make an important presentation at work, start now. Study, create, or prepare a little bit each day to be prepared with plenty of time to spare, rather than trying to cram it all into the day or night before.

Failure is a natural part of life and learning. Everyone makes mistakes and has goals that end up not being accomplished or challenges that are created by not giving 100% effort. We also fail because of things outside our control. The trick is to understand that failure is not permanent. It is not what we will or have become. It is an outcome that we can learn from. It is an opportunity to get better.

We can always start again, learn from our failures, and create successes. No matter how big the failure or challenge, we can start each day anew and create successes by adjusting to what we learned by failing the day before. Instead of making failures a part of our identity, we can make them the keys to our future success. But this is only possible if we take responsibility for our failures. If we pretend they are someone else's fault, then we become victims to the whims of other people. If we own our failures, then we can learn, improve, and take back control of our lives.

"If you make it a habit not to blame others, you will feel the growth of the ability to love in your soul, and you will see the growth of goodness in your life." - Leo Tolstoy

Activity:

1. Make a list of recent failures.

2. Check the box/circle whether you own those failures.

3. Determine what you could have done to make the outcome different.

4. Give yourself a "thumbs up" for admitting and evaluating your failures. They are often a more important part of your happiness than your successes.

Failure	Do I own it?	What I could have done differently	Thumbs Up!

Take Control of Your Life

Chapter 8
Control What You Can Control

Serenity Prayer

God grant me the serenity
to accept the things I cannot change;
courage to change the things I can;
and wisdom to know the difference.

Part of taking control of your life is knowing what you can and cannot control. Your thoughts, your actions, your reactions, and your happiness are always within your control. Everything outside of you is not. We are all comfortable with the fact that we can't control the weather or the performance of our favorite team.

We run into a challenge, however, when we are confronted with the possibility that we can't control the behaviors of the people around us. It becomes even grayer when we start discussing life events and circumstances where we have a lot of influence, but where the ultimate direction includes outside factors.

A lot of confusion is created by our ability to influence but not control outcomes. Where does control end and influence begin? When does our influence become so small as to be ineffectual?

A great example of something we have a significant amount of influence over but can't control is a promotion at work. We put a lot of time and effort into our jobs or careers. We spend time learning and getting the proper training and education. We put in the years to get the experience. We stay late to get special projects done. We attempt to intuit what our bosses want and make sure we deliver. Overall, we work really hard and hope to get rewarded for those efforts. These are all actions that we can take and we can control. Unfortunately, the decision to promote us lies with someone else. It is not something we can control. So we can get ourselves 95% of the way there, but someone else makes the final call. This can be extremely frustrating for most people. People often get angry and take that anger out on their friends, family, coworkers, and company--actions which can sabotage the next opportunity for the promotion they so desperately want.

This is where understanding what we can and can't control really helps, and where understanding the difference between pleasure and happiness is important. A promotion is a pleasure. It is an external event. It is something that is outside of us. Recall that happiness is internal. It is how we think and feel about our lives. We can control our actions and what we decide to do, but we can't control what others do. If we focus on the pleasure of the promotion, we no longer have control of our lives or our happiness. If we focus instead on the satisfaction that comes from doing a good job, learning something new, and being part of a great team, we can feel autonomy and happiness. The good news is that most of the research shows that excitement over a promotion lasts only about 90 days. Feeling good about ourselves for doing hard work, a good job, and being engaged in something challenging lasts as long as we make that a part of our lives. So we are better off finding happiness in the daily activities and challenges that prepare us for the promotion (all things we can control) than being unhappy and counting on the promotion, something we can't control, to make us happy.

Another great example of what we can and can't control is other people, especially those who are close to us. People close to us can have so much impact on our lives that we want to make sure it is positive and happy for them and for us. We want them to know what to do and how to do it so they understand how they can make us happy. They even tell us they want to make us happy. We can communicate and share all that information, and for the most part, they will likely do their best to live according to a plan that will make us and them happier. But inevitably there are areas of conflict where our ideal world and theirs don't match. In those times we discover that we can't control their choices and actions; we can only hope to influence them. They are going to make their own decisions, which may or may not leave us happy and contented.

Have you ever worn a lucky shirt (or other clothing or token), hoping to help your favorite team win a tough game? We desperately want to believe that we can influence the outcome of events that we have an emotional stake in.

When we don't have control, we feel a sense of helplessness.

I was having lunch with a friend and he mentioned the impact traffic and someone cutting him off can have on his life. He could choose to be offended, get really angry, and let it ruin his day; or he could choose to believe that the other person had something really important happening and needed to get ahead. My friend admitted often giving instructions to other drivers under such circumstances--"USE YOUR TURN SIGNAL!" or "GET OFF MY TAIL!" (or worse...). He wondered, "Why do we feel the need to teach other drivers how to drive?" Could it be that we are altruistically thinking of the other driver and we want to help them be safer and more knowledgeable? Or are we concerned for the other people on the road and we want them to be safe? Or is it more likely that we are attempting to control something we have no control over?

If We Can't Control It, Why Try?

The fact that you can't control whether you get a promotion does not mean you won't get the promotion. If you work hard, learn, and become a good team player, the odds are in your favor that you'll get the promotion. The important message, however, is that if you derive your happiness from the daily work, challenges, and activities, then the promotion will be the icing on the cake rather than the sole reward. Plus, being happier on a daily basis will lead to more promotions, raises, and other positive life opportunities. In a meta-analysis of more than 100 research studies, Laura King, Ed Diener, and Sonja Lyubomirsky concluded that "happy individuals are more likely than their less happy peers to have fulfilling marriages and relationships, high incomes, superior work performance, community involvement, robust health, and a long life."

In the success and leadership classes we have taught, we make comparisons to Johnny Appleseed, the American legend who planted apple tree seeds all over the north and southeastern United States. Every day that you invest your time, share an idea, help someone get their job done, or find ways to help someone be happier and more successful, you are planting seeds. Not all of the seeds will sprout and blossom, but many will grow into appreciation, opportunities, and even promotions. Put simply, a lot of seeds and a little patience will lead to good things. Don't forget, though: take happiness from planting the seeds. What they grow into is an added bonus.

Time

"If you ever want to be in a position to choose happiness and take control of your life, then you will need to put yourself in a position where you are choosing what you do with your time." HowtoHappiness

It will help you take control of your life if you become accountable for your time. We each have 24 hours in the day. What do you choose to do with your 24 hours?

"Don't say you don't have enough time. You have exactly the same number of hours per day that were given to Helen Keller, Pasteur, Michelangelo, Mother Teresa, Leonardo da Vinci, Thomas Jefferson, and Albert Einstein." H. Jackson Brown, Jr.

"Does't thou love life? Then do not squander time, for that is the stuff life is made of." Ben Franklin

You have 1,440 minutes every day. You get the same amount of minutes as everyone else, and you get to choose how to use those minutes. Most of us are busy and have a number of obligations. We have to go to work, get the kids to school, buy the groceries, prepare something to eat, do the laundry and the dishes, or help out with other obligations to our friends or families. (Remember that doing these things, no matter how necessary or unavoidable they seem, is a choice). Since you have chosen to do these things, how many of your 1,440 minutes do they take up? Ten hours at work plus an hour of obligations before work and an hour after work is 720 minutes. What do you do with the other 720 minutes? If you need 8 hours or 480 minutes for sleep, you have 240 remaining minutes. Can you find 5 minutes before you go to sleep or 5 minutes when you wake up? What activity can you borrow minutes from? Can you take control of some of your time at lunch? During what activities could you do more than one thing? For example, during your commute, could you work on a plan for better health, walk part of the way, or listen to a book that is interesting or fun? My commute is 45 minutes to one hour long, and I spend much of that time listening to books about happiness and success. Alternatively, I sometimes sit in silence and work through challenges, or simply try to relax.

Start by choosing what to do with one to five minutes of your day. Focus on something you want to take control of--diet, health, exercise, spirituality, career, family--whatever you feel will help you take control of your life. If possible, carve out the same time every day so you can create a habit. If you're working on your diet, take five minutes every evening to write down what you have eaten, or five minutes every morning to plan what you will eat. If you're working on exercising more, take a quick five-minute walk, or do some push-ups or sit-ups. Take the five minutes to write down what you are thankful for or to remember what went well that day. A great way to choose to spend your found five minutes is to decide how you're going to carve out another five minutes (or even an hour) and what you're going to do during that time to take control of your life. I have three kids, work with several charity organizations, and have a demanding full-time job. In an effort to write this book without giving up any of those responsibilites, I've risen at 5 am every day exclusively to write for one hour. I have to go to bed a little earlier so I get enough sleep, but I get to start out every morning with passion and energy doing something I love.

Activity – Finding the Time:

1. Keep a notepad, journal, calendar, or notes on your smartphone or tablet.

2. Write down, in 15-minute increments, everything you do for a day.

3. Review your list. Where can you steal or add time?

Activity – Assigning the Time:

1. Make a list of slots of time you currently control – you probably have to go into work at a certain time every day. That time is already scheduled and focused. But what about your lunch break. What about your commute time? Could you expand the time between leaving work and arriving home, and insert a workout several days per week? What do you do as soon as you get home? Could you get up 30 minutes earlier each day to do something that makes you feel good?

Activity – Using Your Time Wisely:

1. Write a list of things you want to take control of in your life.

2. Choose from these categories or add your own: time, health, diet, exercise, spirituality, career, being mindful, etc.

3. Pick one. It is important to start small. Don't try to change everything at once.

4. Find 5 minutes every day at the same time. Write down that time here. _____

5. Write down in one sentence exactly what you're going to do (for example, "walk in place for five minutes," "plan my day," "think about things I appreciate").

6. Put an index card or small calendar in your pocket, purse, or taped to your mirror. Every day, mark down that you took control of those five minutes. You can use hash marks or you can put checks on a calendar.

7. Reward yourself the first time you complete seven days in a row. Then again when you do three weeks in a row, and then a big reward when you go six weeks in a row.

8. Write down the date, probably six weeks from now, that you will add the next 5 or 15 minutes of time to take control of. Change that date if you have not made the first five minutes a habit. Don't move to your second choice until you have proof through measurement that the first five minutes is a habit.

Don't get discouraged or sidetracked if you happen to miss a day. Just follow up and do it the next day. Keep trying until you feel like you have control of at least five minutes every day.

Side Note: One of the excuses we often hear, is "I already have control of a lot of my time. I just like to watch TV and relax." There is nothing wrong with watching TV or other mind-numbing activities if that is what you choose to do and you feel like you are in control of your life. But consider whether you're choosing that over other areas of your life like health and exercise. Are you overdoing the pleasure and missing the happiness?

Take Control of Your Life

Chapter 9
Gratitude

"Gratitude is not only the greatest of virtues, but the parent of all the others."
Cicero

Jacob Sokol said it well in his book *12 Things Happy People do Differently*: "Express gratitude. When we appreciate what we have, what we have appreciates in value. Being grateful for the goodness that is already evident in your life will bring you a deeper sense of happiness. We can never really be happy if we can't find a way to be thankful for what we already have."

Rabbi Noah Weinberg tells a story about a young man who learned how to appreciate life at an early age:

> A young man with an unusually happy disposition once came to meet me in Jerusalem. I asked him, "What's your secret?"

> He told me, "When I was 11 years old, God gave me a gift of happiness. I was riding my bicycle when a strong gust of wind blew me onto the ground into the path of an oncoming

truck. The truck ran over me and cut off my leg.

"As I lay there bleeding, I realized that I might have to live the rest of my life without a leg. How depressing! But then I realized that being depressed won't get my leg back. So I decided right then and there not to waste my life despairing.

"When my parents arrived at the hospital, they were shocked and grieving. I told them, 'I've already adapted. Now you also have to get used to this.'

"Ever since then, I see my friends getting upset over little things: their bus came late, they got a bad grade on a test, somebody insulted them. But I just enjoy life."

At age 11, this young man attained the clarity that it is a waste of energy to focus on what you are missing, and that the key to happiness is to take pleasure in what you have.

We once had a neighbor who, due to infection, had lost both of her arms just below the elbow. Despite her disability, she was a very happy and joyful person. She had migrated to the U.S. some 20 years before and was appreciative of the life she was now able to lead. She paid her bills by walking and taking care of dogs, so she was constantly surrounded by loving animals that didn't notice or care if she was missing her arms and were excited to see her no matter what the situation. She would openly talk about her arms and how that had changed her life. But rather than being sad and angry, she was appreciative that she could still be independent and still do the things she wanted to do. Her gratitude turned her life from sad to fantastic and added joy and happiness to our lives as well.

Other research on gratitude found that participants who recorded their gratitude on a regular basis or participated in other gratitude exercises:

1. were more successful in attaining their goals

2. had more energy and were physically healthier

3. slept better

4. exercised more

5. felt more optimistic about their lives and were less stressed

6. were more alert, enthusiastic, and determined

7. were more likely to have made progress toward goals

8. were more likely to help someone else with emotional support or in solving a problem

9. had more positive moods

10. felt more connected to others, were less envious, and shared more

Gratitude doesn't eliminate your negative feelings. It provides you with more reasons to feel positive and enhances your normally positive feelings. Spending time with your friends or family is nice. But taking a few seconds to acknowledge how grateful you are to have those people enhances those feelings and brings them to the surface. When you have a flat tire or car problems, you are likely to feel frustrated or even angry. If you take a second to be grateful that you have a car, and grateful that you know someone who can help, then you will have positive feelings that provide a balance to your negative feelings.

The power of gratitude appears to be one of the most common and agreed upon themes in happiness research. The belief in its positive impact is almost universal. Gratitude is also a keystone habit, in that practicing gratitude is foundational and helpful to most of the other habits that improve happiness. Gratitude is geographically universal. Almost every culture has a practice of showing gratitude. In most cases, that includes giving thanks to a higher power or deity. Grateful people tend to find less conflict and more harmony in their relationships and interactions. They appreciate the action that was taken rather than being upset about the action that wasn't taken. Feeling grateful has been shown to help people feel more energized, alert, and enthusiastic. People who are grateful tend to be more spiritual and more agreeable. Grateful people have a higher sense of belonging. They are less stressed, less depressed, and feel like they have more social support. This encourages them to be closer to people and to build harmonious rather than fractious relationships.

The practice of being grateful forces us to find the positive things in our environment and relationships that are applicable and specific to us. It's a method of thinking positively that connects more to our feelings than to our logic. Some of the research showed that grateful people perform better specifically in areas where they practice gratitude. Sixth- and seventh-grade students who were asked to write what they were thankful for about school showed improvement in their performance at school. Gratitude also has a pay-it-forward characteristic that creates a virtuous circle. The more grateful we are, the more we want to help other people, which makes us feel better and more grateful. In turn, the people we help become more motivated to help others themselves.

Activities for Gratitude:

1.　　Spend 10 minutes counting your blessings. Don't stop writing until the 10 minutes is up. Don't stop until you have over 100 items on your list. Most of us have a lot more to be thankful for tian we realize. We take for granted the simple things in our lives, like a bed to sleep on and running water.

2.　　Every morning, think about things you are grateful for and write down three of them. Do this daily to create the habit. Longer term, you will want to vary your timing based on how you feel and what works for you. For some people, doing this exercise weekly created more happiness than doing it daily. You can find the timing that works for you.

3.　　Write a heartfelt letter of gratitude to someone important in your life and read it to him or her in person. The significant increase in happiness comes from actually reading it to them, not just in writing it.

4.　　Write thank-you notes to five people and make sure they get delivered.

5.   Find a gratitude support partner. Someone you can work with for mutual support for regularly practicing gratitude.

6.   Introduce someone to something new that you enjoy. Show a friend your hobby. Show a new co-worker around the office. Show a visitor the great things in your town.

Take Control of Your Life

Chapter 10
Mindfulness

"Yesterday is history. Tomorrow is a mystery. Today is a gift. That's why it is called the present." *Alice Morse Earle*

If today is a gift, how do we make the most of it?

One of our biggest challenges in life is focusing on what is right in front of us. Mindfulness is the ability to remove the distractions of what might happen and what did happen, and focus on what is happening right now, this second. Too often, we're either chasing the happiness that will come if all the stars align, or regretting our past mistakes and things we didn't do that we should have.

Practicing Mindfulness is one way to experience the gift of the present. Observing and appreciating what we have and what is around us today helps us find peace. Having gratitude that we have made it to this moment sets us up for a better future by giving us hope and confidence.

Mindfulness has been shown to improve immune function as well as reduce muscle tension, headache, and other forms of chronic pain. It also has longer-term impacts such as lowering blood pressure and cholesterol levels. Mindfulness has also been shown to help with stress, anxiety, and depression.

Mindfulness can help with diet and weight management. Many of us are caught up in "mindless" eating. We're too busy to pay attention to what or how much we are putting into our mouths. Research by Liesal showed that women who are mindful about eating ate fewer calories, and men who consciously focused on chewing their food at least 40 times ate 12% less than those who didn't.

Mindfulness includes being curious and open to discovering new inspirations and information in the current setting. As a society, we tend to place a high regard on our ability to multitask. The challenge is that, according to an increasing amount of research, multitasking doesn't really work. We tend to shift between multiple tasks quickly and for short periods of time. We are eliminating parts of the task in order to quickly shift in and out of it. The parts we are eliminating include focus, thoughtfulness, and appreciation. Instead of living in the moment, we attempt to live in several moments. Think of one of the most common and rude forms of multitasking: having a conversation with a person while simultaneously receiving, reading, and answering a text while they are talking. We are physically in the same space as the person and we probably get the overall idea of what they are saying, but we miss the opportunity to connect with them, to stop and really think about and feel what they are communicating. Most importantly, we're not allowing time to stop and appreciate the here and now of our lives. We are focused on the message on our phone, which is often trivial in comparison to our feelings about the person with whom we're actually conversing. As a result, we go from activity to activity throughout a day or a week, and our memories reflect not the great moments in our lives, but how busy we have been. We have missed our opportunities for happiness by attempting to do everything, rather than choosing the few things that will make us happy and productive.

Mindfulness has several levels, from being aware of nature during a walk to focused meditation of the mind, spirit, and body.

Have you ever noticed, while standing in line or waiting, that you have a strong desire to either look busy or be busy? We are almost afraid to be alone with our thoughts; waste time; or, worse yet, appear not to be productive or engaged. Next time you get this feeling, you can become productive by being mindful and appearing to do nothing. Observe the people around you and the environment. What parts of your surroundings can you appreciate? Look at the details. What can you notice that you've never seen before? Being mindful requires us to make two choices: we are intentional about our observations, and we are accepting rather than judgmental. In other words, do it on purpose and collect and savor the information from your senses rather than evaluating it as good or bad.

We can be mindful in many different situations. While eating, stop and look at the food. Observe the colors and how they interact. Observe the shapes and sizes. Smell the food and identify the different aromas. How do they smell separately and how do they blend together? Slowly take a bite, paying attention to the whole process of cutting, scooping, or biting. Think about the flavors and aromas as the food enters your mouth. What kind of textures do you notice? How do the colors, flavors, and textures reflect one another?

You can do the same thing while taking a walk. What do you see? Look closely at the grass, flowers, trees, buildings, people, and wildlife. Do you notice a bug or a butterfly you might have walked past? What are the colors and smells? How hard or soft is the ground? What shapes are the leaves on the trees?

When you are spending time with someone else, be mindful of that person and what she is communicating. What is she trying to get across? Does she need to get something off her chest? Is she sending a different message with her facial expressions and body language than what is being expressed through her voice? Is she interested and engaged, or is she distracted by something else in her life? Is she leaning in with intensity, or is she leaning back and relaxed? Is her smile genuine or forced? Look deep into her eyes. What do her eyes tell you? Take time to be thoughtful and think through what she is saying. Focus on her message by being mindful and observing the whole person. Be fully engaged with her, rather than letting your mind wander to everything else in your life or environment. If you are mindful with the people you interact with, they will seek you out and want to talk to you. People want to talk and spend time with someone they believe will listen and pay attention to them and what they are saying.

Recently, I was talking with a student from one of the local colleges where I am part of a mentoring program. We were discussing this young man's future and his biggest life challenges. This was a serious discussion that included decisions about what he would do over the next year of his life, and how that would affect his life and career over the long term. An acquaintance in a study group with him was sending a stream of texts about where and what time the study group would meet. The study group was meeting soon after our meeting ended. This young man continued to look at his phone and texts throughout the conversation. He would be in the middle of a sentence and would pause, pick up his phone, read the text, and then continue, somewhat awkwardly with his train of thought. He unwittingly had prioritized a study group for one class over decisions that would affect the rest of his life. He had chosen the urgent over the important. These discussions were intended to give him a clear path about what classes to take, what jobs to accepts, and what actions to take to reach his goals and dreams. Clear answers would have given him a roadmap of how to be productive and efficient with his time over the next 12 to 18 months. Instead, he chose to be productive and multi-task for that single hour. He traded long-term clarity and success for short-term productivity. His biggest challenge was confusion and lack of clarity on what he should be doing; yet when it came time to create that clarity, he was too busy trying to be minutely productive to work on the longer-term clear path (a likely contributor to the confusion in the first place!). If he had taken a few seconds at the beginning of the conversation and had decided to be mindful and focused, he would have accomplished significantly more than changing times and locations for a study group.

As we go through the activities in our lives, are we worried about the future, fretting and reliving the past, or focused on what we can enjoy, learn from, and appreciate right now? It comes down to what we value. Do we value the text that is planning our next interaction with someone more than we value the present moment? Is it possible that in our next interaction we will once again be looking at texts about yet another interaction and another after that? Are we so busy planning and thinking about what we need or want to do to be happy that we are not finding the happiness available right now in front of us? James Oppenheim said "the foolish man seeks happiness in the distance; the wise man grows it under his feet." Mindfulness is about looking at what is around us and under our feet, rather than missing the "now" because we are worrying about the future.

Mindlessness is the opposite of mindfulness. Ellen Langer, a leading researcher on mindfulness, likens mindlessness to being on auto-pilot: "The past determines the present; your rules and routines govern rather than just guide what you do."

"Children think not of what is past, nor what is to come, but enjoy the present time, which few of us do." Jean de La Bruyère

As children, before we become overwhelmed with the pressures of life and a need to be as productive as possible, we are naturally mindful. When we see a toy or a friend, we stop what we were doing and put our full attention on playing. We don't evaluate or worry, we just start playing. We become completely absorbed in our games and our friends. At some point we learn the concept of scarcity, and we start trying to cram as much into our days as possible. We get so focused on finding productive hours that we forget to actually "be" in those hours.

Our minds are really good at categorizing. Everything we see or are exposed to gets categorized in our brain so we can more quickly understand the world around us. At some point we start believing that since we have categorized it, we have all the information we need. Our natural curiosity wanes, and we see no need to gather more information. Since we think we know everything there is to know about the person or environment in front of us, we get bored and start looking for something more interesting. We get caught in a vicious cycle of being able to quickly categorize more and more new experiences and therefore finding fewer and fewer things to be excited about. Mindfulness is the act of stopping and discovering something more to be excited about. It requires us to realize that we really don't know everything there is to know about what we are eating, where we are walking, or even the person we are with. Reigniting our curiosity gives us more opportunities to be happy as we find ways to re-engage with the world.

Obviously, mindfulness does not dismiss entirely ideas of responsibility or planning for the future. Just as with the young man I was mentoring, time should be specifically set aside to plan for the future; and when that time arrives, we should mindfully focus our full energy on that too.

Think about work and vacation. How many people plan and think about their vacations while they are at work, then go on the vacations and think about work? Use mindfulness to think about work when you're at work and to be on vacation when you're on vacation. Focus on enjoying your current activity. Make time to plan the next activity.

Many of the challenges of finding happiness stem from the problem of comparison. We find people and things we believe are better, and we compare our life to that life. Because of what we choose as our point of comparison, we find ourselves lacking and focus on attaining some holy grail in the future or berate ourselves for the mistakes we made in our past.

"Change the way you see things, and the things you see will start to change" Wayne Dyer

If we focus our point of comparison on growth in ourselves and on what we have instead of what we don't have, we can truly start to appreciate the gift of the present. Are you happy to have a family member or friend? You could be completely alone in the world. Are you happy to have enough money to buy food? You could be going hungry every day. Are you happy to see the green trees and blue sky? They are beautiful parts of nature and should be appreciated because they may not always be within our sight. There can be pleasure in getting up every morning and preparing for a job. There can even be pleasure in getting up every morning and preparing to look for a job. When you eat your breakfast, what aromas, tastes, and sensations do you experience? Take a moment to appreciate what is here and now. It is truly a gift only you are able to experience in that moment.

As a society, we tend to group with people who are similar to us. We typically live and spend time with people who have the same nationality, similar income levels, similar values, similar education levels, similar interests, etc. When we start comparing ourselves to others, we look to the best in our comparison group. We compare ourselves to people who represent our aspirations; and because we tend only to see the aspirational parts of those people while ignoring the harsh or undiscovered realities, we never seem to measure up. We then begin focusing on the future and how we are going to work harder and do more to be prettier, or richer, or drive a nicer car. When we feel we have reached that level, we stop and re-compare, only to find that there is yet another level to chase.

One solution is to expand from a mindset of comparison to a habit of mindfulness and gratitude. What do we have right now that we can appreciate? There are millions of people around the world who are not as well off as we are. We can focus on how our car is not as new or nice as our neighbor's, or we can look at how many people don't have cars to drive to work at all. Our houses are not big enough or close enough to work, but we do have houses when millions don't. How about having running water and bathrooms? Over three billion people--*more than 2/5 of the world's population--*do not have running water and bathrooms in their homes. Are you familiar with the phrase "Stop and smell the roses"? What is your commute like? Are you focused on how long it is, how boring it is, how much traffic there is, or how many people there are? Could you pause and appreciate the scenery along the way--the ponds, the architecture, the trees, the flowers? How about the people? There are thousands of interesting people getting off and on buses and trains every day. What makes them happy? What could you do to make them smile? How beautiful is the sky today? How refreshing is the rain? How exciting are the thunder and lightning?

In the next section, called Positive Relationships, we'll discuss the importance of your family and friends. But in relation to mindfulness, are your kids driving you crazy because they are slow to get going in the morning, or they can't find their shoes, or they need help getting their breakfast? Pause for a short second and imagine if you didn't have them there. Would you miss those hugs, those sleepy looks in the morning, those excited days when they had met a new friend or found a subject or teacher that they connected with? Be mindful of and grateful for what you have. No matter what it's like, there are things we can pay attention to and appreciate in our lives.

> "*Sometimes we develop grand concepts of what happiness might look like for us; but if we pay attention, we can see that there are little symbols of happiness in every breath that we take.*" — His Holiness Gyalwang Karmapa

Mindfulness is about taking a moment to experience and appreciate all the wonderful things in and around your life. You can't wait to be happy in the future, because by definition the future never comes. To be happy, you have to find ways to be happy <u>right now</u>. Practicing mindfulness will help you focus more on being happy today, enjoying the "present."

Connecting Mindfulness

In a previous chapter we discussed Pleasure vs. Happiness and knowing when pleasure was taking away from rather than adding to our happiness.

Mindfulness is a great tool to help us be aware of when that is occurring. If we think about what we're doing and why we're doing it, we can monitor our behaviors and make adjustments. For example, Brene Brown in *Daring Greatly* gives an example of eating chocolate. Are we savoring the taste and texture of the chocolate and really enjoying the sensations, or are we stuffing handfuls of chocolate in our mouths in an attempt to forget about some negative event or thought in our lives? We can use mindfulness as a tool to determine when we are savoring and should continue our activities, and when we are numbing and should probably stop and attempt to deal with our current feelings and challenges.

In a later chapter we will discuss habits and activities you can do every day to be happier and more successful. Mindfulness is one tool that helps create those daily habits. Being aware of what you are doing and thinking is a key to being able to make positive changes.

Being mindful also helps lead to Flow, a state of mind in which we're so focused on what we're doing in the present that we lose track of time and temporarily forget about the myriad other challenges going on in our lives.

Activities for Mindfulness:

1. Be present in the moment – when eating, commuting, etc.

2. Be present in the moment with a person – pay full attention to him or her.

3. Stop multitasking.

4. Meditate – focus on your breathing. Count slowly to eight while breathing in, hold for an eight count and then exhale for an eight count. Focus completely on the breath coming in and out of your body.

5. Designate one meal a day — or even one a week — during which you take the time to notice the aroma, flavor, and texture of what you're eating.

6. Curl up in a favorite chair at some point after you return home from work and spend at least a half-hour reading a book purely for pleasure.

7. Take the time to really listen to someone you love — to give that person the space to speak without interruption, for as long as it takes.

8. Choose a place that interests you – it could be in the city or the country – and spend a couple of hours just exploring it without any specific end in mind.

9. Buy a journal; and before you go to bed, take a few minutes to reflect on what you feel grateful for that day, and what went right.

3rd Concept

Positive Relationships

Chapter 11
Why Relationships are Important

". . . relationships with other humans are both the foundation and the theme of the human condition: we are born into relationships, we live our lives in relationships with others, and when we die, the effects of our relationships survive in the lives of the living, reverberating throughout the tissue of their relationships" Berscheid

How can you be healthier, happier, more successful, and live longer? The answer is positive relationships. Positive relationships form a foundation for happiness and success. We all have relationships we have chosen (our friends), relationships we have inherited (our family), and relationships that are a result of our circumstances (colleagues and classmates). How we navigate and participate within these relationships has a significant impact on our happiness as well as our health, longevity, and success. Creating positive relationships will make us happier, while surrendering to and becoming victims of negative relationships and the related drama will be an obstacle to our happiness. One of the most robust findings in the happiness research is that happy people have better social relationships.

Whelan and Zelenski conducted research in which they showed participants film clips that were positive, neutral, or negative. They wanted to determine if the film clip would change the participants' level of happiness, and if that change would result in more or less social interest. They were able to confirm that by showing participants the positive film clips and making them happier, the participants were also more interested in social contact. Positive relationships help people become happier, and happier people are more likely to be in positive relationships.

We all have a need to belong and to find positive relationships that help satisfy that need. The word positive refers to whether the relationship involves caring and concern. Unpleasant or unsatisfying interactions result in a negative relationship. Delongis's research showed that it is not just having a relationship, but having a positive relationship that creates the benefits of health and well-being.

Hang out with people, even to do little things. Interactions that may seem inconsequential, like making small talk or just enjoying each other's company, are important to a relationship. Making small talk about trivial things helps people feel happier and healthier. But talking on the phone is not enough. Seeing each other in person is more effective than just talking on the phone, which has ramifications because of today's technology. Facebook, texting, and online video chats are better than no contact, but nothing is better than spending time in person. Face-to-face contact and doing even mundane things together can solidify a positive relationship.

Choose happy friends. Hanging out with happy friends instead of sad friends makes us happier. Each happy friend increases our probability of being happy by 9%, while each unhappy friend makes our probability of being happy decrease by 7%. Geographic distance is a proxy for amount of interaction. When a friend who lives 1 mile away is happy, it increases our probability of being happy by 25%. A happy sibling who lives less than a mile away increases our probability for happiness by 14%. (Apparently we often like our friends better than our siblings.) Happy next door neighbors also increase our probability of happiness.

In a survey of 800 college alumni, students who had a preference for close friends and a positive marriage were happier than those who showed a preference for high income and success at work. Active pursuits with other people or going out and working with a charity make us happier than working long hours so we can earn more money to buy more stuff. Research also shows that happy people in positive relationships were much less likely to become criminals.

Relationships are connected to some of our strongest emotions. When the relationships are positive, we feel happiness, elation, contentment, and calm. When relationships are negative or non-existent we feel anxiety, depression, grief, jealousy, and loneliness. Close relationships with our friends and family help us build our self-worth and self-image. They provide support in times when we struggle, unconditional love, and a reason for doing many of the things we do, which all help give our lives meaning. They also provide us with a sense of identity and belonging. Knowing we are part of something bigger in life helps us be happier.

Remember the last time you had a peak experience. A time when you laughed and laughed or got really excited or felt like everything was right with the world. More than likely those times all involved other people and positive relationships with those people. People and relationships are the source of our greatest joys, as well as our most gut-wrenching traumas.

Happier people spend time with their friends and family. They are more likely to have a circle of friends, a romantic partner, and companions for other activities in their lives. They are also more likely to have a strong, long-lasting marriage. As a result, they receive emotional and other forms of support from friends, co-workers, and other people in their lives on a regular basis.

Overwhelmingly, researchers draw similar conclusions about the link between happiness and positive relationships:

> *"Relationships constitute the single most important factor responsible for the survival of homo sapiens"* – Berscheid

> *"Like food and air, we seem to need social relationships to thrive."* – Ed Diener, Robert Biswas-Diener

"The strongest predictor of happiness is not money, or external recognition through success or fame; it's having meaningful social relationships." June Gruber, Yale University

"...70 years of evidence that our relationships with other people matter, and matter more than anything else in the world." George Vaillant

"The number one predictor of happiness is the time we spend with people we care about and who care about us. The most important source of happiness may be the person sitting next to you. Appreciate them; savor the time you spend together." Tal Ben-Shahar

Your happiness affects other people. Christakis and Fowler, in their book *Connected*, found that you influence your friend's happiness by about 15% and you can influence your friend's friend's happiness by as much as 10%. They illustrated happiness connections with network maps that show happiness groups. The colors radiate outward, with the least happy people being on the fringes of the network and the happiest people forming the center of the network. So nurturing positive relationships is not just good for you; it's good for those around you, and even for those around them.

"Friendship redoubleth joys, and cutteth griefs in half." Francois Bacon

People with close friends are happier. Relationships make us happiest when we feel closely connected. Having a lot of friends is important. But having a few close friends we can comfortably share our secrets, small successes, and failures with is a key to being happier. It is not the quantity of friends, but the quality. Having people with whom we can discuss our daily thoughts about what is going on in our lives is what makes the difference. Having the most friends on Facebook is not a good happiness goal. Having a few friends with whom we can share ourselves and be authentic with is much more effective.

We all need our time alone, a break from the world. But the research shows we are happiest when we are with other people. Research on introverts and extroverts found that even introverts who have a natural tendency to be around people less often are still happier when they are with someone they like.

George Vaillant, a Professor of Psychiatry at Harvard Medical School, titled his 2009 article "Yes, I Stand by My Words, 'Happiness Equals Love — Full Stop.'" For 40 years, Vaillant, has been leading a 70-year Harvard project called The Study of Adult Development. He summarized his findings this way: "The only thing that really matters in life are your relationships to other people… It was the capacity for intimate relationships that predicted flourishing in all aspects of these men's lives."

The Harvard study followed and measured various aspects of men's lives beginning, when they were college students in 1940 and through their lives into their 80s.

The results of his study were that men with indicators for strong positive relationships were healthier and made 60% to 140% higher incomes by age 80.

Other findings include the warmth of relationships men had in childhood were predictors of whether they were more likely to become officers or privates during the war. Even better news: the men could change their destiny if they had as few as one loving relative, mentor, or friend somewhere in their lifetime. The men who were less emotionally connected earlier in life could change and adjust to become happier and more successful later in life. Changes could take place as late as their 70s or 80s. In 2009, only 12% of the men with negative relationships are still alive, while 33% of the men with positive relationships are still living.

Other research has shown that social relationships do not guarantee happiness, but that social relationships are necessary for happiness. The happiest participants in the research had more and better relationships and spent less time alone than the average participant. The characteristic that was most consistent in the happiest participants was their commitment to their relationships with friends and family. They made time to be with the people they were closest to.

It is natural for us to doubt ourselves, have fear, and be insecure about our plans and actions. Being in a positive relationship is an antidote for those feelings. Other people can confirm we are on the right track, support our dreams, and help us get through those tough times when we really doubt ourselves. They can offset our negative moods and give us something different to think about instead of spending all our time ruminating over our past mistakes.

Another positive aspect of relationships is providing us a group to identify with. We know more and feel better about who we are when we can identify with other people who have similar beliefs and behaviors. I have two kids in high school and was speaking with one of the school's more experienced teachers. His belief was that every student needed to belong to at least one organization while in high school. We are lucky to have more than 50 school organizations at our local high school, which range from things as common as sports to smaller groups like the chess club. Many are formed and run by the students. The important point this teacher was making was that belonging to some group was a key to surviving and flourishing in high school, because it gave the kids an identity that helped them navigate the ups and downs of their teenage years. Those kids that did not choose to become involved were often isolated and did not have the social support structures that acted as a safety net when they faced the inevitable disappointments of those tough high school years, when they were transitioning from teenagers to young adults. They were less likely to drop out of school or get caught up in drugs and alcohol if they were connected with and could identify with at least one group.

Happiness and Marriage
Relationships are a virtuous circle. The more you have, the better you feel, and the better you feel, the better you are at cultivating relationships. Our romantic relationships are often the most impactful to our happiness. Happier people are more likely to get married. Married people are more likely to be happy. People in positive marriages are on average happier than people who are single. People who are divorced are less happy than married or single people, and people in negative marriages are the least happy of

everyone. So marrying the right person and then working to keep that relationship positive is very important.

Being happier makes you more attractive to other people. Research has shown, unsurprisingly, that people would rather be with someone who is happy than someone who is self-focused, irritable, and withdrawn; so happy people probably more often tend to get married. Also, being committed in a marriage means you have to learn to get along. It gives you someone to share your fears, failures, and successes with. Marriage is daily, rather than weekly, and provides a lot of opportunities for small happiness experiences.

Being married adds up to 10 points to the average happiness score. While marriage doesn't guarantee happiness, happier people tend to get married and tend to be more satisfied with their spouse and marriage. The least happy people are in negative relationships or are divorced. Divorce is strongly correlated with being less happy. To be clear, being divorced does not guarantee you will be unhappy. Some people are much happier after they are divorced and separated from negative relationships. But the statistics show that, on average, divorced people are less happy.

Once a marriage ends through death or divorce, people are much less happy. Research indicates it may take as long as five to seven years to recover after the death of a spouse.

For most people, marriage creates an environment conducive to sharing, intimacy, and the bond of connectedness that supports happiness. It matters who you are married to, what you are giving to the relationship, and what you are focused on getting out of the relationship. Those people who find joy in giving to and appreciating their spouse are happier than those who focus on what they need and are not getting. As with other aspects of happiness, it is the giving that provides the lift much more than the getting. If your spouse enjoys doing some little thing for you, acknowledge his or her gift and show appreciation. Your appreciation will support your spouse's happiness.

Another great point is that being single in no way indicates you will be unhappy, or even lonely. Many single people have close, intimate, non-sexual relationships. They have close friends they can share their ups and downs with and with whom they feel comfortable sharing intimate details.

Relationships are about giving. Once you are focused on giving and not receiving, it becomes much easier to cultivate great relationships.

Our Happiness Impacts our Children

The children of happy parents are happier throughout their lives, and happiness in children was related to being able to keep jobs, lower rates of suicide, and lower levels of substance abuse as long as 20 years later.

Unfortunately, negative relationships also have serious negative impacts for our children. The results of children being around adults in negative relationships can include depression, withdrawal, poor social competence, health problems, poor academic performance, and overall bad behavior. Children exposed to parents with negative relationships have more trouble expressing and controlling their emotions and aggression. They also have a harder time focusing. When these kids grow up, they report more stress and less satisfaction with life and their families. Their bodies even create more stress hormones than children exposed to positive relationships.

Children of parents with positive relationships are better socially, better in school, and have fewer behavioral problems.

The best possible scenarios for the children are parents who stay married in a positive relationship, or who change a negative relationship in a marriage to a positive relationship. But the research also shows it is better for the children if the parents get divorced instead of staying in a negative relationship.

Habits and Relationships

One of the best known researchers on marriage and romantic relationships is John Gottman from the University of Washington. Using analysis techniques he has honed over several decades, he has developed the ability to determine the health of a relationship and its potential future within the first five minutes of observing the interactions of a couple. His methods have resulted in an ability to predict which couples will get divorced with better than 90% accuracy.

Most people are not aware of the habits and patterns they have formed in their relationships. Gottman recommends habits we can practice or avoid in order to create and maintain positive relationships.

Fight the negative habits.

1. <u>Don't criticize</u> or point out flaws in your partner's character or personality.

2. <u>Try not to be defensive</u>. Listen and consider the meaning of what your spouse is saying rather than potentially hurtful words he or she is using. Avoid denying responsibility, blaming someone or something else, whining, or being the victim. Negative statements that begin with "You always…" and "You never…" are indicators of challenges if the accompanying tone of voice is also negative.

3. <u>Don't use contempt or disgust</u> – talking down to your spouse as if you are superior. Don't insult, use sarcasm, mock the other person, show disapproval, judgment, or hostile humor, or communicate that the other person is incompetent. The amount of disgust shown on a partner's face can be used to predict the health of the relationship and the amount of time a couple will be separated.

4. <u>Stonewalling</u> – withdrawing emotionally. Don't exit the room or the conversation. Don't start watching TV, looking at your phone, or reading a book during the middle of a serious conversation.

5. <u>Whining</u> – statements that blame the other person and make you the victim as if you did not have any control. Don't complain when you can make a request.

Create good habits that nurture positive relationships:

1. Use "we" instead of "I" to show you are in this together and to help reduce the perception of blame.

2. Have a sense of humor – be able to laugh at yourself. Insert humor into tense situations to hint to your partner that, no matter what, you still care about him or her.

3. Start every conversation with something positive rather than jumping into negative statements.

4. Listen to and support each other's hopes and dreams. Our hopes and dreams give us a true sense of purpose; and at the same time, they are areas of great sensitivity and low confidence. Knowing our hopes and dreams are honored and respected gives us renewed strength and makes the relationship extraordinarily valuable. Not supporting the other person's hopes and dreams can lead to a slow death of the relationship as the other person slowly builds the confidence to pursue his or her dreams and leave the non-supporting partner behind.

5. Start discussions by clarifying what you do agree with before jumping into what you don't agree with.

6. Say small positive things often: Thank you, I love you, I respect you, I like you.

When relationships are happy, people are constantly finding and thinking about what is good about them. When relationships are negative, people do just the opposite: they constantly identify and review the negative aspects.

Conflict is a normal part of a relationship. We all grow and learn. We find different interests and discover new areas of excitement. As our lives change, we need to confront and address the issues created by two people changing in different ways. It is not the number or emotionality of the fights that is an indicator of a negative relationship as much as the balance of positivity to negativity and whether the fights are constantly about the core issues and sensitive areas of the relationship.

Many couples fight about money. It turns out that the amount of money is not what causes the fights; it is each person's perception of whether they have enough money. So more money does not stop the fighting, while gaining an understanding on how each party judges how much money is enough does.

Indicators of a positive relationship include how two people talk about how their day went, or how they try to have an enjoyable conversation. People in positive relationships celebrate the small wins with their partners.

Activity:

1. Create rituals that give you the opportunity to connect

   a. Dinner with the family

   b. Annual vacations

   c. Nightly walks

   d. Activities related to common interests: exercise, diet, gardening, bowling, saving money for a big purchase

2. Talk a lot

   a. Talk about things you appreciate about the other person

   b. Talk about small things the person is going to be doing each day

   c. Share and discuss the positive aspects of experiences

My wonderful wife and I have been married for 25 years and we have 3 great kids. It has taken a lot of time to learn how to make the marriage work. One of our rituals is walking the dog every night. It gives us the opportunity to vent and get out the frustrations of the day. It also gives us the opportunity to talk about the little things that are going on in our lives. I am not much of a talker, so it gives me the opportunity to open up on a regular basis. Also, the short time away from the kids gives us the opportunity to actually complete sentences and thoughts without being interrupted by kids who need help with homework, shirts for soccer practice, school paperwork signed, permission to watch TV or play on the Wii, or directions on how to fix their newest kitchen concoction.

Positive Relationships Make You Healthier

Research shows that social relationships are an independent predictor of health. Positive relationships improve our immune system, while negative relationships make it weaker.

Cohen and Wills reviewed a wide expanse of research and concluded this: "Numerous studies indicate that people with spouses, friends, and family members who provide psychological and material resources are in better health than those with fewer supportive social contacts… Social support is a causal contributor to well-being."

Additional research indicates that relationships actually alter the cardiovascular, endocrine, and immune systems, contributing to better health and longevity. More optimistic cancer patients can be less stressed, less fatigued, and have less disruption of their normal life because of their willingness to reach out socially. Several other studies have confirmed that cancer patients with strong relationships, both personally and in support groups, live 50% longer on average. The strength and happiness that come from positive relationships keeps them going.

Positive Relationships Help You Stay Smarter

"Frequent social activity may help to prevent or delay cognitive decline in old age." Bryan James, PhD.

Visiting friends, attending parties, and going to church will help keep your brain healthy. Bryan James and his team tested seniors over a five-year period and found that those who spent more time in social activities reduced their rate of cognitive decline by 47%. Social activity included playing bingo, trips with friends, volunteer activities, visiting relatives or friends, participating in groups or organizations, and going to church.

Positive Relationships Help You Live Longer

A nine-year study in California found that people with four types of relationships--marriage, friendships, church relationships, and informal groups--lived longer than those who did not have those strong relationship ties. Marriage and friendship were the strongest predictors. The strength of prediction increased with age.

The Evolution of Heroes

> *"It is within relationships with others that most people find meaning and purpose in their lives; that they typically experience the positive emotions of love, joy, happiness, and contentment; and that they successfully overcome the physical and psychological challenges to well-being and survival all humans encounter. "*   Berscheid

In order to survive, humans had to form social groups to become more effective at hunting and gathering food, and to protect against other more dangerous individuals or groups. As a result, people who were best at forming social bonds were more likely to survive and more likely to pass down those genes to their offspring. This leads many researchers to believe that over time we have evolved to be more social, and to be happier when we are connected to other people. We are also physically healthier when we have positive relationships. We recover from disease faster and have lower blood pressure. We are biologically wired to feel good when we meet new people and to feel bad when our relationships don't work out.

It is instinctual for people to want to belong to a social group. Being part of a social group meant you had a better chance of survival because you had access to and shared responsibilities for food, shelter, and protection from enemies. Our ancestors found that it was easier to care for and protect children in groups, that hunting with three or four people was more successful than hunting alone, and that banding together made it easier to fight off enemies.

Our brains are wired to be social. We use the pre-frontal cortex of our brain to simulate social situations and the impacts of our actions and decisions. For survival, we need to know what is going to keep the people in our tribe happy and functioning effectively.

It is common for scientists to talk about an instinct for self-preservation. New research and analysis is showing that we really have an instinct for group preservation. We survived and thrived as a species because we were able to work cooperatively to gather food, grow food, and hunt food.

There was some recognition of the importance of social relationships that caused the hunter to risk his life to kill food, yet bring it back to share with his family or tribe. A social group would be much more successful at working together to protect themselves from overly aggressive individuals who were only interested in self-preservation. Humans didn't survive and evolve as individuals. They survived and evolved initially as small family groups, then as small tribes, and eventually as larger communities.

Research shows that people will form social relationships without economic or other motives. We are simply internally driven to form positive relationships that provide regular social contact and a feeling of connectedness. As a result, much of our thinking has evolved around how we become part of or remain part of a social group. We interpret events, actions, and communications based on their impacts on our belonging to the group. We also form many of our responses with the reaction of our social group in mind.

If we evolved to be social, why would we choose loneliness?

"I can tell you without a doubt that virtually everyone I see comes to me because of some deficiency of human contact. Indeed, I am increasingly sought out because people feel lonely, isolated, or confused at work. They feel cut off." Hallowell

People withdraw and retreat into isolation to protect themselves. In the modern era, it is to protect themselves from negative emotions and feelings, but early on it was to protect themselves from physical dangers in the unknown world. Since they didn't know if other people were going to take their food and resources or physically harm them, they had to remain distant, guarded, and vigilant for signs of danger. This withdrawal was accompanied by a host of negative emotions that supported their survival instincts. Once they found a group where they were safe and felt comfortable, their instincts and their supporting emotions switched gears, and they became more positive and open. Positive emotions and happiness are a reflection of a more open and social outlook. There is more trust, more venturing out to meet new people, and more comfort with characteristics that we initially thought indicated potential dangers.

Positive relationships have many benefits, one of which is helping us avoid loneliness and its related negative consequences. Instinctually, loneliness is a sign of a harsh or dangerous environment. So loneliness automatically triggers stress levels related to increased vigilance for threat and heightened feelings of vulnerability. Loneliness interferes with our sleep and has been shown to increase blood pressure. It increases the risk of heart attack and stroke, and impairs kidney function. Loneliness creates a downward spiral. When we are lonely our instincts compel us to find a positive relationship, because it will be safer. So we have a need as well as a desire to find a positive connection. But we also worry about being rejected, not being good enough, and not being able to handle the disappointment of not making that connection. So we don't want be lonely, but our self-doubt prevents us from taking the risks to initiate or reignite those relations we not only crave but physically need. As humans, we need relationships because they make us feel safer and give us the opportunity to let our guard down and reduce our stress levels. It is important for our happiness and our health that we push through our social fears and self-doubt to build positive connections to other people.

Deci and Ryan developed a theory of human motivation called the Self Determination Theory, or SDT for short. They determined that well-being results when a person's needs for autonomy, competence, and relatedness are met. Relatedness is the feeling of being connected to other people in a positive manner. Feeling connected helps motivate us to do more in our lives. For example, children are more likely to venture out and explore if they feel a strong connection to their parents. Relatedness helps us feel more secure to move outside of our comfort zone. The research showed that children were more intrinsically motivated when their teachers were warm and caring and paid attention to their work.

Relatedness also helped the evolutionary process by providing a reason to pass knowledge down from one generation to the next. Feeling connected to and caring about their tribe members would have motivated them to pass down any information that would help them survive and flourish.

One of the most reasonable arguments about social or group preservation vs. self-preservation is a parent's reaction in the face of a threat to his or her family; the automatic, unflinching reaction would be to sacrifice his or her life to save the family. Even the smallest social ties lead people that are nearly strangers to risk their own lives to save others. As stories come in about a recent tornado, we hear about teachers who thought nothing of using their bodies to protect their students from falling debris. The stories are inspirational; but everyone wants to believe that is, of course, what they would do and how they would react. My wife was telling me about the daydreams of one of my sons, which included common thoughts that we have all had about what we would do in a life-and-death situation. We almost always imagine ourselves rising to the occasion and risking our own lives to save others. Positive daydreams never include us slinking away and leaving other people to face certain death. We want to be heroes; we want to do what feels right for the group.

As I am writing this book, we have had a series of weather-related tragedies, acts of terrorism, and horrific accidents. Everyone I speak with has an itch to help. They have some unknown force that makes them want to help other people in need. It brings people together and reinforces the community. It also brings tremendous relief and satisfaction when people can find a way to help, even if it is something as small as donating a few dollars or bringing in a few canned goods. It is in our nature to help other people survive, and if there are even the smallest ties to family or community, we will put their survival ahead of our own.

Positive Relationships

Chapter 12
Nurturing Positive Relationships

Nurture close relationships. Spend time with people who want to "celebrate when you were born, care about you as you live, and miss you when you are not around."

Life and relationships are made up of small moments and fleeting opportunities. John Gottman, considered one of the foremost researchers on relationships, tells a story about a time when he was walking by his wife and he saw her looking into the mirror sadly. He knew he had two choices: he could keep going and go read a book that he was very interested in, or he could stop and listen to a story he wasn't sure he wanted to hear. Understanding that relationships are based on the trust that is built during these tiny moments, he stopped and listened and connected with his wife.

To nurture positive relationships, we can take advantage of those small moments and fleeting opportunities. We should build trust when we can. Brene Brown, in her book *Daring Greatly*, used the analogy of marbles in a marble jar. Each time we take a moment to connect, we are putting marbles in a marble jar. The marbles represent the good will we may need later when our actions are less than positive and we need forgiveness and understanding from our partner or friends. It is like our positive relationship savings account. We are saving for later when the relationship will need the trust and forgiveness that we have built up over time.

Find and Build

Many people are focused on finding the right romantic partner, rather than nurturing the right relationship. The assumption is that if you find the right person, then you can just be yourself and you will live happily ever after. Finding the right partner is a very important beginning, but it is only a beginning. It must be followed up with a commitment to doing a lot of little things on a regular basis to maintain and improve the relationship. Finding opportunities to feel and show appreciation and gratitude, sharing successes and failures, having a sense of humor, working as a team, bringing positive energy to conversations, and regularly saying the small things like "I love you" and "I respect you" all help maintain those positive relationships over time. Positive relationships require effort and commitment. Much of that comes naturally because of our love for the other person; but at some point as the bloom on the rose fades, a conscious effort is required to build and sustain what can become one of your most important sources of happiness.

Activity: Make a list of the relationships you would like to nurture

Name	Relationship

Gratitude

People who practice gratitude are more empathetic and are able to see things from another person's point of view. Others see people who practice gratitude as more helpful and generous. Gratitude for what you have reduces your need to accumulate "stuff" and therefore results in less judgment and jealousy about other people and what they have, which means less friction in relationships.

Feeling gratitude toward a person improves your relationship with them. Gratitude is a habit you can form that will help improve your relationships. To make a relationship more positive, seek out aspects and opportunities where you can show gratitude. Make a list of the things about that person that you are grateful for.

This will help bring to the surface all the small ways someone else has supported us. Spend lots of energy and effort communicating your gratitude to that person. Do it often. Every day, share and be specific about why you appreciate them. Don't expect any reaction in response. Embrace whatever reaction they have. New behaviors create discomfort at first, but eventually they settle in. Be sincere and push through the challenge of "it feels awkward" or "it's too much." Once they realize you are sincere, they will relax and begin to accept, if not look forward to, your expressions of gratitude. (See the **earlier chapter on gratitude** for more information and exercises.)

Activity

1. Write short notes of gratitude to your partner or spouse and leave them in strategic places on a daily basis. Start with at least seven--one a day for a week's worth of gratitude.

2. Write a heartfelt letter of gratitude to someone important in your life and read it to them in person. The significant increase in happiness comes from actually reading it to them, not just in writing it.

3. Write down three things you are grateful for. Find something to be thankful for every day.

More Positive Than Negative

We often take for granted that our partners or friends know we love them. We have said it hundreds of times and we show it through the many things we do with and for them. But they still need to hear it said out loud and often. Relationships require constant confirmation that things are going well. We tend to get into a habit of assuming the good and talking about the bad. "Of course he knows I love him. That is why I married him. We need to talk about why he doesn't open up to me." We think about and appreciate the unique and wonderful traits about the other person, but we don't always give voice to those thoughts. So even though we are thinking them and they are a part of our internal conversation, our significant other doesn't get to hear them. They only hear the part we have time (or decide to make time) to talk about, which can often be the problems or challenges rather than the things we are grateful for.

Research on several different levels has shown that relationships need more positive input than negative input. It is what is called your "Positivity Ratio." John Gottman found that personal relationships need at least five positive comments, actions, or statements for every one negative comment. The real challenge is that our habits are usually to voice the negative and assume the positive. We love and appreciate the other person, and we assume they know it. It is not bothering us, so we don't feel the need to make sure we express those positive feelings. On the other hand, we seem to need to express the negative feelings. We need to get them out, hash them out, or somehow expel them from our mind. So once we get comfortable in a relationship, we tend to speak the negative and assume the positive.

By consciously focusing on the positivity ratios, we realize that we have to work to get to a five to one. We can rebuild the habits of positivity that will make our relationships stronger. I have a 17-year-old son; and his job, car, messy room, homework, and interactions with his brother and sister give me a lot of opportunities to point out areas for improvement and future success. Since the number of conversations we have is limited by our busy schedules, our interactions can become dominated by my giving him direction on areas where he can get better, rather than my sharing how proud I am of what he has accomplished. It is hard to maintain the five to one or better positivity ratio. But reading about Gottman and Frederickson has helped me make a conscious effort to spend more time on the good things; which means I sometimes let the areas for improvement slide for a while, or at least find examples of when he did it right, rather than finding when he wasn't quite at the top of his game.

Activity

1. Give more positive feedback than negative feedback. For one day, use an index card or your Notes App on your smartphone and add a little tick mark every time you say something positive about the other person in your relationship. Count how often you tell them you appreciate them, or they dress well, or you really value their advice. Then make a tick mark every time you discuss something negative with them. Try to add five more positives every time you add a negative. It is surprisingly difficult, yet unbelievably important. NOTE: This is something we give to someone else. Expecting our friend or partner to do the same is unfair and will lead to disappointment. (See the 100/0 Principle below for further explanation.)

Thinking our way to Positive Relationships

Positive thinking can help make relationships stronger. Approaching a relationship as if everything is positive and the other person believes in you and supports you helps you take actions that encourage positive results, rather than actions that put the other person on the defensive. Positive thinking also provides you with more perseverance and the ability to get through the rough times, rather than give up.

Diener and Biswas-Diener, in their book *Happiness*, discussed how thinking positively about a past event actually changes your memories of that event and makes you happier. Thinking back and focusing on the best parts of an experience enables you to enjoy that experience again today and remember it even more fondly in the future. This is especially true of relationships. Thinking positively about all the great times and experiences you have had together actually shapes your memories to be happier and more positive. You are much more likely to stay in a relationship with lots of happy memories.

We have the power to make people great just by how we think about them. All people are human beings. They all have problems and flaws. They all have good points. It is what we focus on that makes the difference. We can spend our time listing their mistakes, or we can think about the things we love and appreciate about them. Most of us are reasonably good people that sometimes make bad decisions. We all know we are not perfect, so it is unfair to expect others to be perfect and spend our time focused on those imperfections.

Another part of the problem is not loving or appreciating ourselves. We know all our flaws. We see those same flaws in other people; and because we hate them in ourselves, we judge and hate them in others.

There are a lot of bad behaviors, and I'm not saying that we have to accept those bad behaviors. We should hold people accountable. We should spend less time with people who consistently exhibit bad behaviors. But we can also feel sad for them, rather than judging them as a bad person. Most people we would categorize as bad are just sad, unhappy, or angry people who need love but don't know how to find it in themselves or in others.

People are what we make them. No one is perfect. Why are the people we love so great when we first meet them, but seem not so great later on in the relationship? Do they change? Not necessarily. It's just that we tend to create a "halo effect." When we like someone, we notice all of their good points. When we don't like them, we notice and focus on all their negative points. We create how wonderful people are in our own minds. We retain the information that supports our judgments and makes us feel "right," and reject the information that disproves our judgments and makes us feel "wrong." Our friends and family members also tend to respond to our expectations. If we have low, unhappy expectations, they tend to live down to them. If we have high, positive expectations, they work to meet those. The power to choose how great the people around us are is a fantastic power. A little positive thinking, and you can make people great!

Addressing Our Anger

We are often angry with other people for various things they have done. What we can realize is that the anger is more related to what is going on with us than related to the other people. Pretending the emotion does not exist is not productive. It is important to admit we feel anger and to identify it as anger. Once we feel and identify it, we can manage it. The existence of the anger doesn't mean we have to act on it and lash out at other people. Instead, we should explore what made us feel that way and why. What was the trigger? What did the other person do that bothered us? Once we can understand the origin of our feelings, we can discuss them patiently with other people and improve our relationships through those discussions, rather than ruining them by lashing out in anger.

Show respect, honor, empathy, kindness, and love, even during a fight. It is okay to feel the anger. It is not okay to make your friend or partner feel demeaned, disrespected, or belittled because of how you feel. It is common to want the people closest to us to feel our pain and to sometimes want them to pay for making us feel that way. But in the long run, making them feel worse is not going to make us feel better. It just hurts our ability to connect and be comforted by that person. It is easy to read and logically understand these concepts, but in the "heat of the battle" you forget everything but the pain and anger. Somewhere in the back of your head you have to listen to that little voice that will tell you, "This is how I feel, but I choose how I will act. I can choose to love them or hate them, but what I need most now is their love." You can explain to them what type of behavior you will accept and what type you will not accept, but you don't have to make them feel like less of a person because of your pain. An Alcoholics Anonymous saying captures the message: "Anger (or hatred) is like swallowing poison and expecting the other person to die."

Close your eyes and imagine you could feel better about all of your bad relationships. Imagine you could stop being angry and upset and could get past whatever event or memory is preventing you from getting along with that person. The good news is you can. You choose to be angry and upset. You choose to let that past wrong interfere with your relationship. You decide that what they have done is so horrendous that you have to keep them out of your life for whatever amount of time. So make a different decision. As hard as it may seem, forgive them. Understand that whatever they did was an insult, inappropriate, and unforgiveable; but your relationship with them is more important.

Practice Forgiveness

A skill helpful for creating positive relationships is learning forgiveness. Being able to forgive ourselves and others frees us from the burden of maintaining negative emotions. It also releases all parties from being victims. By forgiving ourselves we can stop being victims of our own overly critical judgments, and by forgiving others we can stop being victims of the perceived wrongs they have inflicted upon us. We imprison ourselves by wallowing in and ruminating about what others have done to us, constantly reliving those negative emotions. Having those original feelings of pain or betrayal is not bad or uncommon. The challenge comes when we choose not to let them go, and we relive them over and over again. As the AA saying goes, It is like taking poison and expecting the other person to die. We are hurting ourselves and having little or no effect on them. We have given our power to be happy to them. If we forgive them and let go of the pain, then the relationship can move forward in whatever new form it takes; and we can spend our time finding more positive emotions and experiences.

So how do we shed all that negative emotion and create a space of forgiveness? One idea is to become the observer and pretend you are giving advice to a friend in the same situation. What would you tell them to think about or to consider? Another idea is to evaluate the relative value of the relationship against the value of getting to keep your negative emotions. What do you gain by staying angry or upset? What do you gain if you forgive and rebuild the relationship?

Be smart about it. If they are in any way a danger to you or your family, or if they are abusive, you can choose to forgive them but still not subject yourself to danger or physical or verbal abuse. Choose to manage that kind of relationship from a distance via phone, email, or Google Hangout. If you do visit them in person, when their actions become inappropriate, forgive them, but let them know that you choose not to be around them. Rather than nurturing the hate that is created by the pain they cause, nurture the forgiveness and pity you have for someone who is unable to control his actions and his life, or someone who does not understand the negative impacts his actions create.

"Forgiveness is the feeling of peace that emerges as you take your hurt less personally, take responsibility for how you feel, and become a hero instead of a victim in the story you tell." Dr. Fred Luskin

Get Excited About Good News

Respond well to good news. It can make your relationship stronger and help it last longer. Research has shown that our happiness is magnified when we can share it with others, and magnified even further if the other person had a positive and enthusiastic response to our happiness. How your partner responds to good news is a better predictor of the longevity of the relationship than how he or she responds to bad news. Celebrating small wins is ideally something you encounter daily, or at least much more often than you encounter hard times. Sharing small wins with the people who are close to us increases our level of happiness associated with those wins. When others share with us, it is important to respond positively and enthusiastically. We can often dampen their level of happiness by responding negatively or even by responding in a neutral manner.

Good news is an opportunity for someone close to you to share their excitement about big and small accomplishments. People who are really good with children do this naturally. When a child walks up and proudly shows them how they tied their own shoe or finished a puzzle with six pieces, they get noticeably excited and share their feeling of accomplishment with the child. It is a celebration for something that may seem small to an adult observer, but the children love it. They work to find more accomplishments they can show off. When we become adults, we don't lose that need or that desire to share our great news and little wins with other people. We look for that joyous feeling and sense of accomplishment. So how we handle those opportunities in a relationship is important. Dismissing them as menial or something that should have already been accomplished takes away that joy. So does talking over their news and telling them about our lives, because we just can't wait to get it out. Taking time to appreciate, compliment, and celebrate their little successes and news is just as important for adults as it is for children. Those close connections are formed in the small interactions around good news and small accomplishments. These small acts show them that we value them, and that what happens in their lives is important to us.

Remember the things they have told you about and ask them about the outcomes. Check in to find out how things went. If they took the time to tell you about it, it had some kind of a special meaning or importance to them. Follow up in a positive and participatory manner to show them they matter to you.

In later chapters we will talk about finding our purpose. Supporting someone else's purpose or dreams is another great way to nurture a relationship. The more your partner feels like you are an integral part of his or her purpose and dreams, the closer the connection you will form. We all have something we are striving for or wish we could strive for. We seek out the company of those who will help us get there and avoid the people who interfere or don't believe in our ability to one day fulfill our dreams.

Smile More

"A smile is the shortest distance between two people." Victor Borge

One way to improve your close relationships as well as those in your extended network is to smile more. Smiling is the original example of something going viral. When you smile, other people catch it and they spread it to more people.

Ron Gotman, in his "Ted Talk, The Hidden Power of Smiling" video, talks about smiling being a built-in mechanism to help us determine how safe another person is. It also gives us the opportunity to quickly determine their emotions. Researchers who suppressed a subject's ability to smile found they also reduced their ability to read the emotions of others. We automatically mimic someone's smile to determine its authenticity. Smiling is like our internal radar. We send out a smile, and they send a smile back. We mimic that smile and automatically interpret the results. The results enable us to intuitively know whether this person is friend or foe and what kind of mood they are in.

One research study showed that by measuring the smiles of people in their yearbook photos, scientists could predict how long-lasting and fulfilling their lives would be, how they would score on measures of well-being, and how inspiring they would be to others. Other researchers found that measuring smile intensity on a Facebook profile could predict the life satisfaction of college students three-and-a-half years later.

Research has also shown that smiling sends positive messages to the emotional centers in the brain. So by forcing our faces to smile, we can activate the areas of our brain that make us feel better. In other words, we don't just smile as a result of being happy; smiling actually makes us happier. Smiling also increases mood-enhancing hormones like endorphins and decreases stress-inducing hormones like cortisol, so you become healthier as well as happier. Smiling makes you more attractive to other people and has been correlated with a longer life.

Babies are born smiling. Children smile more than adults. As we get older, we start finding reasons not to smile. We are often so busy trying to be successful and so caught up in being disappointed by the world's lack of perfection and cooperation with our pursuit of success, that we believe we have a lot of reasons not to smile. Stop for a moment and consider this: what would you say if a child asked you why you don't smile a lot? Although your answer may be serious and real, is it really a good reason not to smile?

Hugs

Somehow in our politically correct world, touching people has become associated with negative consequences. We are overly cautious about offending someone or invading their space. Positive relationships are enhanced by appropriate touch. In other words, we must respect boundaries; but we can also reach out with appropriate gestures like a handshake, a pat on the shoulder, or a touch of the elbow. In our more connected relationships and with those people who are more comfortable with touch, we can add various levels of hugs and embraces, or even light kisses on the cheek. Touch is good for connection, and it is good for us physically. Touch is a physical need, just as sleep and exercise are. One study showed that premature babies who were kept in a ward where they were touched more grow more, both mentally and physically. They found premature babies who were touched for 45 minutes a day put on 47% more weight than those who weren't. These babies also showed better cognitive development several months later. A tragic experiment also took place in 1989 under Ceausescu, the dictator in Romania. He took children away from dissidents and raised them in group homes where they did not receive any touch. Touch deprivation resulted in stunted physical and cognitive development. There is a famous quote by Virginia Satir, who was known as the "Mother of Family Therapy," that "we need 4 hugs a day for survival. We need 8 hugs a day for maintenance. We need 12 hugs a day for growth."

In our personal relationships, touch is a requirement to feel closer and to improve communication with the other person. Touch, and specifically hugs, help us build trust with the other person. Hugs have also been shown to improve memory. They reduce stress and provide a feeling of safety. This is not just an emotional reaction; it is also a physical one. Hugs release oxytocin, which is like a relationship hormone. It is found in increased levels between moms and their newborn babies and in people with positive romantic relationships. Hugging also increases serotonin levels, which helps us feel happier and more relaxed. Hugs help improve the immune system and the production of white blood cells, and they help us release tension.

Hugs are another way of communicating the importance of people in our lives. Hugging sends the message that they are important to us and matter in our lives. Hugs open us up when we are feeling constrained and up tight. It gives us permission to start a dialogue about what is bothering us and opens up channels of communication. Have you ever seen someone so tense from emotional challenges that they looked like they were about to burst? Then with just a hug, the flood gates open and their emotions come pouring out? Hugs create the opening to release the pressure that has been building up.

Remember, hugs are a gift that give much more than we realize. But they are still a gift that some people might not want to receive. So offer hugs often, but only follow through if the other person wants to accept your gift.

Activity

1. Try to give eight hugs per day. Hugging releases oxytocin, which helps you feel even more connected to people.

2. Keep a post-it note on your desk, write the name of each person you hugged, and share your list with others. Sometimes at dinner my daughter will review her hugs from that day. We all enjoy listening to and thinking about who got and gave the hugs.

Be Mindful

When you are with someone, be mindful of them and what they are communicating. What are they trying to get across? Do they want you to learn something? Do they just need to get something off their chest? Are they genuinely interested in your opinion or learning about your experiences? Are they sending a different message with their facial expressions and body language than what is being expressed through their voice? Are they interested and engaged, or are they distracted by something else in their lives? Are they leaning in with intensity or are they leaning back and very relaxed? What are they doing with their hands? Is their smile genuine or forced? Look deep into their eyes. What are their eyes telling you? Take time to be thoughtful and think through what they are saying. Focus on their message by being mindful and observing the whole person. Be fully engaged with them rather than letting your mind wander to everything else in your life or environment. If you are mindful with the people you interact with, they will seek you out and want to talk to you. People want to talk to and spend time with someone they believe will listen and pay attention to them and what they are saying.

Be Authentic

> *"Be real. Try to do what you say, say what you mean, be what you seem." Marian Wright Edelman*

The research we have discussed so far overwhelmingly shows that positive relationships contribute to your happiness. In order to develop and maintain those positive relationships, it is important that we are authentic. Positive relationships require disclosure about who we are. We have to share our personal hopes and fears. Two different studies found that relationships are closer when people share their personal feelings and challenges. It is about opening up and sharing who you are, the good and the bad, as opposed to simply talking about the weather. It is funny how we are most guarded with the people we are most eager to meet. Going out on a date or meeting with someone we have a tremendous amount of respect for causes us to be on our best behavior and do everything we can to hide our flaws. We go to what sometimes seem like ridiculous lengths to make sure the other person doesn't meet the real us. Usually, that is because we think if they do see the real us, they won't like us. Brene Brown says we are the "most in debt, addicted, obese, overmedicated adult cohort in US History." We think we can selectively numb ourselves. But when we numb the pain, we also numb the joy. Yet, when asked about our closest relationships, we often explain they are people we can be ourselves with. They are people who accept us for who we are. They are people with whom we can experience our full range of emotions. I am not suggesting we should show bad behavior or flaunt our flaws when we meet someone new. It is a good idea to make a great first impression. But we should be careful not to overdo the act and pretend to be someone we are not. It can be fun, mysterious, and probably even wise to reveal our secrets and more in-depth thoughts and feelings a little at a time. It is probably a good strategy to show our best qualities first and let them learn about our lesser qualities later. But it is important not to step over the line and pretend to be something we are not. We should be authentic and proud of who we really are, and let that new person decide if they like the real us; if they don't, it is their loss and not ours. Dare to be vulnerable. Be authentic.

Positive Relationships

Chapter 13

Give 100% and Expect Nothing in Return

The100/0 Principle

> *"Some of the biggest challenges in relationships come from the fact that most people enter a relationship in order to get something: They're trying to find someone who's going to make them feel good. In reality, the only way a relationship will last is if you see your relationship as a place that you go to give, and not a place you go to take." Anthony Robbins*

A foundational element to creating and improving positive relationships is a concept Al Ritter writes about called the 100/0 Principle. Most of us go into a relationship believing that it should be a 50/50 distribution of commitment. The assumption is that two people giving half each adds up to a 100% commitment to the relationship. As long as everything is even, then it will be a great relationship. The challenge is, 50/50 doesn't work a lot of the time. If one person is giving 50% but the other person is only giving 30% because of some challenge they are having that may or may not be related to the relationship, the relationship suffers. We all experience situations where someone has had a bad day, is stressed from work, or has something going on in a different relationship that makes them not want to or unable to participate in your relationship. When that happens, do you just ignore them, or do you put forth a little more effort to comfort and empathize with them? For most of us, the answer is that we reach out to them. We give more than our 50%, because we know that is what the relationship needs. We put out extra effort, and we feel good doing it. We inherently know that it is much better to extend ourselves than to let the relationship lapse. It makes us feel better, and it makes the other person feel better.

Now let's look at that from the other side. How do you feel when someone reaches out to you? When they give 70% or 80% because you are just not able to give right now? Think of a time when life was really bad for you and someone was there to support and help you. For most of us, that is a person we describe as a real friend. "She was there for me when I needed her most." Often, it is not even the person we thought it would be. What did that person ask for in return? What did he or she want from you in return for being there and giving you the extra love and attention you needed? Most likely, the answer is nothing. That person just felt good about it and gave what he or she felt you needed, and the reward was being able to give.

So if it is good to give a little extra, if that is how we define our "true" friends, and if giving extra makes us feel good and more connected, what if we became that person? What if we became that person in all of our important relationships? What if we became the person who gave what people needed and expected nothing in return, because the reward was in the giving?

That is the key to the 100/0 Principle and to great relationships. We give 100% and we expect nothing in return. They can give 0% and we will still be there for them, because we want to give and because we believe that relationship is important. How would the people in our relationships react? How did you react when your friend gave more than 50%? You were grateful beyond measure, and you were willing to give your friend more than 50% whenever he or she needed it. As a matter of fact, you probably looked forward to the opportunity when you could give back. As a result, the most likely scenario is that both people will end up giving more than 50% to the relationship, and it will thrive.

If we give 100% and expect nothing in return, how many of our relationships would be successful? The answer is, all of them. Every single one will work, because we are 100% committed and the other person doesn't have to do anything. We have no expectations that they will call us, or bring us flowers, or remember our birthdays, or behave in any particular way. So we never have a reason be disappointed in them and they don't feel pressure to be someone different from who they are. Most likely, and even though we are okay if they don't, they will respond in kind. They will appreciate our efforts, and they will give more than 0%--and often more than 50% back to the relationship.

How good would you feel if you took control of all your relationships? If you had the opportunity to give to people unconditionally? If you had no expectations and therefore could not be disappointed, but instead had true appreciation and gratitude for everything the other person did? How good would you feel if you knew you were the person that people said "She likes me for me. She lets me be myself and loves me for it." By following Al Ritter's 100/0 Principle, you can be that person.

Why does it work? Not having our expectations met is one of the biggest challenges to relationships. We spend time thinking and planning how we are going to make someone happy. We put ourselves out there and become more vulnerable than we may be comfortable with. Often we don't communicate our expectations, or if we do communicate them, the other person doesn't agree to them or doesn't remember, understand, or focus on them. As a result, their reaction is not what we expected. Our actions don't make the other person as happy as we had hoped, or they don't do the things we wanted them to do, so we are disappointed. Our natural reaction to our disappointment is to communicate to the other person how they should behave next time, so they will meet our expectations. Now they are disappointed. They want to be accepted for who they are, and they don't want to have to think about how to react when they are around us, especially when they don't understand the rules. As a result, the relationship becomes stressed and uncomfortable.

We can change that by giving 100% and having zero expectations. Whatever reaction they choose is ok. We appreciate any positive reaction and are not upset that it did not meet our dreams of the perfect reaction. They are happy, or at least contented, with our gesture and hopefully appreciate our acceptance of them. The relationship stays strong.

The 100/0 Principle takes discipline to implement. We have developed habits throughout our lives to protect our feelings and to protect how we think about ourselves. We often spend our early years and well into our teens getting what we want. When we cry or get upset, our parents try to comfort us. In middle school and high school, our friends and first loves forgive our outbursts and demanding nature. So we develop bad habits and expectations that other people will change and adapt for us. We lose track of the positive feelings created by giving, because our hormones and other factors create a world where we are focused only on fulfilling our own needs. We incorrectly start to believe that getting is what will make us happy. It takes focus and discipline to discover that fulfillment in the relationship comes from what we can give rather than what we can get. The good news is that it becomes a virtuous circle. The more we give, the better we feel, which makes us want to give more. It is hard to practice and remember during times of stress, but those times happen less and less often as we become happier from sharing more and more of ourselves.

Practicing the 100/0 Principle requires us to move from judging other people to accepting them. We have to treat everyone with dignity and respect, no matter what we believe their shortcomings are. By judging other people, we give ourselves permission, either consciously or unconsciously, to treat them poorly. We place ourselves on a level higher than the person we are judging. Instead of judging, we can observe their behavior and choose what we would or would not do in those situations. We can choose to act differently without judging them as good or bad people, or as worthy or unworthy of our efforts.

The word "should" is one of the most toxic words to positive relationships. I have seen people drive themselves crazy in work and personal relationships focusing on what someone else "should" have done. "Should" is a judgment that requires us to believe someone else thinks, believes, and understands all circumstances exactly the way we do. We all know that is impossible. We like people because they are similar to us and have similar values; but they all come from different environments, cultures, backgrounds, and parents. So they are going to evaluate a situation differently than we do. If we change our language to "we ask" or "we would like," then we own it instead of making a judgment or blaming it on them. "Should" is a great warning sign. If you are thinking about what someone "should" have done, then you are not practicing zero expectations; and your relationships will suffer.

There is a difference between not having any expectations, which can make our relationships better, and hiding or not sharing our expectations, which will strain our relationships. If we are repressing our expectations, they will fester and create problems down the road. So how do you handle those expectations? You know it would be better for the relationship if you didn't have them, you just don't know how to let them go. Focus on what you like and appreciate about the other person. Why do you like being around them? How do they make you feel? What do you admire about them? What are the great things they do for you? Focusing on the positive and what you appreciate will help you let go of what they don't have or are not doing.

There is a line between not having expectations and allowing someone to abuse us. Giving us flowers, fixing us dinner, remembering our birthdays, or turning off the TV to talk to us, are expectations of things that people do <u>for</u> us. We can eliminate these expectations and improve our relationships. But we can't eliminate the expectation that other people will treat us with respect and dignity and not do harm or negative things <u>to</u> us. The key differentiation is the distinction between what people do "for us," which is good and which we should allow them to control, and what people do "to us" in a negative form, which is against us or could hurt us. Our tolerance level for verbal, physical, or any other kind of abuse should be something close to zero. For example, we may not like that someone around us uses curse words in their language, but that is their choice. We should not start setting expectations that they can or can't curse. We could choose to be around it or not, and we can communicate to them how we feel about cursing. But they get to choose whether or not they want to curse. If someone is cursing at us in an abusive way, our tolerance level changes. They are doing something negative "to us" and causing us harm, and we need to immediately remove ourselves from that situation and spend a lot less time with that person.

Always keep in mind that we are talking about giving freely. Giving freely is never painful. We give because we want to and we are excited to share ourselves and our feelings. Giving 100% does not mean we give someone our car when we need that car to get to work. Giving means we help them find a ride or we give them a ride, not that we sacrifice our own happiness and success for theirs. Building positive relationships means building something that works for both parties and leaves both parties better off.

As we mentioned before, one skill for creating positive relationships is the art of forgiveness. Often, when we feel we have been wronged or treated unfairly by another person, we choose to hold onto that feeling and simmer in it. We even share it with other people so we can marinate in it together and be mutually offended by the action. Most likely, the offense was that the other person did not meet our expectations.

They did not do what we thought they "should" do or hoped they would do. We believe they have purposely hurt us because they "should" know or they "should" have acted differently. They may feel they were in the right, not care that you are offended, or most likely be completely oblivious to how you feel. So we simmer in our disappointment and sometimes let it churn into anger and hate. We not only put unnecessary stress on the relationship, but we may even cut them out of our lives completely. The challenge is, the feelings are all within us. The other person is not feeling the same pain we are, and may not be feeling any pain at all. The saying that we are "taking poison and expecting the other person to die" is applicable here. We are wallowing in our anger, hatred, and disappointment, and they are continuing to live their lives. They either don't know they hurt us or wish they hadn't hurt us, but there is nothing they can do to change our feelings. That responsibility is within us. By forgiving them, we can reclaim that relationship. By allowing them to be who they are with all their faults and challenges, we allow ourselves to stop "taking the poison" and to once again enjoy and strengthen the relationship. Practice forgiveness. Make it the solution that replaces your disappointment, anger, and hatred.

"Seek first to understand, then to be understood." Stephen R. Covey

One step to finding the ability to forgive is asking questions. We often create a running dialogue in our heads about what is going on, what happened, what the other person did, and why they did it. We make assumptions and jump to conclusions; and because of our strong emotions, we jump to the conclusion that we are right. Since we feel this anger or disappointment so strongly, we must know why they acted that way. Try to turn that internal discussion about the facts to a series of questions. "They love me; why would they act that way?" "Why would they make that statement?" "What is going on in their lives that would cause them to have that reaction?" Once we start to ask questions and dig deeper into the real cause of the pain, we often find the answers are not as obvious or clear as we had originally assumed. Many times the reactions are based on events and feelings that are completely separate from the interaction we are focused on. If we understand them, we can forgive them and move on. The relationship will stay stronger.

Another benefit of the 100/0 Principle is that it helps you realize you are in control of your relationships. You get to choose to make them work and what you will give to them. You also get to choose which relationships you want to give your energy to. Some relationships, like friends, we choose and develop; while others, like family, we are anointed with. So how do you make a family relationship, which you can't sever except in the most extreme cases, work for you? The answer is "thumbs-up" and "thumbs-down." You may not get to pick those family relationships, but you can choose how much time and energy to put into them. When you have an interaction with a difficult family member and you have given 100% with zero expectations, but they still create an atmosphere that is mostly negative, that is a "thumbs down" experience. As a result you will choose not to spend as much time with them, or to implement a longer period of time before you interact with them again. You don't have to be angry, disappointed, or upset; just choose a different schedule. If you interact with them and it is a "thumbs up," meaning most of the interaction was good, you can choose to see them more often and for longer periods of time. Regulate your schedule of interaction with a "thumbs up" for more time or a "thumbs down" for less time, rather than being upset or cutting them out of your life completely.

Holidays are a great time to practice the 100/0 principle. We spend time with those friends and family members whom we may not have as much fondness for. We can re-hash all the baggage and problems and let them push our buttons. We can dread the encounters and go over and over in our heads how horrible it will be or what catastrophic scenarios could occur, or we can forgive them for all of their past transgressions and accept who they are with no expectations for better behavior. If we give them a chance with an open mind, we might be surprised by how pleasant they can be; and if things start to go south, we can excuse ourselves and go spend time with the family members we are more able to accept and appreciate.

Perfection and Apologies

We are human beings, so we are not perfect. We can't always give 100% and make all our important relationships work. As a matter of fact, it is difficult to get it right more than 50% of the time. Relationships are emotionally charged and full of surprises and difficult moments. But that doesn't mean we give up. We try to be the best person we can be today, and then we build from there. When we make mistakes, we forgive ourselves, apologize to the other person, and work on doing better. It is hard to apologize, because the other person always had some form of involvement in what went wrong and we don't want to move forward without them recognizing their role. But that is counterproductive and doesn't fit with the 100/0 Principle. We are giving 100%, so we have to own it and apologize for our actions, no matter what the other person does. Over the years we will improve and get better, but we will always have times when we are imperfect and we need to forgive ourselves, apologize, and try to do better. Knowing we will be wrong and will fail sometimes will also help us accept those missteps in everyone else. We can forgive them, help them forgive themselves, support them, and help them move forward.

Don't give up. The 100/0 Principle will not feel natural at first. You will have to work at it, and you might not see results immediately. But if you have the patience to stick with it, you will begin to feel differently about yourself and your relationships; and those feelings will motivate you to do more and more. Once giving 100% becomes natural rather than forced, you will start to notice other people appreciating what you are doing, and reciprocating.

"Life is an echo – what you send out comes back." Chinese Proverb

Activity

1. List your important relationships.

2. What can you give to those relationships?

3. List your weak, challenged, or severed relationships that would be important if they worked. What can you apologize for? (It doesn't matter who is at fault. What matters is the relationship.) What can you give to that relationship? Remember to use the "thumbs up"/ "thumbs down" guidelines.

4. List at least three positive points about this person.

5. What are your expectations? Can you let go of them?

6. What are your unmet expectations?

7. What are your judgments about this person? How can you accept them anyway?

8. What are your questions about how the other person feels or why they are acting the way they are?

Positive Relationships

Chapter 14
Work Relationships

"…work relationships are central, not only for how work gets done, but also for the quality of our lives." Dutton and Ragins

Not only are relationships important for happiness in our personal lives, they are also important for happiness at work. For most people, happiness at work includes dynamic interpersonal relationships, which include ongoing respect and recognition for accomplishing something meaningful for the team or company. Given that most of us spend 50% or more of our waking hours at work, it would be impossible to ignore the impact of relationships in that area of our lives. In the past, relationships at work have been a taboo subject because of how complicated they are and how complicated they can make productivity and work life in general when they go from good to bad, which seems to happen often.

Unfortunately, relationships are a vital part of our work lives and productivity, and ignoring their existence is no longer productive. Our best solution is to understand the nature of work relationships and teach employees and team members how to create and sustain positive relationships. Most everything we do at work runs more smoothly when we have positive relationships and the related support at work. In the workplace, happy people receive more emotional and task support than less happy people. We can get more done because we have team members who can add knowledge or lend a hand. We are happier because we have people to commiserate with and to discuss and test our feelings with. Our relationships with vendors and clients determines our ability to bring new ideas and get raises and promotions. In the age of the knowledge worker, having other people to help us focus and expand our knowledge allows us to be more productive and more creative.

Most of this book addresses you, the individual. As we talk about workplace happiness, let's get into the mindset of you the informal leader, you the team leader, you the supervisor, and even you the executive or organizational leader. Take the perspective of what you can change about you, but also what you can change within your team or organization. I have personally witnessed small actions by individuals ripple through teams and organizations and become rituals and defining characteristics. We had a team member whose sister taught at a school full of lower income students. Her and her sister's idea to rally our team to help those children around Christmas became a defining example for our company and for many of our careers.

It helped us realize what we could do to help someone else, and it also clarified what was really important to us as individuals and as an organization. There are many examples of people sharing their passions, leading by example, and just showing their caring side to others in the workplace and creating a positive ripple effect throughout the organization. This can be something as small as bringing in cupcakes, organizing a walking club, or inviting a group to happy hour.

Working with and for people you like will have a short-term and long-term effect on your cardiovascular system, in the form of lower heart rate and lower blood pressure. Research has shown that positive relationships help people learn faster, because they have a safe environment in which to learn. If they are worried about how the group will react to failures and mistakes, they will not venture out of their comfort zone and take new risks. If, on the other hand, they feel supported by their peers, they will explore new areas and help increase the knowledge level of the entire organization.

How you feel can affect your team members. Gallup's research of 1,740 people across 105 teams found that one team member's happiness can increase by as much as 20% over a 6-month period if their other team members are happier. It is a virtuous circle, in that each team member has a positive effect on the other. Happier supervisors who are trusted by their employees can increase their employees' happiness by as much as a 15% over a 6-month period. Employees who agreed that they could connect with their supervisor or someone at work were more productive, contributed more to profits, and were significantly more likely to stay with their company long-term.

Research shows it is better to sit in large groups at lunch during work, because you will be connected to more people and more areas of the organization. The more diverse the group, the higher are your chances of success. The diversity makes you more innovative and productive. Having a group you can trust to share your positive and negative feelings with is important. It provides an outlet for negative feelings as well as a source for productive information exchange. It also doesn't have to be limited to lunch. Bumping into people in the hallway and at the coffee machine can result in similar connections. Maintaining a few high-quality, high-contact connections is key, but don't overlook expanding your secondary network to a larger and more diversified group.

Results of a Gallup-Healthways poll showed that the two best determinants of job satisfaction are having a good boss and having a best friend at work. A good boss is defined as one who is approachable, provides regular feedback, establishes clear requirements, delegates, practices good listening, offers recognition, is trustworthy, and considers your best interest.

Our relationship with our supervisor is the number one predictor of our willingness to stay in our jobs. Research indicates that the supervisor can influence the employee's job satisfaction based on what he or she communicates about the job. In one study, supervisors in one group told their employees how difficult and involved a job was, while in another group they did not make any special comments. Both groups of employees did the same job, but the group whose supervisor made the comments felt like the job was more involved; and they were more satisfied than the group that heard no such comments. Research by Eisenberger and colleagues confirmed that "employees who believed that the supervisor valued their contributions and cared about their well-being" stayed at companies longer and had more faith in their company.

As individuals, if we want to enjoy going to work every day, we can find ways to improve our relationships with our supervisors. As organizations, we can recognize the influence our supervisors have on the happiness of our employees, their retention, and their productivity, and emphasize programs that help them become more aware and supportive of their team members. We can create an environment of accountability and building on strengths to increase success, rather than an environment of policing and constantly focusing on the failures.

Our antiquated management models were built to manage people's butts and hands. Their purpose was to make sure their butts were in their chairs or at their stations on time and that their hands were continuously busy with their assigned task. Now, in the age of the knowledge worker, we need to change our management practices to focus on managing people's brains. We need them to be engaged, excited, and creative. We want them using their resources to solve the challenges of the company. I have spent the majority of my career in companies that do not produce anything tangible. My companies have always provided some kind of service or digital product. As a result, we are completely dependent on our employees' brains rather than their butts and hands. Unfortunately, many supervisors believe we should focus on what time the employees sit down in their chairs rather than how much work is produced. A person can sit in a chair for a long time and not produce anything. We need people whose brain is engaged and focused. It is imperative that we create positive, trusting relationships and healthy environments that provide opportunities for what Daniel Pink calls mastery, purpose, and autonomy. We have to teach our supervisors how to manage their brains instead of their butts.

Our opinions about how much we like our jobs can be heavily influenced by our peers and supervisors and what they think of the company and their jobs. The implications are that nurturing, teaching, and creating opportunities for positive relationships in the workplace should be a priority for organizations. It has a domino effect of leading employees to become more satisfied and happy, which makes them more successful and productive, which leads to more of their peers becoming satisfied and happy, which again results in more productive and more successful employees, which benefits the organization.

When Times are Tough, Make Relationships Your Priority

"We need to feel wanted, accepted and loved...We need support from friends and family...We need to feel a part of the human race, to have friends. We need to give and receive love." Davidson & Stayner

Unfortunately for many of us, our natural inclination when things start to go wrong is to abandon our relationships and go it alone. We do this for many reasons. Stress clouds our thought. We focus on the goal of fixing the problem and don't have time to reach out for other opinions. We don't want to admit our challenges or failures. We don't want to involve the people we love in our biggest challenges; often, we think it's for their safety and to keep them away from stress, but really it's because we don't want to deal with their judgment or disappointment. The problem is, during a crisis is when we need other people the most. It is when we need a clearer, more objective point of view to help us make decisions, and we need their emotional support because the stress and worry exhausts our emotional resources. Shame, embarrassment, or anger cause us to shut out the people we love just when we need them the most.

One of the fallacies most of us embrace is that there will only be one crisis, one failure, or one tough project we have to power through. So we think that if we focus all our attention on the situation and temporarily give up the things that matter to us, like time with our friends and family, we will get past this hill and be able to get back to our normal routines. But that small hill is part of a mountain range, and one hill will lead to a bigger hill. Our reward for climbing the hill so successfully is a bigger hill, then an even bigger hill, and eventually a mountain. There will always be tough times; they are an important part of our lives. But if we make our relationships a priority, we will always have the support we need to keep pushing and keep enjoying the good times in life that will also always be there for us.

I once saw a story about a mountain climber who was in a dire situation. He had lost his partner to a fall and now had to get out of a crevice by himself before dark, or risk being buried by falling snow or possibly freezing to death. He had made it to a ledge and only had about 20 more feet to climb. He had often completed similar climbs using only his hands, without any ropes or support, on the climbing walls in the gym. Climbing free hand should only take 5 to 10 minutes. If he took his time and invested in fastening all of the supports and safety techniques as he had been taught, it could take as long as an hour to make the same climb. The risk was, without the support system, if he slipped, he would fall 500 feet to his death in the chasm and no one would know.

Which have you chosen? Do you have the patience to build the support system or are you risking everything to get there as fast as possible? What if you knew there would be another challenge at the end of that climb? Your positive relationships are your support system. If you ignore them, your happiness and level of success are constantly at risk. If you take the time to build those positive relationships, you will have many opportunities to successfully reach the peak of happiness and success.

Missing time with our family and friends becomes a routine that we don't even realize we have created. The Internet, e-mail, social media, and globalization, where we have teams of people working in every time zone, create the potential to do work 24 hours a day, 7 days a week, 365 days a year. There is never a time when everything stops and we can re-focus on our relationships. We have to make a concentrated effort to create time for our friends and family. If we don't place a high value on our relationships and the support systems they provide, they will get lost in the vortex of the "always on" crisis. Stephen Covey, in his book *The Seven Habits of Highly Effective People*, talks about placing a higher priority on doing what is important first, then doing is what is urgent. The research proves that strong personal relationships and their resulting support systems are associated with, and may be our best investment in, both happiness and success. That makes them one of the most important things in our lives. We often take them for granted and sacrifice them on the altar of the urgent needs of our job in an effort to ensure speedy career advancement. But that sacrifice comes back to haunt as when we get stuck trying to climb a higher mountain that may be just beyond our capabilities. We end up slipping with no support to keep us from falling 500 feet down the mountain. Covey would recommend we take the time to create the important social support structures first, rather than urgently climbing the mountain without them.

The climber also chose to build the support system, mostly because the past warnings of his fallen partner still rang in his ear. He made it to the top, only to lose his grip just as he was climbing over the edge. Luckily, the support system he had taken the time to create did its job and kept him from falling more than a few feet. He was able to regain his grip, climb over the edge, and live to tell his story.

Improving Work Relationships

High Quality Connections, or short mutually positive interactions in the workplace were first defined by Dutton and Heaphy. They can occur in very short periods of time, but they leave people feeling energized and important. People with High Quality Connections show less negative impacts from stressful situations. They seem to be able to weather the storm more calmly.

People with High Quality Connections also live longer. They are sick less often and have lower blood pressure. High Quality Connections release oxytocin, which is like a relationship hormone that reduces stress and increases a person's willingness to cooperate. High Quality Connections also reduce blood pressure. High Quality Connections improve how people work together by improving their exchange of information. They help people explore and confirm roles within a group so they have an identity that matters to them and is of value to the team. High Quality Connections help get things done because of better connections to other people's knowledge and the way teammates learn from each other. High Quality Connections between supervisors and employees lead the supervisor to spend more time developing the employee, while motivating the employee to be more loyal and committed. The research confirms that people with High Quality Connections have more physical zest, energy, and vitality. They have more resilience, and they learn faster. They are better at identifying who they are and how they fit in, which helps them be more effective change agents.

To create High Quality Connections, engage with people when they come into your workspace. Stop what you are doing and give them your full attention. Don't fall victim to what Dutton calls "disrespectful engagement." She cited a recent poll that 90% of respondents believe workplace incivility is on the rise. It makes you less energized, less motivated, and less committed. Use mutual positive regard, trust, and active engagement to help team members feel more open, competent, and energized. Give them your attention, be authentic, listen attentively, and actively respond to the discussion. If you don't have time, let them know when a better time will be.

Listening skills can be learned or taught. High quality connections can be created in short, focused interactions. By recognizing the value of positive relationships and their significant impact on productivity and making it a priority to create such relationships, we can encourage our team members to pause and focus on the person who is requesting their attention. Stop your work, look up from the computer screen, and acknowledge the presence of another human being. Listen intently to what they are trying to communicate and respond actively and positively. A 30-second interaction can have an impact on their psyche that will last all day long. You can make that impact positive and productive or negative and de-motivating. A series of positive, people-focused interactions will build good will that will help the team push through future challenges.

Employees and supervisors can find ways to help each other be successful. Rather than focusing on what needs to be done differently, focus on what can be done to reach their goals and get to the next level. Hold them accountable--it shows you care. But tie that accountability to why it hampers their goals vs. why they are wrong. Show them the big picture. You are part of a team trying to accomplish the same thing. An adversarial relationship helps you both fail.

You can't control your supervisor. People are going to act the way they act. You can only show empathy and respect. If your supervisor gets angry, that is something you can't control. It is his or her failure, not yours. Find the truth behind the anger; there is always something to learn there. But don't absorb the anger as your fault, or even something you are going to try to control or avoid. Let it be your supervisor's problem, which it is. Do the best you can, control what you can control, and let go of the things you can't control.

A great way to be happier at work is to expand your network of friendships. Most people focus on a few really close relationships that they form early on in a particular workplace. Those are the people they go to lunch with and spend most of their time talking to. Unfortunately, those people usually have similar circumstances, as far as supervisor, workload, or location. So they also have similar perspectives and feelings. By including people with different experiences, you can get different perspectives and have a broader base of support when things are not going well in your area.

Ask your friend to invite one of his or her friends to lunch with you. If you are in the kitchen getting coffee, take a minute to talk to an acquaintance and find out more about that person. If you are on a project, get to know the people on your team on a more personal level.

One of the best predictors of job satisfaction, engagement, and retention is your relationship with your direct supervisor. The outdated notion that you can't be friends with your boss should be thrown out the window. Your boss is a necessary part of your success and happiness. Boss/employee relationships are difficult, but it is important that they are strong and positive relationships. If you have a bad boss, find out and write down the things that are good about them. At the very least, it is good to know what not to do with your employees when you are a boss.

Another area for building positive relationships at work is introductions. How are employees treated on their first day? Do they have an assigned mentor or welcoming committee? Do they have a desk and computer prepared and waiting? Has someone been assigned to take them to lunch and give them a tour of the building and work areas? Are we introducing them to the key people they will be working with? You begin creating positive relationships from the first meeting. Plan to make it a positive experience and build from there.

What about vendors and other visitors? Do we treat them like slaves who have to do business with us? Do we take advantage of their need for our continued patronage or their desire to make us one of their new customers? Do we make them wait constantly and miss scheduled appointments? They can become valuable partners in the success of our business. They can bring creativity and resources that help motivate our employees and solve problems for our clients. Creating and maintaining positive relationships with all potential partners is good for our business.

Another aspect of positive relationships in the workplace is emotion. To build high quality connections, we have to feel and even show emotions. Emotions seem to have been banned from many workplaces because they "make things messy." But it is fallacy to believe that because they are well-hidden, the emotions don't exist and are not a part of our activities and decisions. By building positive relationships, we create an environment where both positive and negative emotions can exist in a safe environment. Positive relationships include room for a wider variety of emotions, more flexibility in dealing with stresses and strains, and more openness to new ideas and creativity. They create higher levels of engagement, facilitate cooperation, promote learning ability, strengthen commitment to the organization, enhance resilience and growth, and improve performance. We want our teams to bring their whole person to the office, because that is when they are most engaged and creative. There will be stresses and strains as we go through the work day; and the stronger our relationships, the more resilient and effective our teams will become.

Jeff Haden writes about how blaming can interfere with our positive relationships at work. In every work environment there are things that go wrong and things that go right. There may be challenges with our employees, our boss may not behave as we like, or the vendors may not come through on an important project. We can focus on blaming someone, or we can focus on fixing the problem. Often we blame people simply because they didn't do what we would have expected them to do or what we would have done. More often than not, we never give those explanations to them, nor do we spend enough time to give them the tools to get it done. We may have years of experience packed into our brains; and we expect that everyone else has the same perspective, even though they may have only been at the company a few months. We don't realize how much we know just from experience and how much a newer team member may not have learned yet. Very few people want things to go poorly at work. Part of creating positive relationships is realizing that and doing whatever is necessary to help the other person continue to learn. Rather than wasting our time blaming someone, we can accept the situation and take action to improve it now and in the future. This is part of taking control of our lives. When we blame someone, we give them control; we become victims. When we accept and find solutions, we become empowered to create our own happiness and success.

A great habit for creating positive relationships at work is providing recognition. Recognize people for great work, for taking the first step, for making a great effort, and for anything else we can find. Sometimes we think that because it is work we should only point out what people are doing wrong.

My wife and I coached each of our kids' soccer teams when they were five to eight years old. When kids are five, they don't know anything about soccer; so we don't wait until someone scores a goal to get excited. We are excited when they just touch the ball. Then we get more excited when they actually kick the ball. We recognize them when they kick the ball in the right direction, and then we recognize them again when they kick the ball in the right direction two or three times in a row. If we only pointed out that they didn't score, they would never learn. Many of the kids don't score any goals their first season. We would never think about not recognizing the small accomplishments they did make. Adults are no different.

They try hard to learn new things and will make mistakes early in the process. We can recognize what they did well, or we can wait until they get everything perfect. The first method encourages them to continue working hard to get better, and the second method leaves them discouraged and unhappy. Some people have been beaten down so much in their lives that they are uncomfortable with recognition. They dodge it and sometimes appear to shun it. But it is lighting a small fire inside them that even they might not recognize; and in time, they will come to appreciate and even expect to hear a few positive words from you. And they will be loyal and more hard-working because of it. Recognize people for the little things and recognize them often. It is one of the best ways to create positive relationships.

Baker and Dutton offer five areas that can help improve positive relationships in your organization. They include hiring for relationship skills, including employees in the hiring and selection process, teaching positive relationship skills, rewarding for positive relationship behaviors, and education on positive relationship meeting practices.

Think about someone in your office who highly encourages the culture. They help plan events and parties, and seem to take responsibility for people getting to interact and getting to know one another. Help and support those people; they are extremely valuable.

Positive relationships are a key to success at work. They provide us with intellectual, physical, and emotional resources that help us be more productive and more efficient. They help us reduce stress, become happier and healthier, and live longer. Our supervisor-employee relationships are especially important, because they have the most impact in determining our satisfaction with work and our willingness to stay and be fully engaged.

Activity

1. The next time a new person starts at your office, offer to take them to lunch in their first week, even if they are not in your department.

2. Pick a day and focus all your attention on every interaction. Put down your phone, turn or close your computer screen, and don't look at or answer your phone. Look only at them, and pay attention to what they are saying and how they are saying it.

3. Write a list of what you appreciate about your supervisor. What is he or she good at, what are you learning from your supervisor?

4. Get to know your supervisor personally. Go to lunch together or schedule time on both of your calendars to get to know each other; ask about his or her kids, careers, and lives in general.

5. Go to lunch with someone at work who is not part of your core two- or three-person network.

6. Practice recognition at work. Find team members and tell them what a great job they are doing. Send an email to their boss or their team. Recognize your supervisor or his or her boss as well. All levels of team members need recognition.

Positive Relationships

Chapter 15
Community, Giving, and Charity

"The Master has no possessions. The more he does for others, the happier he is. The more he gives to others, the wealthier he is." Lao Tzu

Being kind to others actually makes us happier. Helping people requires you to see them in a good light. If you reach out to help people rather than avoid them, you have to make the transition in your mind from judgment or fear to empathy and compassion. It also creates a reciprocal reaction in them in the form of a smile or eyes that are bright with appreciation, which then makes you happier, creating a virtuous circle. That circle continues as they move to the next person, still thinking positively about you, and share that smile with someone new. Think about a woman in business attire walking towards the same building as you. She has a sour or put-out look on her face. Your initial thoughts might be that she is mean or angry and you should avoid her. But a thought flashes through your mind: what if she has had a bad morning, or what if she is concentrating on what she has to get done at work today? So you open the door for her. She looks up, at first confused, and then recognizes the kindness you are offering. Her look changes from sour to a smile as her mind clicks away from whatever was bothering her to appreciation of this small gesture. Her smile makes you smile, and you are both likely to carry that smile into the elevator and the office. This doesn't work every time; but you will become happier as you find new ways to be thoughtful and kind to people, whether they reward you with a smile or not.

Practicing acts of kindness releases serotonin into your brain, which makes you feel happier. People who observe an act of kindness also have serotonin released into their brain. So doing something nice not only makes you happier; it also brings happiness to anyone that happens to be watching.

Helping others gives us the opportunity to use our strengths or hobbies that we don't get to use at work. Cooking for others or building a house with Habitat for Humanity could be two examples. Helping others also serves as reinforcement that we are good people. We all like to think that we are, but helping others is the concrete proof that we should feel good about ourselves. It connects us to people in ways we might not expect as we get surprised by other people's positive reactions to what we are doing. Helping others helps us find a sense of meaning, and helps us see how fortunate we are.

Kogan and team found that giving without expecting anything in return significantly improves our mood. Also, the more authentic we feel about our motivations (in other words, the more we truly feel we are doing it for them and not for ourselves), the greater the improvement in our mood. If we make giving and helping others a habit, something we want and choose to do, then we become happier ourselves, but if we give to people because we want to feel happier rather than because we want to help them, it doesn't work. Focus on making it a habit to help others. We all have natural inclinations to reach out and help. We are often just too busy or too shy to take action. If we can overcome our reluctance and reach out whenever we hear that voice inside our head telling us to help, it will become a habit. Once it becomes a habit and you are not calculating the benefits to yourself, you will become happier.

Volunteering to work at a charity or help others makes you happier. The effects don't just last during your volunteering; you could actually become happier for months afterwards. The key word is volunteering. Your motivation has to be an intrinsic desire to help someone, rather than being focused on what you are going to get out it. Participants in studies who worked at a charity to fulfill some other obligation did not become happier. Also, seniors seem to benefit most from volunteering for a charity and helping others. Caring does not have to be connected to an organized charity. Reaching out to a friend or someone at work or school also makes you happier. Interestingly, it is also important to get the people you are helping to participate. People who help others help themselves also get a bump in happiness, while people who do not actively participate in improving their situation can actually become less happy because of their feeling of dependence on someone else.

Volunteering for a charity or helping others also builds our self-confidence. It helps us feel competent and worthwhile. We feel better because we are contributing to something bigger than ourselves and helping our community, as well as the individuals who are directly affected by our efforts. It can even reduce our stress levels by taking our mind off of our own challenges and providing us with reasons to be grateful for the abundance in our own lives.

People who volunteer physically feel better. Research by Luks with more than 1,700 female volunteers showed that giving to others releases endorphins, which provide us with a "helper's high" similar to a "runner's high." The better news is that even after the chemicals dissipate from our bodies, we still have a long term sense of well-being that can last for several months.

Functional magnetic resonance imaging (fMRI) shows that the same regions of the brain light up when a person is giving as when they are experiencing pleasure or receiving a reward. Can giving to a charity have the same mood-enhancing effects as cocaine? Research by Harbaugh, Mayr, and Burghart found that giving away money activates a region of the brain called the ventral striatum. That portion of the brain also happens to light up when people have cocaine in their system.

Volunteering doesn't just help us be happier, it can make us smarter and contribute to longer lives. Several research studies have shown that giving money to a charity or to help someone else made people happier, and that happier people gave more money to help others--suggesting that there is a virtuous circle of giving and becoming happier, which leads to more giving. The research included giving people $5 or $20 and then assigning them a task of giving it away or spending it on themselves. Those people who gave the money to someone else were happier when contacted that evening than were the people who spent it on themselves. In an organization, this can be multiplied. One person who is passionate about a cause can recruit others to contribute to that cause. The opportunity to give back makes the team happier. Participating with friends and co-workers makes the team happier. The belief that the organization supports charities and passions makes employees happier and more likely to stay. The combination of these benefits creates a more productive workforce and a more successful company. Finally, and most importantly, the community benefits from the generosity and help of the employee volunteers. Organizing charitable opportunities at work creates happiness and success on multiple levels.

Charity at work brings teams together and boosts morale. It makes people feel like they are part of a team—something bigger than themselves-- and gives them a sense of making a difference. It also improves how they feel about the company, and their willingness to stay.

Research from a 2011 Deloitte Volunteer IMPACT survey showed that employees who volunteered in workplace causes were more engaged and had a higher opinion of the company's culture. Among the younger generation (those under 35), those who participate are twice as likely to be satisfied with their career development as those who don't participate. Research by Cone Communications shows that more than 75% of employees want to be involved in giving and volunteering programs, including volunteer days, with as many as 81% willing to participate in company matching programs.

Let the employees choose the programs that are important to them. Most likely there are passionate people on your team with causes that have real meaning to them. They can tell their stories and share their passions with their other team members, who will feel great being able to help. Don't make the first effort too big, however; a lot of small opportunities are more effective at getting people involved. Once you have established a group that is committed to helping others, you can branch out to bigger and bigger projects. Participation is always an option. Doing good has to come from the heart. Also, no one wants to deal with a disgruntled participant when they are trying to help make other people happier and better off.

Activity

"...Doing a kindness produces the single most reliable momentary increase in well-being of any exercise we have tested." Martin Seligman

1. Pick one day a week to practice Random Acts of Kindness. Pick a number to shoot for, like five in one day.

    a. Tape money to a vending machine

    b. Help someone in need cross the street

    c. Open a door for someone

    d. Buy a friend a Coke or a coffee

    e. Help a friend through a stressful time at work or personally

    f. Bring donuts to the office

2. Find a charity or cause that matches your values. Find ways to help, even if it is for only a few hours each month. Share the opportunity with your team members at work.

"Our happiness is dependent on the happiness of others, and so the only way we can be happy is if others are as well. In this way, we can still serve ourselves while serving others. If we take action to make others happy, even if that action does not in itself provide us with happiness, the happiness we caused in those others will ultimately make us happy." Jonji from ProjectHappiness.org

Higher Purpose and Meaning

Chapter 16
Higher Purpose

"Focusing your life solely on making a buck shows a certain poverty of ambition. It asks too little of yourself. Because it's only when you hitch your wagon to something larger than yourself that you realize your true potential." Barack Obama

Part of happiness is having a Higher Purpose--something to strive for that is bigger than you. We all want to matter and to make a difference in the world, at work, or in someone else's life. Our Higher Purpose is how we find deep meaning and fulfillment in our lives, by contributing to someone or something that is bigger than ourselves.

"Many persons have a wrong idea of what constitutes true happiness. It is not attained through self-gratification, but through fidelity to a worthy purpose." - Helen Keller

Based on research by the Center for Disease Control, only 21% of adults strongly agree that their life has a clear sense of purpose. In two other studies, 90% of alcoholics and 100% of drug addicts thought their life was meaningless. In several polls spread across several time periods and countries, when people were asked what was very important, "having a purpose or meaning in life" was chosen by 80% to 90% of respondents, while money was chosen by around 16%. Having purpose and meaning in your life has been connected to happiness, life satisfaction, physical health, and self-esteem. According to recent research by Fredrickson and Cole, having purpose and meaning actually increases our health at the cellular level, providing us with a better immune response profile. Purpose and meaning are important and better for us emotionally and physically, but for many of us, they are also elusive.

It is that nagging feeling that you are not on the right course or that something just isn't right. You get a sense that your hard work and effort may be directed in the wrong places. Does your work give you energy so you feel excited and pumped, or does it suck your energy so you feel worn down and depleted? Is it possible that you believe that being unhappy today is the sacrifice you need to make to be happy tomorrow?

These are all signs that you are going through the motions, but don't have a good understanding of why. Without a Higher Purpose, your daily trudge can often feel mundane and pointless. In the Greek story of Sisyphus, King Sisyphus is punished by the gods, forced to roll a boulder up a mountain all day every day, only to watch it roll back down at the end of the day. No matter how hard he works, the rock never stays at the top of the mountain; and his work is pointless. Our lives often fall into the trap of becoming like Sisyphus. We do the same thing every day with little progress.

This Sisyphean pursuit often starts after the honeymoon of our careers has ended. Initially we work to gain something for ourselves, such as buying our first car or our first apartment. Focusing on our own personal gain can be motivating for a while. But once we reach that goal, the reward and internal feeling of satisfaction are fleeting. We move on to the next bigger goal, often not even stopping to celebrate our accomplishment. After several months, or whatever timeframe it takes to accomplish those first basic goals, we lose our excitement and focus and fall into a routine. Over the years, we settle deeper and deeper into that routine. Prying ourselves out of that routine requires a Higher Purpose--something we can work toward that makes us want to get up every day. That usually includes something bigger than ourselves. Focusing on giving to someone else or helping our team achieve a bigger goal actually changes our brain chemistry. We get more internal satisfaction. The feeling is consistent and ongoing, rather than fleeting, as it is when we are focused on ourselves.

Also, when we only focus on ourselves, we easily move into negative thinking. The majority of people are naturally self-critical and tend to think about what is wrong with themselves, rather than appreciating what is right with themselves. We often try to silence those thoughts and bury those feelings with more and more pleasurable experiences, but that voice always comes back and attempts to fill us with self-doubt and sometimes even self-loathing. If we choose to spend our time focused on helping someone else, we have an answer for those doubts. It is a like a proof point for our own internal conversation. When we naturally criticize ourselves, we can counter those negative thoughts by internally referencing our good deeds related to our Higher Purpose. They are concrete examples of the good things we do. If your internal voice says "You are lazy and not good enough," it can be countered with the example of "but I am building a life for my kids, and that is important work," or "I contributed to my team reaching their goals, so I am working hard and I am good enough," or "I have a reason to get up every morning, because I am helping someone accomplish his or her goals."

Defining Terms

Throughout this section we will use three key terms to discuss the science and concepts of striving for more than just mundane, day-to-day actions. They are purpose, Higher Purpose, and meaning.

Purpose is a connection between what you are doing now and a positive result in the future. Planting seeds is a mundane activity. It gains purpose when you know those seeds will grow into beautiful flowers.

Higher Purpose is a purpose where the positive result is for someone else or contributes to something bigger than yourself. A purpose of planting seeds and growing flowers becomes a Higher Purpose when you plan to share the joy of seeing the flowers with someone else or when the flowers contribute to making your neighborhood a more beautiful place.

Meaning is the feeling of contentment and confidence that comes from having a purpose, or even better, having a Higher Purpose that contributes to something bigger than yourself. A meaningful life is one in which you believe that you make a difference, that you matter, and that you are living in harmony with your core values.

A Higher Purpose is related to finding meaning in your life. Your Higher Purpose is something you strive for, and that striving results in a more meaningful life.

It is important to note that these are not the most scientifically accurate definitions; they are simplified to help with clarity and understanding of the concepts in this section.

In his book *Man's Search for Meaning*, Viktor Frankl writes about living in concentration camps and trying to help his fellow prisoners stay alive. He found that those prisoners who could find meaning in the midst of all that suffering were far more resilient than those who could not. Frankl provides two illustrations of how men found meaning and a purpose to keep living while enduring the horrors of the concentration camps. One prisoner focused on his young child and staying alive so he could once again see his child. Another prisoner focused on his work as a scientist and writing books that would share his knowledge.

Finding our "Why"

"He who has a "Why" to live for can bear almost any How." Nietzsche

Have you ever had the feeling that something is missing? Everything should be good. You have great relationships and/or a great family, a great job where you are doing well and moving up, and everything in your life seems to be in place. But you can't shake that feeling that there must be more. Not having a Higher Purpose can lead to this feeling that something is missing. You need a Higher Purpose to help you understand where to go from here. It serves as your answer to the question "Why?" Why am I doing these things? Why should I get up in the morning? Why should I put in this level of effort? Once you understand your "Why," you can get the "what" and the "how" in order. You can take action that will fulfill your passion and feel meaningful in your life. Your "Why" provides clarity for taking that next step.

Dennis Waitley provides an analogy of a suitcase with a million dollars in it. The story explains that all you have to do to claim the one million dollars is drive across town and pick up the suitcase in under one hour. You would probably make two decisions: you would start immediately, and you would overcome any obstacle, traffic problem, or even a natural disaster to get to that suitcase in under an hour.

The decisions you would make and the actions you would take are probably very different from what you would do if you were driving across town for a meeting, a doctor's appointment, or some other mundane activity. The one million dollars is a clear and motivational "Why." You can clearly visualize how it will impact your future, and you would push yourself to extreme measures to claim that prize. We can tap into that same motivational current by finding a clear "Why" for our lives. Knowing and understanding our "Why" will help us start early every day and overcome obstacles that would otherwise deter us from our goals. Find your "Why" for everything you do, and you will discover the ability to overcome any obstacle that is thrown in your way.

Knowing our Higher Purpose helps us understand why our actions are meaningful and why they matter. It provides confirmation that we are not experiencing a random set of events in our lives, but that we are purposefully headed in a general direction. It may not be a straight path, but at least we are headed in what we judge to be the right direction. Our Higher Purpose serves as our guide when we come to a fork in the road and need to make decisions.

Having a Higher Purpose helps guide our priorities. We can focus on goals and actions that will keep us motivated and energized, rather than following the path of least resistance, feeling de-motivated and bored.

A Higher Purpose will also help keep us on track when unexpected negative events occur, like family in the hospital, or other tragedies close to home.

My wife is very clear on her Higher Purpose: it is our children. She would give her life to save one of our children without a second thought. She would go hungry so they can eat and be cold so they can be warm. This Higher Purpose includes all the characteristics we have discussed. It fits with her values of children first, empathy, kindness, and integrity. She has someone else to focus her efforts on, the children. She has a strong sense of self-worth in helping them grow to be healthy, thoughtful, well-mannered, industrious, and independent. Finally, she knows she is making a difference in their lives and the lives of the people they help and interact with. She has not always been able to articulate that our children were her "Higher Purpose."

She explored graduate school and a career in insurance first. She always knew she wanted to stay home and take care of her children once she had them. She always knew that taking care of the children was a priority in her life. But it took a lot of thought and self-reflection to identify and fully embrace that as her Higher Purpose and eliminate the feeling of guilt for not having a job and a career. Once she identified the values she already lived by and identified the experiences that made her happiest, she was able to get comfortable with her Higher Purpose and become much happier and more satisfied with life. It was not as much about search and discovery as it was about identifying the clues that were already a part of her life.

When I was younger and first studying success, I was referred to a couple in a nearby town. They did not have any children, were not wealthy, and had low-paying jobs. But I found them to be extremely successful and happy. They had created a Chinese garden in their backyard, and their Higher Purpose was taking care of each other and that garden. They went to work at 7 am each morning and left work by 4 pm. They were happy with their work and talked positively about it. But their real love was being at home and with each other. After work they would go straight home, have a cup of coffee or a glass of wine, and sit and talk or work on their garden. They were deeply satisfied with their life together and always had smiles and positive things to say.

What do you want to do? What is meaningful and fulfilling to you? Don't try to impress or meet the expectations of others. Don't do what you think the people you know would want you to do. Do what really matters and is important to you. A good test: if you took action related to your Higher Purpose, and no one knew you had taken those actions, would they still be meaningful? For example, if your Higher Purpose were to feed the hungry, and you dropped off $100 worth of groceries to 10 different families, and no one knew it was you, would it still feel as meaningful? If the answer is yes, then congratulations; you have found something that fulfills you, rather than trying to impress other people.

My nephew Ben works at a mortgage company, on a team that handles homebuyers who have been unable to make their payments, are experiencing foreclosures, or are caught up in bankruptcies. He was unhappy with his job because he didn't like the constant flow of calls from unhappy people, and he felt like changes in their bonus system had resulted in him losing a significant amount of money. He had no interest in putting in extra effort or working extra hours. He had a form of a career, but it was not going well; and he we was not getting the promotions he wanted and the consideration he thought he deserved. He had a career orientation. He wanted the money and the satisfaction of moving up in a career. This was enough to keep him somewhat motivated and minimally happy.

Ben worked to identify his Higher Purpose and discover how he was using his strengths for this job. As it turns out, his strength was in taking the angry callers and converting them to happy (or at least happier) callers before the call was over. He also found satisfaction in helping some of the clients save their houses. So he set a goal and started tracking the number of houses he saved on a monthly, then weekly, and eventually daily basis. He also started tracking the number of people he could turn from angry to happy. This gave him a noble Higher Purpose to pursue. It was no longer about money or working to grow his career, or even to keep his job; it was about saving homes. The initial impact was almost immediate. Within a week, he was enjoying work more and having better interactions with his executives and teammates. He moved up in team rankings, qualified for top bonuses, and became a source of inspiration, rather than an average employee. He had a different perspective on the same job. Answering calls from angry homeowners all day can be draining and surely does not seem like a long-term job for happiness. Saving homes and helping angry callers become happier, however, does reflect a "Higher Purpose." It is a great reason to get up in the morning and go to work. It is a reason to look forward to those calls, rather than resenting them and wanting to avoid them. It turns a career into a calling and results in your interactions with peers and executives becoming more positive as you reflect a positive attitude about what you are doing, rather than seeming downcast and defeated.

During this process, Ben also discovered an additional purpose. It turns out that he often takes calls from clients assigned to other members on his team or the organization. He found that if he can successfully handle those calls and do everything possible to help out his teammates, it will also make them successful. So his list of Higher Purposes now includes helping to make his teammates successful. How do you think those kinds of changes will affect his success? Can happiness and success result from having a Higher Purpose of helping people save their homes, turning callers from angry to happy, and helping your teammates become more successful and make more money?

I want to clarify that, even though Ben saw immediate success, it took a lot more time and investment to confirm that these Higher Purposes were a good fit for him. It also took time to change the old habits of distaste and inward focus so that he could enjoy his job every day and not just on certain days. Identification of your Higher Purpose and changing the habits related to living it is hard work, but it is worth it because of the happiness and success it eventually brings.

Why Do We Need a Higher Purpose?

People yearn for stability in their lives and the concept that life is not just a series of random events that are not connected and have no real reason for occurring. We distinguish ourselves from other animals by our intellectual ability to connect events across time and understand how they will impact other people, our future, and the world in general. It is one of the things that enables us to make progress in our lives and across time and generations. Identifying our Higher Purpose ties our past and present with our future, helps explain how we matter in the world, provides validation that our values are correct and that we are making the right decisions, and gives us confidence that we have a reason for being and that we are adding value to the world.

A Higher Purpose provides resilience. You are able to endure countless more challenges and obstacles when you know your "Why" and you are clear on your direction. Your resilience is even stronger when you know your sacrifices are going to benefit someone else.

A Higher Purpose can seem overwhelming and too big to take on. You don't have to be trying to solve world hunger to find meaning and fulfillment. A Higher Purpose can be as simple as "Sharing my music" or "Teaching others the joys of surfing."

Here are a few examples of Higher Purpose that were posted on the Internet. (See Kimberly Pichot's web site – Complete Success, Inc., http://completesuccess.wordpress.com/2011/05/10/examples-of-life-purpose-statements/)

My life purpose is to energize, connect, and inspire purpose in others.

My purpose in life is to be a mom: to empower independence, self-reliance and confidence in others through being a positive, supportive role model.

My purpose in life is to grow continually and use my wisdom to help others grow through teaching and encouraging them while making a difference in their lives and the lives of those around them.

To be a positive role model & help people.

Your Higher Purpose can be simple and attainable. The important concepts are that it provides a "Why" for your daily activities, it gives you energy and enthusiasm for getting up and getting started in the morning, and it helps you feel like you matter and can make a difference.

Higher Purpose and Meaning

Chapter 17
Finding Purpose

"When you walk with purpose, you collide with destiny" Bertrice Berry

From a happiness standpoint, the next step down from a Higher Purpose, is having any purpose. Purpose means we are able to connect what we are doing today with some benefit in the future. It is part of having meaning. If we know why we are doing something and how it connects to the future, we can endure the mundane or difficult challenges we run into. Without understanding that purpose, we have no reason to endure the pain or be disciplined about completing a task. The difference between purpose and Higher Purpose is who is being helped. A Higher Purpose requires something bigger than yourself. If you have a purpose, you know how what you are doing is going to help <u>you</u> in the future. If you have a Higher Purpose, you know how what you are doing is also going to help the team, the company, or someone else in the future.

One interesting study showed retirement-aged people with a "purpose in life" lived longer than seniors who did not have purpose. They defined purpose as the sense that life has meaning and direction and that one's goals and potential are being achieved or are achievable. They evaluated 1,238 people in two studies and found that seniors who had a "purpose in life" had a mortality rate that was more than 40% lower than those who did not have a "purpose in life." These conclusions held true even after controlling for factors like gender, race, depressive symptoms, disability, neuroticism, chronic medical conditions, and income. In their questionnaire, they found three questions that particularly related to mortality. "I sometimes feel as if I've done all there is to do in life," "I used to set goals for myself, but that now seems like a waste of time," and "My daily activities often seem trivial and unimportant to me." Another study showed that "purpose in life" was one of six factors that increased the release of chemicals and other indicators of stronger immunities and lowered the risk of heart disease for women over 65. Yet another study of 950 people with an average age of around 80 showed that those with a "purpose in life" were half as likely to suffer from Alzheimer's, and were better at housekeeping, managing money, and getting up and down stairs. Having a "purpose in life" and setting and pursuing meaningful goals on a daily basis is good for your happiness, health, quality of life, and longevity.

Purpose works across time. Describing something as it exists today does not provide purpose. Understanding how it connects across time helps it have a purpose. "I wrapped a box in colored paper" is not purposeful. It is a description of an action that only impacts one point in time. Understanding the result of that action, "I wrapped a present that Tina will be so excited to open," provides purpose. Our brains become engaged emotionally and chemically at the thought of Tina being excited to unwrap her gift. We connect what we are doing now with how it will impact us (or even better, someone else) at a later point in time.

Your purpose could be linked to a fundamental challenge or crisis you endured or observed someone close to you endure. Deep emotional experiences create a strong empathy for others in similar situations and motivate us to go to great lengths to help them. Many people who have someone close to them die from cancer, or a car accident, or some other tragedy find a Higher Purpose in helping raise money or change laws to support those causes and prevent someone else from enduring similar pain.

Write Your Sentence

Daniel Pink, in his book *Drive,* uses the story of Clare Boothe Luce to provide an example of finding purpose. Clare Boothe Luce, a US Congresswomen in the 1940s, later gave President John F. Kennedy some advice. She told him that "a great man is a sentence, and it is always a sentence that has an active verb." For Abraham Lincoln it was "He preserved the union and freed the slaves." For Franklin Roosevelt it was "He lifted us out of the Great

Depression and helped us win a world war." What is your sentence? Is it focused at home? "I raised two kids to be healthy, happy adults." Is it focused on your work? "I kept patients and their families healthy and comfortable." Is it focused on one of your charitable efforts? "I helped less privileged children have happier holidays." Is it a result of your hobby? "I created art work that will inspire my great grandchildren." It doesn't have to be big; it just has to be yours--something you believe in and are passionate about.

Activity: Write Your Sentence

Examples:

1. Lincoln - "He preserved the union and freed the slaves."

2. Franklin Roosevelt - "He lifted us out of the Great Depression and helped us win a world war."

3. Parent - "I am raising two kids to be healthy, happy adults."

4. Health Professional - "I keep patients and their families healthy and comfortable."

5. Faith Based – "I will live a life that reflects positively in the eyes of my God."

6. Volunteer - "I help less privileged children have happier holidays."

7. Artist - "I create artwork that will inspire my great grandchildren."

8. Mine – "I help others become happy and successful."

Now You Try It

1. Start with "I."

2. Add an active verb that describes what you do or want to do – help, create, design, provide, lift, build, etc.

3. Add the "who." Who specifically fits into your Higher Purpose?

4. Add in any details that help make it unique to you.

5. See if it fits and make changes until you are comfortable.

My Higher Purpose Statement:

I _____

(Active Verb)(Who)(Details)

This is <u>your</u> Higher Purpose. It can be anything you want it to be, and you can change it at any time. Like a finely tailored suit, it needs to fit you and make you feel proud when you show it to others.

Some purpose statements that have been posted on the Internet include:

I will energize, connect, and inspire purpose in others.

I will enliven, encourage, and re-inspire the love of music for children in public schools.

I will create an inviting environment for shop visitors so they can leave behind their daily challenges for a few minutes.

Higher Purpose and Meaning

Chapter 18
Your Higher Purpose and Work

"The two most important days in your life are the day you are born and the day you find out why." Mark Twain

Most of us spend close to half our waking hours working. If we can understand how to tie our Higher Purpose to work or how to find purpose and meaning in our work, we can make half of our life that much better. Having a Higher Purpose helps you understand your "Why." You wake up in the morning glad to see and experience another day. You may even be excited and enthusiastic about what is ahead for you. You go to work with a clear understanding of what you will get out of work and why you want to go. It is important that on most days, going to work is a mental "thumbs-up" vs. "thumbs-down." Your work may not always be your Higher Purpose, but it often helps to provide your living wages so you can pursue your Higher Purpose outside of work.

Meaning connects work and happiness. People find meaning in their lives when they can leverage their strengths and experience their passions. Often their work enables these two to come together. People who find meaning in their work are more motivated, miss less work, are more engaged, feel empowered, have less stress, have better job satisfaction, and experience more personal fulfillment. Charles Kearns' research on happiness

and performance in the workplace revealed that one of the characteristics of the top-performing employees, what he termed as the Happy High Performers, was that they found purpose and meaning in their work.

Many people will tell you they work for the money. But when surveyed, most people say they work because of the relationships, autonomy, and learning. They work because they believe they have something to contribute, and work is a method to fund that contribution or an outlet for that contribution. Research by the iOpener institute revealed that employees under the age of 30 are willing to stay at a company or recommend that company to friends based more on how fulfilled they are at their jobs than on how much they get paid.

Dan Ariely did some interesting studies related to meaning and work. He paid participants to assemble Bionicles, which are Lego models that look like robots. Each participant was allowed to build and get paid for building as many Bionicles as they wanted. With one group, as each Bionicle was completed, the researchers would place the built Bionicle under the table and give the participant a new Bionicle to build. With the second group, the researchers would disassemble the Bionicle in front of the participant and give it back to them to reassemble. The second group assembled far fewer Bionicles than did the first group and rated the joy that came from assembly as very low. By disassembling the Legos in front of the participants, the researchers were able to suck the meaning and the enjoyment out of the task.

"What man actually needs is not a tensionless state, but rather the striving and struggling for a worthwhile goal, a freely chosen task. What he needs is not the discharge of tension at any cost, but the call of a potential meaning waiting to be fulfilled by him." Viktor Frankl

Historically we have managed people like machines, looking for ways to make them more efficient and productive in a stable environment. Continuously improving how fast they could complete the same task was our measure of accomplishment. The challenge is that the migration to a knowledge worker economy has brought with it constant and accelerating change. Peter Vaill uses the metaphor of continuous white water. We are always in the rapids and in danger of drowning. Solving one challenge just clears our vision long enough to see five more coming toward us. We need something constant to strive for. A Higher Purpose in our work gives us that one constant. It is the point high above the rapids that we can use to re-orient ourselves after each challenge. When all the things we can't control seem to conspire against us, we can realign with our Higher Purpose to determine our next course of action.

It is no longer reasonable to expect that we know the exact outcome of every decision. There is no "right answer." There are too many variables in a constantly changing world. The best we can do is to use our Higher Purpose as our North Star so we will know we are generally heading the right direction and can make constant course corrections along the way.

How do you make progress in meaningful work?

> *"Of all the things that can boost emotions, motivation, and perceptions during a workday, the single most important is making progress in meaningful work."* Amabile and Kramer

Meaningful work uses your strengths and aligns with your values. Find work that matters or find meaning in your work. Your happiness will be improved by your willingness to find how your work can help other people, how it can best utilize your strengths, and how it can align with your values.

A few ways to find purpose and meaning in your work include:

1. Identify how your company is helping its customers or the community. If you work at a restaurant, you could conclude that "I put up with grumpy, complaining people," or you can believe that "I provide a much needed enjoyable experience with friends and family." Are you more motivated to "put up with grumpy people" or to provide a much needed positive experience that will help your customer be happier?

2. Support a good cause. Recruit your friends and peers to support your favorite charity or focus on a cause you believe in.

3. <u>Apply today's lessons to your future.</u> What are you learning that can be applied later in your career or in other parts of your life? Are there other forms of personal growth that are available through your work?

4. <u>Ask your family to support you.</u> Family can influence the meaning in you work either positively or negatively. They can put strains on the work due to demands for time, energy, or money. Your family can be focused on a desire for more money, which moves work farther from meaning, or your family can be supportive and proud of your work, which helps to give it meaning.

5. <u>Focus on what you are accomplishing.</u> Every day when you are ready to leave the office, write down what you accomplished for that day. It can be directly related to your work--how many customers you helped--or it can be an indirect result of your work--how many people you made smile or helped be more successful at their jobs. Keep track of the good things you are doing and focus on those. Happiness can be as much related to what you think about and remember as it is to what actually happens. Focusing on and thinking about the positive things you are accomplishing opens your mind to finding the purpose and meaning in your work.

6. <u>Help someone else.</u> Who are you interacting with? How are you positively impacting people? Who are you helping succeed? For some people, interacting with and helping the people they work with provides purpose and meaning. Is there meaning and purpose in helping your team complete a project or accomplish a goal? Who can you help today? Deepen and strengthen your relationships at work.

7. <u>Connect what you are accomplishing to the company goals.</u> Purpose and meaning are related to how much you think you are contributing or making a difference at work. Understanding your company's or group's goals and how you contribute helps you find meaning. You may also want to ask or determine how your work will help a person inside or outside of the organization. If you can connect your work to how it is better for society in general, it will be more meaningful.

8. <u>Be authentic.</u> In other words, identify how the organization reflects similar values to yours. Identify how you are using or how you can

use your strengths. How do your values and the values shown by your company or peers match up?

Jobs, Careers, and Callings

Campbell, Converse, and Rodgers found that work satisfaction can account for up to 20% of life satisfaction, and work satisfaction can be improved by having a Calling. Amy Wrzesniewski and team have done significant work around how people relate to their work. They classify these "work orientations" as people feeling like they work at a Job, feeling like they are building a Career, or feeling like they have a Calling.

If you have a Job orientation, working is a chore and your paycheck is compensation for your effort. If you have a Career orientation, your work and long hours are an investment in your potential advancement and success. They are related to your social standing and self-esteem. If you have a Calling orientation, your efforts are part of a Higher Purpose. They are done for the betterment of your team or society in general. People with a Calling feel that work has meaning and a purpose, which helps them feel like they are making a difference. They put in longer hours with more energy because their work is inherently rewarding. These are the people who are more likely to get ahead and succeed. People with a Calling orientation are also more satisfied with their work.

As an employer, you probably want more of your employees to have a Calling orientation. In workgroups where a higher percentage of the membership had Calling orientations, there was stronger identification with the team, less conflict, more faith and trust in management, more commitment to the team, and better communication. Employees are more satisfied with their coworkers and their work. Workgroups where a higher percentage of the membership had Career orientations had the opposite results. More conflict, less identification with the team, less faith and trust in management, and less job satisfaction.

The most interesting part of Wrzesniewski and team's research was that the work orientation was determined by the person and not the work. Part of their research included 24 staff assistants who all worked for the same company. So it was basically the same job in the same company. Those 24 staff assistants self-selected evenly into all three categories. One-third had a

Job orientation, one-third had a Career orientation, and one-third had a Calling orientation. It was the person's attitude toward the work, and not the work itself, that determined his or her work orientation. Individuals define whether they have a Job, a Career, or a Calling. Being a teacher is only a Calling if the person teaching believes it is. Some could also look at it as a Job. It doesn't matter what type of job you have, it only matters whether you see it as a Calling or as a Job. A doctor could have a Job orientation, while a janitor could have a Calling orientation. It's all in your perspective.

If you identify your work orientation, it can help you perform better and improve your happiness at work. This awareness can help you choose to perceive your work differently. You can craft a better work situation in the current job, rather than going on a search for a new job where you may or may not change your work orientation. It will also give you insights into your peers and employees, and into why some of them are more successful than others.

How do you know if you have a Job, a Career, or a Calling? (Note: You could have characteristics from multiple orientations. Look for the one that best fits your feelings about your work.)

Individuals have a <u>Job</u> orientation if:

1. They need the money for something outside of work.

2. They would change jobs if they didn't feel trapped by their circumstances

3. The job is a necessity.

4. They can't wait to leave work. They live for the weekends.

5. They would not choose this line of work again or would not recommend it to friends and family.

People have a <u>Career</u> orientation if:

1. They enjoy their work but are always looking for the next big thing.

2. They are focused on several goals related to future, more important positions.

3. This is a waypoint, and they just need to do well enough to get promoted to the next position.

4. A promotion is the ultimate recognition, and it scores big points in the competition with peers.

5. Self-esteem and social standing are very tied to work and level of accomplishment.

People have a <u>Calling</u> orientation if:

1. Work is the most important part of their life.

2. They love their work.

3. They have a lot of their friends at work.

4. They feel their work matters and makes a difference.

5. They would recommend their work to anyone.

6. They would prefer to continue working rather than retire.

Jobs, Careers, and Callings are not permanent situations. People can transition from one to the other, based on how they choose to perceive their work. What is going on in their personal lives, how their job is changing, their relationship with their supervisor or peers, the success of their company, and how their company is embodying certain values can all have an impact on those perceptions. It is important to note, however, that these are work orientations, which means it is not the characteristics of the job but how the person perceives those characteristics that results in them falling into one of the three orientations.

You also have the option to maintain your current work orientation. Some people choose a Job or Career orientation because their Higher Purpose is not related to work and they are not interested in making that connection.

For them, there may not be a reason to identify a Higher Purpose at work. If you have a Job orientation, you might identify the purpose and meaning your job enables. In other words, making money at this job allows me to take the time to teach surfing. If you have a Career orientation, it is important not to confuse your advancement goals with meaning.

Having a Career orientation and being motivated by external promotions, raises, and recognition are good; but they are external, pleasurable, and fleeting, as opposed to having meaning and offering fulfillment. We often think we are finding meaning because we are always chasing that next raise or promotion; but once we get them our sense of joy and excitement are only temporary, and we are quickly chasing the next raise or promotion. With a Career orientation, you may want to identify the Higher Purpose your advancement will enable. If it will help you raise your family, invest in your church, or provide some other form of intrinsic satisfaction, it will be more fulfilling in the long term.

If you would like to change your Job orientation into a Calling orientation, you might try re-writing your job description as if you're trying to entice someone else to do it. What is the list of tasks or experiences that are fun, interesting, or challenging about your work? How does your work impact others in a positive way? What are the bigger picture things you can choose to do? Can you re-write the work of "cleaning up after kids" to "giving children a safer, healthier place to learn"?

Activity: Finding Purpose and Meaning in Your Work

1. On one side of a page, make a list of tasks that are related to your work.

2. For each task, draw an arrow to the other side of the page and write a possible meaning that could be found in that task.

For example:

Task	Changes To	Meaning
Fill out a spreadsheet	====>	Improving organizational decision-making
Wait on a customer	====>	Change the customer's day with a wonderful experience
Go to a meeting	====>	Create new ways to make the company successful

Purpose and meaning come from how we purposely choose to perceive our work and its importance to other people.

In the next section we will review Job Crafting and how you can craft your work to help you create a Calling orientation.

Job Crafting

Wrzesniewski, Berg, and Dutton wrote about improving your work satisfaction by changing aspects of your job. They call it Job Crafting. You can change your tasks, relationships, or perceptions about the work, and it can improve your satisfaction with that work. Changing how you see your tasks changes how much meaning you find in them. You can add more meaning to your job by how you construct the tasks, interactions, and descriptions of your job. Chefs don't cook, they create works of art. Stewardesses became Flight Attendants focused on safety instead of glorified waitresses.

In my current job, our janitor Linda is one of the happiest people at our office. It was her goal to help make sure the "kids" (her name for our employees) had a wonderful, productive place to work. She crafted her job to be much more than being a janitor. Every morning she makes sure coffee is prepared and ready for quick brewing. Since my travel schedule is rough on

the plants in my office, and I am a detriment to any plant I touch, Linda voluntarily takes care of my plants. She waters them, fertilizes them, and even moves them to bigger and bigger pots because they are growing so profusely. She added these and other tasks to her job, which helped her redefine her role from "cleaner of the bathrooms" to "preparer of the productivity palace." As a side note, I use the term janitor because it has a universal meaning that everyone can understand. Linda is far more than a janitor: she is a valued and productive member of our team. She just happens to do a lot of the duties we would hire a janitor to do. Her positive attitude and ability to see her Higher Purpose led us to hire her away from our old office building to be a permanent part of our team when we moved to a new location. By re-crafting the tasks of her work, Linda changed her Job into a Calling.

Building and extending relationships is another route Wrzesniewski and team recommend to improve your work satisfaction through Job Crafting. Sandelands & Boudens concluded that when people talk about their work, they mostly describe their relationships with other people. What kinds of connections can you make with your peers so you know the real people behind the job descriptions? Non-work discussions about families, hobbies, and vacations enable positive feelings that help create an open dialogue when discussing the opportunities and challenges at work. Many people come to work because they enjoy the social interaction and team support of the people they work with. A Higher Purpose can often be focused on your relationships at work or can be identified through those relationships. For example, a peer may have connections to a charity you would be excited to work with.

A third way you can improve your work satisfaction through Job Crafting is by changing how you perceive the purpose of your job. We spoke earlier about my nephew Ben who changed his perception of his job from spending all day on the phone with unhappy people to helping them save their houses and helping them go from angry to happy. He even started measuring the number of people who said thank you and showed appreciation at the end of the call. His job didn't change; his perception of what he was doing changed. He found a Higher Purpose.

Wrzesniewski, Berg, and Dutton's research showed that Job Crafting helped people become more engaged and more satisfied with their work, show more resilience, and achieve higher levels of performance in their organizations.

Activity: Become a "Job Entrepreneur"

How can you make your work more satisfying and start identifying your Higher Purpose?

1. Write down the purpose of your work. For example, instead of cleaning bathrooms, you are preparing a productivity palace. Instead of handling phone calls you are saving houses. Instead of creating spreadsheets, you are preparing the foundation for organizational decision-making. Note: You may need family, friends, or peers to help you think differently about what you do. Focus on the areas of your work you are passionate about, that you think make a difference, or that you are excited about or at least interested in.

The purpose of my work is:	

2. List the tasks of your job and divide them into like and don't like. How can you make the tasks you don't like more fun?

Tasks I Like	Tasks I Don't Like

3. What tasks can you add or change that will help your job better reflect the purpose you wrote in Step 1?

New or Enhanced Tasks

4. What relationships can you create, nurture, or change?

Person	New way to interact with that person (e.g. introduce yourself, mentor, ask about his or her family, etc.)

5.   How can you change your perceptions of your job?

Negative Perception	Changed to Positive Perception Supporting Your Purpose

Cues

Finding meaning in your work can be broken down into three main questions: What activities are you doing and how valuable are they? What is your perceived position in the organization and social structure? Why are your unique talents right for the job, and how do your peers and the organization value those unique talents?

To answer those questions, you interpret cues from your peers, supervisors, and the executives of the organization. Cues are the subtle meanings taken from the actions of the people in each of these groups. For example, when your colleagues say hello in the morning, that is a cue that you are personally valued.

When your supervisor uses your work as an example, that is a cue that your work is valued. When you observe a cue, you assign a motivation to it. Did they intentionally forget to say hello or did they just not see me? The motivation you assign is related to how you feel about the person and how you feel about yourself and the value of the work you are doing.

Most of the cues you interpret and place importance on are not provided consciously by the giver. For example, your supervisor may not include your work as an example because he or she already had enough examples, or

because there had not been time to review it yet. It may not have anything to do with how they value you or your work. Noticing and interpreting these cues is an important part of identifying our meaning and value in the workplace, but it is also a subjective and biased process.

We choose which cues we want to pay attention to, and we determine what level of importance we want to place on each cue. For example, we may place a lot of importance on whether a visiting executive remembers our name and stops to talk to us during her visit. The executive, however, may have other things on her mind and may not take the time to stop and say hello. It is not a reflection of how she values our work, but a reflection of what challenges are occupying her mind at that time. Cues are a one-way communication where we interpret the message without any confirmation from the other side. As a result, if we are feeling bad about the value of our work, we are probably going to pay attention to and place more importance on those cues that support that negative belief.

A few examples of the cues we experience daily include:

1. Do our peers, supervisor, and colleagues say hello to us or ask about our day?

2. Does our supervisor review and provide feedback on the work we have done?

3. Do our peers and supervisor pay attention to our meetings and presentations?

4. Are we given the autonomy to make decisions and use our best judgment to get the job done?

5. Do we receive help from our supervisors or peers when we are under a tight deadline or don't understand how to do something?

Being aware that we are gathering cues will help bring more objectivity to our thinking process. We can use other information to validate our interpretations. By beginning with a positive mindset that includes a list of reasons why our work has meaning, rather than a list of reasons why it doesn't, we can be more aware of the positive cues and assign positive motivations to our interpretation of them. This process of positively interpreting the cues will help us find meaning in our work and help us be happier, which will create a positive spiral of better work performance, additional positive cues, and more affirmation of our value.

Finding your Higher Purpose at work can add happiness to a significant amount of time in your life. Jobs, Careers, Callings, Job Crafting, and Cues, are just a few of the tools you can use to identify and focus on your Higher Purpose at work. In the following chapters we'll discuss activities to help you add more clarity and definition.

Higher Purpose and Meaning

Chapter 19
Identify Your Higher Purpose

"Don't ask what the world needs. Ask what makes you come alive, and go do it. Because what the world needs is people who have come alive."
Howard Thurman

Finding meaning in your life and your Higher Purpose requires you to identify it, not search for it. Quitting your job and leaving behind your obligations so you can search for meaning on a trek through the wilderness will most often result in disappointment. Search implies evaluating thousands of options to see what fits best. The assumption is you will "know it when you see it." Evaluating thousands of options does not give you the opportunity to thoroughly explore each option, and unfortunately you might not "know it when you see it." You may toss out the meaning that works for you because of a few minor challenges you don't yet understand, or because of a rush to get to the next option to evaluate.

Understanding that you are already living according to your values (with some exceptions for mistakes and errors in judgment) and that you are already attempting to do the things that bring you joy and happiness (with exceptions for lack of discipline or knowledge) can make it much easier to identify your Higher Purpose. You already have the hints and indications of your Higher Purpose embedded in what you do every day.

Identify the values you are living by, or at least aspiring to live by. Identify the areas that are providing you happiness in the short term and long term. Give yourself a break for the mistakes and bad judgment. They are a part of your past but don't have to be a part of your future. The hints and clues and sometimes clear answers to what your Higher Purpose is will be found in your current and past life. Make elements of how you are currently living the foundation on which you start; then you can make short, strategic explorations into unknown areas for potential clarity of your Higher Purpose.

I was working with a mentee, Austin, who was considering a different job. He was not progressing as quickly as he would have liked and thought there might be better opportunities at other companies. He started working on his resume and interviewing with other companies, none of which seemed like a good fit. The job search was distracting him from his current job, where his performance was quickly sliding to levels that could result in his being fired. His challenge was not having a clear focus on his Higher Purpose.

He thought he was unfulfilled because of his job, when in reality, without a clear Higher Purpose, it would be difficult for any job to give him that sense of fulfillment. With a little effort, he was able to identify and focus on his Higher Purpose and find ways to become fulfilled at his current job. His performance improved significantly, and his peers and superiors took notice of his renewed energy. He was able to switch his direction from trying to leave a situation he didn't like to finding a good fit for his Higher Purpose. This gave him more time to find the right position, rather than just another position. Fortunately, he seems to have identified that his current work is actually a good fit with his Higher Purpose.

"Man is capable of changing the world for the better if possible, and of changing himself for the better if necessary." Frankl

One of our challenges is feeling comfortable with the status quo. We know there may be another path for us. But it is scary to think about making major changes in our life. Following a path that meets the expectations of our friends and families can be very safe. Thinking about straying outside of that path to do what we really want to do can be overwhelming, especially when we are not sure what is a dream and what is a realistic assessment of the possibilities. It requires time (days, weeks, and months) to clarify our values and our purpose. Once we gain that clarity, the decisions will be much easier.

Once we are sure that "this is what I want to do with my life," then we can find ways in our current life to fulfill that purpose. That may include taking a new perspective on our work, finding a charity to work with, or playing in a band. Once we are clear on our values and our purpose and we can find ways to live them in our current lives, we can start looking at what obstacles we need to overcome to make our purpose an even bigger part of our lives. We can look for jobs or companies that match our values and enable us to live our Higher Purpose. We can find ways to live more conservatively and reduce our expenses so we will be ready for opportunities to pursue our Higher Purpose. We can also find creative ways to make money doing what will fulfill our Higher Purpose. We don't have to jump off a cliff with no safety net. For some people, that may work and be a good option; but for many of us, we need to find ways to thoughtfully move toward making our Higher Purpose more prevalent in our lives. I met a friend while vacationing with my family in Wyoming. His first love was art, and his second love was surfing. The problem was, he couldn't make enough money at either to pay his living expenses.

He found several jobs where he could work enough hours to live conservatively and still make time for his art and surfing. Eventually he was able to turn his art into a business creating collectible duck decoys that sold for thousands of dollars. He found a niche that provided a healthy income and engaged his passion for art, as well as leaving time for surfing. It didn't happen all at once, but by having clarity on his purpose and values, he was able to overcome obstacles and find creative solutions that led to a fulfilling life. As a side note, he met his wife while he was on the beach painting. Life came together for him when he pursued his passions.

Religious and Spiritual Beliefs

In the search for a Higher Purpose, religious or spiritual beliefs and practices may be one of the best places to start. Spirituality and organized religion provide people with perspective, hope, and a deeper sense of meaning. They provide people with an outward focus instead of an inward focus. They give people something bigger than themselves to make the center of their attention.

They provide a perspective that there is more to life than what is impacting us at this moment; and life's ups and downs are part of a bigger picture, so they are not as catastrophic or miraculous as they might seem at the moment. They help us understand the "Why" in our lives. They also provide clarity around values, which is a key ingredient to finding purpose and meaning in life.

Religious and spiritual beliefs encourage many happiness-building behaviors. They provide a plan for an idealistic future and specify positive behaviors today that will ensure we attain that future. They provide hope when events in our lives are going horribly wrong and help us build resiliency. They provide an opportunity and incentives for connections and positive relationships. They provide direction and opportunities to be grateful and to pray, meditate, or otherwise spend time being quiet and calm. They teach us to help other people and support our community. Religious and spiritual beliefs also teach us that we are worthy. Most religions promote that even the most seemingly insignificant individual has value and is worthy of love.

Science confirms the benefits of religious and spiritual beliefs. Religious people are happier, healthier, and recover better after trauma. People whose religious beliefs prescribe healthy diets and discourage smoking and alcohol use also live longer.

Research with 103 seniors aged 58 and above found that an intrinsic belief in a religion gave people purpose and meaning in their lives and made them happier. A similar study with 182 people reached comparable conclusions: religious commitment helps provide meaning in life, which in turn helps people be happier. Being authentically committed to religious and spiritual beliefs can provide you with a Higher Purpose.

Finding Purpose and Meaning in Your Current Actions

"Hard work is painful when life is devoid of purpose. But when you live for something greater than yourself and the gratification of your own ego, then hard work becomes a labor of love." Steve Pavlina

In a conversation with a mentee about his internship, I was told that the work was boring because all he does is complete spreadsheets. Completing a spreadsheet lacks purpose. When we discussed how the spreadsheet would help the company significantly reduce expenses over time, the spreadsheets started to gain purpose and interest. When we connected that purpose to how his unique abilities to produce the spreadsheets made an impact on the organization, he was able to find meaning in his work and a new level of interest. Restating your current tasks to show impact on others and how your unique skills make a difference brings meaning to situations and helps them move from boring to interesting, or even inspiring.

Activity: Find the purpose and meaning in your actions

1. In column A, write actions you take every day at work or at home.

2. In column B, write who they impact, and how it impacts them.

3. In column C, write the impact of those actions over time.

4. In column D, write why you are uniquely suited to make that contribution.

As you can see in the first example below, the current action of "I have to make the coffee" can turn into "I contribute to the success of the company by helping my friends be more awake and get along better because I make great coffee first thing every morning."

A Action	B Who and How	C Impact over Time	D My Contribution
Making Coffee	Friends at work are more awake and in a better mood, so they get along better.	Better collaboration at work leads to better ideas and a more successful company.	I am the first one in and make the best coffee.

Tips for Finding Your Higher Purpose

Higher Purpose and the resulting happiness come from being connected to something bigger than yourself. It is about giving rather than receiving. Many people looking for meaning in their lives find it by losing themselves in causes greater than themselves, such as family, country, team, company, religion, or anything you can identify with and find ways to personally support.

Start by asking, "How can I be of service or how can I help someone else? How do I help others with the talents, experiences and skills that I have? How can I make the world a better place? How do I plant seeds of greatness in the lives of those around me? How do I make an impact in the circles of influence where I find myself? How does what I do impact people?" A video game programmer helps people have fun. A food service worker helps people have a relaxing, enjoyable meal. A school janitor helps create a clean and safe learning environment for the kids. What are the positive impacts you can have on other people?

"This is the true joy in life, the being used for a purpose recognized by yourself as a mighty one..." George Bernard Shaw

Focus on what's inside vs. outside. A paycheck is external motivation. Helping a coworker is an internal motivation. External motivation, such as getting a paycheck or recognition from our peers, is an important part of our lives; however, the key is to make sure that is not the only form of motivation. What makes you feel good inside? What makes you feel peaceful and fulfilled? Helping another person or making an impact on the goals of your company or team provide internal rewards and fulfillment that lasts.

Another opportunity to find your Higher Purpose is to meet the people you are helping. If you work at an agency, meet and get to know your clients. At a restaurant or store, meet and get to know your customers. If you work at a large business, go sit with the customer service team and listen to customer calls or ride with a salesperson.

Our Higher Purpose can be related to our dreams. We all have dreams of what we want to be or do, but we often ignore them or hide them away because they seem impossible or unreasonable. We should uncover them and explore them. Find out how they are related to other people. Knowing our dreams can help us define what will provide meaning in our lives.

Don't limit your thinking to one Higher Purpose in only one part of your life. You can have more than one Higher Purpose, and each can be related to your work, family, religion, hobbies, etc. Creating a great environment for your kids and contributing to team accomplishments at work can both fit into your life. Experiment with different types of Higher Purposes in different areas of your life.

Your Higher Purpose can also change. Life events, like getting married or divorced, having kids, or changing jobs, can be catalysts for stopping and reconsidering your Higher Purpose or asking yourself "Why?" As your life changes, so will the ways you find meaning.

"If you can't figure out your purpose, figure out your passion. For your passion will lead you right into your purpose." Bishop T.D. Jakes

Combine your passions, strengths, and values to find meaning and purpose. Your strengths are what make you unique and what you uniquely bring to the table. Martin Seligman writes that a meaningful life includes a lot of positive feelings, the ability to amplify those feelings, the use of your signature strengths to obtain abundant gratification, and the use of your signature strengths for something bigger than yourself.

To help you find your Higher Purpose, identify those times when you feel truly happy. When you are contented rather than excited and thrilled. What are those things you do every week that you are passionate about? What are the things that give you an almost irrational sense that you can't give up. For what types of activities do you say "I love to do that; it gives me such joy and fulfillment"?

Activity: (Pick Two)

1. Pretend you are 100 years old and explaining to your great-grandchildren what is important in life. What would you tell them about your life? What lessons would you tell them you learned?

2. Find someone who you feel has meaning in his or her life. Where does the meaning come from? How can you use that person as an example?

3. What does your gut say? When you take the time to think deeply, what idea or concept keeps popping up and then gets buried again because it is not realistic? Who is that one person you can share this crazy idea with?

4. Make a list of your values. What can you do that will help you fulfill those values?

5. What are the things in your life that give you energy? How can you do more of those?

Here are some more examples of Higher Purposes that were posted on the Internet:

My life purpose is to live and mentor an authentic, adventurous, spiritual life, while being a catalyst for positive change.

With friendship and affection, I will interact with others to improve my home life and obtain pleasure and recognition.

My purpose in life is to serve others in a balanced and flexible manner in areas of health in such a manner that I get feedback on improvement.

I want to be a spokesman for wildlife issues and help people connect their daily actions to saving the wildlife on this planet.

My purpose is to teach under-privileged children the keys to success and how to become young and successful entrepreneurs by igniting their ambition to change their lives.

My purpose is to grow nutritious, organic food that helps people grow and thrive and have vibrant health. I want to use my skills as a grower to build a sustainable farm that educates as well as feeds people, and builds a community of like-minded organic growers and consumers.

My purpose is to build awesome custom bikes that win mountain bike and speed competitions. I will use my talent for design, prototyping and customizing to dream up, develop, test, refine, build and sell world-class cycling equipment.

My purpose is helping distressed homeowners refinance their mortgages and become better financial consumers by understanding the real details behind home buying, credit ratings and approvals, and secured debt. I want to use my analysis and coaching skills to help people stay in their homes and keep their dream of owning their own home alive.

My purpose is to design and build beautiful wood desks, elegant computer cabinets and amazing dining tables. I will use my eye for detail and my intuitive sense of old-world styling and craftsmanship to make custom furniture that evokes traditional styles with modern functionality.

Remember, you are looking for your Higher Purpose and not someone else's. You don't have to impress anyone or get anyone's approval. Your Higher Purpose doesn't have to be related to your work, and you can have more than one. Most importantly, you can change it if it doesn't feel right or if your life circumstances change. Don't stress over it, and don't worry about getting it perfect. Just try something and keep trying until you feel good inside and can smile when you think about it.

Review your Higher Purpose statement from the previous chapter. Make any changes or adjustments and start trying it out.

My Higher Purpose statement:

I _____

(Active Verb)(Who)(Details)

5th Concept

 Defining Success

Chapter 20
Defining Success

Let's transition from our focus on building happiness to discussions about building success. Everything in the happiness section will help you become successful. Creating and developing those habits will lead to success.

If you know the difference between pleasure and happiness, you will not only be able to focus on what really makes you happy; you will also be developing the discipline to practice the things that will bring you long-term success, rather than short-term excitement. If you learn to take control of your life, you will be able to take ownership of your success and make it happen, despite the many obstacles you will encounter. If you build positive relationships, those relationships will catapult you into multiple opportunities for short-term wins and long-term success. Lastly, if you have a purpose in your life, you will recognize success with every step that gets you closer to that purpose. That idea leads us into our next concept: how do we define success? How do we leverage our definition of success to clearly understand when we are successful and when we are off track?

"If you don't know where you are going, any road will get you there."

Lord Krishna

Many people know they want to be successful, but few have a good definition of what success is or what it looks like. As a result, their actions take them in many different directions—some toward success and many away from success. We want to define success so that every day we can choose actions that are making us successful and avoid actions that will disrupt our success. We want a guiding concept that keeps us on the path we have chosen.

On the other end of the spectrum, defining success helps you know when to pause and celebrate the milestones that confirm you are living successfully. Many people are successful every day and don't realize it. Or they reach certain goals they have set, then quickly move on to the next goal without stopping to appreciate what they have done or accomplished. When we stop, review, and appreciate our success milestones, it builds our confidence and gives us proof that we can tackle the next big challenge. It helps us create our own success manual of what we did that works and what we did that didn't work.

Defining success so that we can recognize it, pause, and appreciate it, also helps us be happier. The most mentioned concept in the definitions of happiness we analyzed was contentment, which also includes satisfaction and fulfillment. Pausing to recognize and appreciate success allows us to feel the contentment, satisfaction, and fulfillment we are searching for. It helps us be happier, which helps us further build on our longer-term success.

Bali worked for 12 years building his company. He risked his life savings, maxed out his credit cards, and unhappily let his wife raise his two little girls, since he was at work or traveling most of the time. He was dedicated to his employees and clients and to their success. He was dedicated to building and selling his company to the right people. It was a long and arduous process, but that day finally came.

He completed the maze of requirements required to close the sale of his company and received tens of millions of dollars. He had enough money to retire, spend time with his daughters, and reconcile with his wife. After a week and a half, he came back to work looking for the next challenge. Within three weeks he was on the road again and had taken on another challenge in the new combined and larger organization.

Although he had enough money to live on for the rest of his life, he still negotiated hard for an unusually large salary and bonus, which he received. Bali had never defined success. He had never learned to live successfully. Even though he had reached a massive financial milestone that many would consider an indicator of success, he was still searching. Bali aimed at one goal and gave up everything to get there. He knew and even talked about how different his life would become once he reached that financial pinnacle—how when he was finally able to sell the company, he would retire and spend time with his kids and reconcile with his wife. Building and selling the company had taken much longer than he had planned, and he had said he was committed to making up that time. He had always wanted a different life, but he believed that life was not possible until he had reached his goal. He had always assumed there was a moment in time when he could declare himself a "success" and switch to the life he really wanted. What Bali never discovered is that there is not a pinnacle or end point. Life marches on. If you can't find success in what you are doing today, it will not miraculously materialize when you reach even your most coveted dream scenario. Bali never defined success. He kept assuming it was just over the horizon.

We should define success so we can live it daily and recognize and appreciate it when we hit the milestones that mark our progress. We also need to know what success includes for us so we don't succeed in one area, yet fail in other, possibly more important, areas. Most importantly, if happiness includes feeling content, satisfied, and fulfilled, we need to define success so we can be content in our accomplishments and feel happier, which will help us become more successful.

Definition Builds Perseverance

"If you know where you are going (definition of self) you will try harder when you fail. If you fail at something that is not in your "definition of self," you don't try harder."   *Brunstein, Joachim, Gollwitzer*

Brunstein and his associates did studies that showed people who had committed to a direction--"I am a technology person" or "I am a doctor"-- will keep going even after they fail. If those who were clear they were technology people failed on a technology-related paper, they would redouble their efforts. Those people who were not as clear would more likely blow it off and chalk it up to bad luck. This is relevant to defining success; because once you have defined it, you will choose actions to fulfill that definition that you would not have chosen without the definition. Your choices and actions will be directed toward fulfilling success.

Write It Down

Defining success in your head doesn't work, because you unconsciously change your definition to fit your current circumstances, rather than creating and maintaining a vision of future possibilities. It has to be in writing on paper. You can always change it by re-writing it, but you have to write it down to make it real. It forces your subconscious to commit to it, as if it were a foregone conclusion.

Writing your definition of success on paper activates several physical and neural processes that will bring you much closer to actualizing your success. The first process is created by using your fingers to write. The process of moving your hands and fingers across the page creates spatial relationships in your brain that signify importance. Writing also requires you to activate your working memory and use up more of your brain's resources for the task than would be used by just thinking about it. By writing it down, you are telling your brain that this is something that is important to remember and to focus on it.

A study by Karin Harman James at Indiana University, using an MRI to monitor neural activity of children who had written letters of the alphabet, showed a significant jump in their brain activity when they were shown those letters again. Basically, the act of writing down your definition of success will activate more areas of the brain during recall then are activated just thinking about a definition you didn't write down.

The other process taking place in your brain is visualizing or mentally practicing your success. As you consider, evaluate, organize, and finally write your definition of success, your brain is cycling through what it looks and feels like to reach that success. Since your brain is unable to distinguish between what you mentally rehearse and what happens in reality, it believes you are successful. In the future it will favor choices that support that memory of being successful because it wants to reconcile what you do with who it thinks you are.

As a side note, studies show that the process of writing is actually more effective than typing, because forming the letters is a more involved process then hitting the keys on the keyboard.

Another process spurred by the act of writing is the mental evaluation and organization required to move your thoughts from images in your brain to forming letters into words and words into sentences that can be read from the paper. It requires your brain to spend more time processing and organizing the information when you have to convert it to something in writing. Writing activates the RAS (reticular activating system), which is your brain's way of clearing traffic to reduce distractions, because what you are writing is really important. The brain is sending a signal that we should pay attention to now and in the future. As a result, your awareness will be increased and you will be more open to and notice cues in your environment related to fulfilling your definition of success.

Your written definition of success will become your touchstone, which you can refer back to each time a new opportunity or a tough decision comes up. My definition of success is "helping others become successful and happy." Every time I am unsure what to do, I can refer back to that definition and ask myself, "Will this action help them become successful and happy?" It is especially helpful when I am emotionally charged up. I would love to give someone a piece of my mind, but I refer back to "Is this going to help them be successful and happy?" It gives me a reason to re-think and re-word my responses, and provide more helpful and supportive feedback. It also helps me feel confident in the decisions I am making. If I know what I am doing is helping people be successful and happy, then it calms my doubts and fears and gives me the courage to move on, even when the next step seems impossible or filled with risk.

A written definition of success also helps you set your priorities. Refer to it as you start your busy day. You should do the activities that support your definition of success first. A point could be made that you should only do activities that support your definition of success. That is definitely something you can aspire to.

Your written definition of success will help you navigate the obstacles you encounter. Immediately after you have defined success, you will face roadblocks to achieving it. It could be old habits; expectations of peers, bosses, or close relations; a lack of confidence; or a lack of resources and know-how. These challenges will knock you off track and send your mind wandering down unproductive paths. Referring back to your written definition of success will help you push through these obstacles and create new ways to be successful.

Once you have your written definition of success, be sure to share it. Research by Dr. Gail Mathews from the Dominican University of California shows that sharing your goals with friends and meeting with them weekly significantly improves your chances of achieving those goals. The same is true for success. Sharing your definition of success with your friends and having regular conversations about your progress and challenges will increase your opportunities, and their opportunities, to be successful.

Lastly, your written definition of success provides you an evaluation tool at the end of each day. Take a few minutes at the end of the day to read it and contemplate your progress. You can take a few minutes to feel good about the small steps you took to fulfill your success and brainstorm new methods for dealing with the challenges that knocked you off course.

Concepts Found in Success Definitions

As we discussed in chapter one, we collected over 240 definitions of success from various sources. Based on the key words used in each definition, we categorized the definitions into one or more representative concepts.

1. The top concept mentioned was contentment, which includes satisfaction and fulfillment.

2. The second-most mentioned concept was others, which includes building positive relationships and creating a better world.

3. The third-most mentioned concept was achievement, which includes reaching your goals.

4. The fourth-most mentioned concept was happiness.

Happiness or concepts related to happiness were mentioned 68% of the time in the definitions of success.

The concept of wealth, which includes financial stability, was only mentioned 6% of the time.

Concept	Success Rank	Happiness Rank
Contentment (contentment, satisfaction, and fulfillment)	1st (tied)	1st
Others (building positive relationships & creating a better world)	1st (tied)	2nd
Achievement (and accomplishing goals)	3rd	4th
Happiness	4th	NA
Be the best you can be	5th	Not Mentioned
Other	6th	6th
Do things I am passionate about	7th	5th
Wealth (and financial stability)	8th	Not Mentioned

When we take time to define success or happiness, contentment, satisfaction, and fulfillment come up a lot. This is often contrary to our actions, where we are constantly chasing the next opportunity or attempting to juggle as many activities as possible. It is part of the over-the-horizon syndrome where we believe if we can just get past this next hill, we will be content, satisfied, and fulfilled. Writing our definition of success will help us recognize if we are looking for contentment so we can pause and appreciate it in our daily successes rather than waiting for that one pinnacle moment.

We all want to matter and make a difference in the world, so we often include the concept of others in our definitions of success. This concept includes building positive relationships with friends and family, contributing to the community, and helping make the world a better place. Others gives us something to aim for that is bigger than ourselves.

The concept of achievement, which includes achieving or accomplishing goals, was the third-most mentioned concept in the definitions of success. It was also mentioned often when we examined the definitions of happiness. Achievement is part of success and provides something objective and measurable we can identify. We are also happier if we are achieving.

The concept of acquiring wealth or financial stability was a distant 8th for the definitions of success, mentioned only 6% of the time and not mentioned at all in the definitions of happiness. This is contrary to what we would expect, based on observations of people's actions and what is emphasized in the media. It often appears that acquiring wealth is the number one reason and often the only reason for success. It turns out that wealth is just a means to an end. Many of us pursue wealth because we believe that it will bring us contentment, satisfaction, and fulfillment, which are often our ultimate goals. What we find is that contentment results from the daily process of pursuing our dreams, rather than being something we experience at a single point in time somewhere in the future.

Definition of Success – Examples

"Success is peace of mind, which is a direct result of self-satisfaction in knowing you made the effort to do your best to become the best that you are capable of becoming." John Wooden

"Success is being content, happy, and satisfied with who you are, and continuously striving and challenging yourself to be the best person you can be."

"Success is knowing at the end of each day that I did my best and I made a positive impact on those around me."

"To me, having a successful life is being able to do things independently for myself and not always having someone there to do things for me. It's achieving my goals on my own terms and at my own pace." High school student with mobility impairment

"My definition of success is achieving true self-fulfillment so that I can feel happiness and peace of mind about my past, present and future situation."

"Success is personal satisfaction of giving all of your effort and ability, no matter the task or outcome"

"My definition of success is to encourage growth and passion in all of my pursuits, relationships, and myself."

"A feeling of peace of mind and genuine happiness based on having lived up to one's potential." Bob Burg

"For me, success is about making a positive contribution to the world and sharing my best self."

"Success is making the best of the opportunities that are presented to us in order to do good things for ourselves and for those around us."

"Success? That's an easy one. BE HAPPY!" High school student with a learning disability

Make It Your Own

We have provided a lot of guidance and thoughts around definitions of success. But the most important rule about your definition of success is that there are no rules. It is your definition and it needs to be something you own and are comfortable with. It is something you can change, adjust, and adapt until you have a phrase or sentence that you can aspire to and that fits your dreams and life situation. We have provided guidelines to help you understand what your definition of success might look like and how to create it, but they are only guidelines. It is your definition of success, and it can be anything you want it to be.

Write a definition that sticks with you. You need something you can remember and contemplate each day. Our strongest motivations come from within. Our definition of success should reflect our internal beliefs and dreams rather than the expectations of others. It doesn't work if you don't own it. If you are doing it because it is what you should do or what is expected of you, then you will at some point become disenchanted and will not reach your full potential.

Your definition of success should probably be applicable to your whole life, not just your work life. Think of what makes you feel successful as a person, not just in your career.

Your definition of success should be about things you can control vs. things you can't control. For example, winning the lottery is probably not a good definition of success.

It is okay for your definition of success to change. As our lives change, as we gain a better understanding of what we want, and as we discover new potential in ourselves, we may need to change and adjust our definitions of success.

These are guidelines for writing a definition of success. To be successful and happy, you have to own it. You have to believe it.

Activity: Define Success

In previous chapters, we discussed your strengths, values, and Higher Purpose. Re-visiting these concepts and your answers to the related activities will provide a good foundation for creating your definition of success.

We're talking about a definition of success, and not a group of goals. We will address goals in the next chapter. So keep your definition of success at a higher level. Make it something you can apply daily in many different circumstances. It should be something against which you can evaluate your day at work, your day with friends or family, or your day of relaxation.

1. What is your Higher Purpose? (From Previous Chapter)

```
┌─────────────────────────────────────────────┐
│                                             │
│                                             │
│                                             │
│                                             │
└─────────────────────────────────────────────┘
```

2. Why do you want to be successful?

```
┌─────────────────────────────────────────────┐
│                                             │
│                                             │
│                                             │
│                                             │
└─────────────────────────────────────────────┘
```

3. What are some success scenarios you dream about?

```
┌─────────────────────────────────────────────┐
│                                             │
│                                             │
│                                             │
│                                             │
└─────────────────────────────────────────────┘
```

4. What do people say about you when you are successful?

```
┌─────────────────────────────────────────────┐
│                                             │
│                                             │
│                                             │
│                                             │
└─────────────────────────────────────────────┘
```

5. What contributions are you making to other people's lives when you are successful?

```



```

Take a few moments to imagine yourself as successful. Sit back, close your eyes, and really immerse yourself in what success feels like. What are those feelings? Where do they come from? How are you interacting with the people around you? What have you done or accomplished every day to get here? What happened today that made it a successful day?

6. Write your definition of success. Make it something you can evaluate your actions against daily for a long period of time. Note: If you can achieve it in three months, it is a goal, not a definition for success.

```



```

Write something in the box. Don't try to make it perfect or make sure it fits certain parameters. Just write something down so you have a place to start. Use this definition until you can craft a better one.

Refine and Adjust

It is important that you feel comfortable, determined, and hopefully a little excited about your definition of success. Often though, people feel a little unsure. "Is it what I really want?" "Is it realistic?" "Is it bold enough?" These are common questions to ask upon seeing success defined and written down for the first time. The solution is to live with it for a while and continue to test and refine it. Write your definition of success down on a piece of paper, an index card, or as a daily reminder on your electronic calendar. Read it every day and challenge its fit for you. Below are some ideas to help you test and refine.

1. Think of how you will feel at the end of each day. Think of what you will want to have accomplished at the end of each day. Who will you want to have been with each day? Will living your definition of success support that?

2. Meet with your friends and family. Ask them to give you their definitions of success. Share your ideas about your definition of success and get their input. You don't have to change it to make them happy, but they may provide insight that helps you understand how you really feel.

3. Who do you know that is successful? What can you learn from them? What do you think is working for them? How do you think they are defining success?

Every day, see what you can do to work toward fulfilling your definition of success. Success doesn't come from innate skill or ability. It comes from hard work done every day, and some scientists say that means doing it every day for as long as 10 years. So how do you stay focused so that every day brings you one step closer to achieving your goals? How do you enjoy today and feel successful today? Having and knowing your definition of success course-corrects you every morning. You start out the morning and end the day knowing what you should be doing to be successful. It is a journey where you take one more step each day. So instead of waiting to reach that one pinnacle moment in your life you can call success, you can take satisfaction each day that you are moving toward and even implementing your definition of success. You are successful each day. You can feel good about your accomplishments on a daily basis, knowing you are doing the things that fit your definition of success. By stringing a lot of moments of success into days and eventually years of success, you will live a successful life.

"The greater danger for most of us lies not in setting our aim too high and falling short; but in setting our aim too low, and achieving our mark."
Michelangelo

6th Concept

Clarify and Prioritize

Chapter 21
Clarify and Prioritize

> *"First, have a definite, clear, practical ideal; a goal, an objective. Second, have the necessary means to achieve your ends: wisdom, money, materials, and methods. Third, adjust all your means to that end."*
>
> *Aristotle*

The next two chapters are about how we "…adjust all your means to that end."

Now that we have defined success, we can clarify and prioritize the steps necessary to be successful. Remember, success is what we take steps toward every day. It is not something that happens one day in the future, it is something we work on every day. Our goals are milestones along the journey that help us confirm that our daily path is on track. We will create three to five major goals and then a list of actions we can take that will have the most impact on reaching our milestones and living our definition of success. There may be more than five areas of your life you that would include in your definition of success. We want to prioritize the top three to five so we can focus on a few things and do them well, rather than trying to

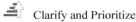

take on too many actions and not succeeding at any of them. Research by Latham and Locke showed that the probability of reaching your goals decreases when your workload is too heavy. In other words, if you don't prioritize and focus on the important goals, you may end up with too much to do and not reach any of your goals.

We can also add, change, and make adjustments to our goals as we establish daily habits that put one area or another on track. A friend of mine pointed out that his faith was an important part of his definition of success. But he already practiced his faith through daily and weekly habits that he was unlikely to change. His question was, should faith be one of his top three to five goals. The answer will be different for everyone, but since he has already established solid daily habits for his faith, he can move on to other goals that will have an impact on his definition of success. At the same time, he can periodically confirm that he is on track for his faith and its impact on his definition of success, and prioritize it higher if he feels it is getting off track.

We use the terms goals and milestones interchangeably. Since success is a daily process, rather than something you wait to reach, the term milestones more accurately reflects the signs of accomplishment on your journey of success. Goals are the more common nomenclature and are the same as milestones.

Goals add purpose and meaning to our lives by helping to clarify the connection between what we do today and what will happen in the future. They give us responsibilities, deadlines, timetables, opportunities for mastering new skills, and reasons to have social interactions. Setting goals helps us connect today's actions with the future. Goals provide clarity for our sense of purpose. They are something we can visualize, and they provide support for our beliefs that the actions we are taking today will lead to reaching our milestones. Goals that we create and own are more motivating than goals we pursue to please someone else. People are happier if they pursue goals that are consistent with their interests and values, rather than goals that are a result of work, peer, or family pressure.

Goals have an impact because we are creating conflict in our brain. Setting a goal sends a message to our conscious and sub-conscious minds that we are dissatisfied with our current condition and that a specified aspect of our lives should be different. The bigger the difference, the more motivated our brain is to change, so it can resolve the conflict.

Having goals gives us something to focus our attention on. Without goals, we meander through life experiencing random events that don't lead us down any discernible path. There is activity without progress. Goals focus our actions to a self-chosen path and bring a pattern and clarity to what would otherwise be a haphazard menagerie of experiences.

Guidelines for Goals

Make your goals specific and challenging, yet achievable. Have a set date for accomplishment, and make them measurable so you can objectively evaluate your progress.

Goals should be specific. Being specific gives you a clear picture of what you need to do. Writing "I will exercise" paints a fuzzy mental picture with too many options to know exactly what you are going to do. Writing "I will run two miles on Monday, Wednesday, and Friday at 6 am" gives you an objective and concrete action you can take at a designated date and time.

We want our goals to be measurable so we can get feedback and see how we are doing. We also want to be able to say definitively whether we accomplished the goal or not. The obstacles and roadblocks we encounter trying to reach our goals will be significant. Most roadblocks are consciously and even unconsciously created by us. Stating our goal as "I will exercise" gives a lot of wiggle room for the less motivated part of our brains to accept walking to the car from the restaurant as exercise. If our goal is stated as "I will run two miles on Monday, Wednesday, and Friday at 6 am," then we can clearly measure whether we ran, on what days we ran, and whether we ran far enough to qualify as exercise.

The most effective goals will challenge us and push us beyond our comfort zone. Locke and Latham's research showed that goals that provided significant challenge were achieved more often because they required significant conscious and subconscious commitment.

Challenging goals offer a higher level of achievement, and that potential achievement provides the extra motivation you need to push yourself a little harder. There is, however, a limit to how challenging you should make your goals. You have to believe that with significant effort you can achieve them.

If you can envision the possibility of reaching your goal, but there is some concern about how difficult it will be, you probably have a good balance of challenge and achievability.

Write It Down

Just as we discussed in the last chapter on defining success and writing it down, writing down your goals is the first step to achieving them. Writing your goals on paper activates several physical and neural processes that will increase your chances of reaching your goals. Active engagement of your fingers and hands and activating your working memory help reinforce in your brain that these are important objectives that should get focus and priority. Writing also helps you visualize, evaluate, and organize your goals, which creates clarity. Writing activates the RAS (reticular activating system), which sends a signal that we should pay attention to opportunities related to these goals. As a result, your awareness increases, and you become more receptive to cues in your environment that will help you reach your goals.

Written goals can be more easily shared with your friends. Research by Dr. Gail Mathews from the Dominican University of California shows that sharing your goals with friends and meeting with them weekly significantly improves your chances of achieving those goals.

Most importantly, written goals give you something to refer back to that refreshes your memory. As our lives get busy, the goals get pushed to the background; and we need to re-read them to bring them back to being part of our conscious intentions. We should also evaluate our progress in reaching those goals on a regular basis.

One of the key aspects of successful goal-setting is feedback and evaluation on our progress. Written goals provide an objective system for measuring our progress.

Creating our Goals and Milestones

Let's start by building clarity around what our milestones for success will be and what we specifically want to accomplish. In order to reach our goals or milestones, we need to have a clear picture of what they are. We need to see the shot so we can make the shot. Begin by closing your eyes and imagining what the milestones of success look and feel like. Are you married or single? Do you have children? What kinds of things are you doing? Who are you spending your time with? How are you helping others? Are you traveling to a foreign land, or sitting on a beach? What kind of car do you drive? What kind of house do you live in? How healthy are you? What have you accomplished? What activities make your days great?

Why Visualize?

Visualizing our dreams and setting goals provides us with clarity and focus. A clear picture of what we want to accomplish opens up our minds to the opportunities we will encounter that can move us forward in reaching our milestones. Also, a clear plan helps us measure our progress and determine what actions will help us reach our goals and what actions will distract from our goals.

Visualize your goal and then the steps it will take to reach the goal. Rather than focusing on the completed goal, focus on what it is going to take to get there. This helps you prepare your mind for the obstacles you are going to face and will help you fight through them. Visualizing a completed goal without including the steps you will take gives you a sense of fulfillment, but reduces your motivation to achieve that goal.

Visualizing our goals and milestones will not make them easier, it will make them inevitable. Reaching the goals that create success is difficult. It takes a lot of hard work, mistakes, challenges, and perseverance. Visualizing helps you keep your eye on the prize so you can push through the tough times and overcome all the obstacles. Knowing the challenges you will face on your way to reaching a goal will prepare you for the battles to come so you can face them with confidence and determination because you can visualize a clear picture of the result of your efforts.

I have three teenagers--two boys, and my youngest is a girl. Having kids is the most rewarding and fun challenge I have ever experienced. But it is really hard. It is incredibly hard to watch them be sad or hurt and to feel their pain, while you can't do anything to stop it. It is even worse to see them learn hard lessons, feel their pain, and choose not to take action, because it is better they learn the lessons now rather than later, when the consequences will be much worse. But I stay focused on my goal of raising three happy and healthy kids, as well as the steps I need to take as a parent to get them there. By visualizing both, I am able to fight through the challenges and make decisions that will prepare my children for success and happiness every day, and not just today.

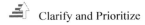

Specifying our goals will also give us something to prioritize. If we have a lot of goals and milestones rattling around inside our head, it is hard to know what comes first and what actions keep us on the path of accomplishing those goals.

As an example, we can use the analogy of a map and real destination to substitute for goals. If we are in Texas and we want to get to New York, we need to know where New York is and stay on the path to get there. We need clarity in our priorities and goals so we don't turn toward Georgia on a whim or follow some "red herring" idea that will distract us for a while, but not result in reaching any milestones. We should only go to Georgia if we make a conscious decision to substitute Georgia (our new goal) for New York (our original goal).

Once we set our goals, we need to build a plan of action that will get us there. Most importantly, we always need to know our next step. If we want to be president of our company someday, our action plan might include getting an MBA, getting experience in various areas of the company, and getting promoted in our current job. Our next steps might include reading about various company presidents and what types of education or experience they had. Even better, we might schedule lunch with or find other ways to interview presidents of companies to get their advice. A next step might include making a list of schools where we could get an MBA and researching what it might cost. Make a list of actions and always have a next step.

Step 1: Activity - Create a Dream Board

On the following page, cut pictures out of magazines that reflect your dreams and what you want to accomplish, and then paste them into the box. They don't have to be in any particular order or structure. Be sure to find at least one image to represent every milestone that represents your definition of success. Find images that reflect who you want to be or what you want out of life. Categories could include physical, intellectual, career, financial, creative, adventure, relationships, charity, and many others. You can use Microsoft PowerPoint or similar presentation software programs to collect and arrange digital images, then print out the collage and paste it onto the following page. As you choose pictures, keep repeating your Higher Purpose and your definition of success, then finding images that represent them.

Dream Board – A Reflection of What I Want to Be and Accomplish

Step 2: Activity – Make Your List of Goals and Milestones

On the chart below, make a list of the pictures you included on your dream board. But don't write the name of the picture, write down the goal or milestone it represents. Put the picture into words. For example, if you included a picture of a Tesla, your list would include: "Own a Tesla Model S." Be specific, and be sure to add a date for when you want to accomplish this milestone. If you included a picture of a healthy person, your list might include "Be physically fit with a cholesterol level below 140 by December 31st, 2017." For this exercise we are going to write more than five goals. In the next step we will prioritize and narrow down to the top three to five.

Goals/Milestones	Date
1.	
2.	
3.	
4.	
5.	
6.	
7.	
8.	
9.	

Once you have your list of goals based on your dream board, check it over to make sure there is nothing else you want to add.

Step 3: Activity – Prioritize your goals and milestones

Now let's re-order the goals from Step 2. On the next page, write your goals from the most important to the least important. Start with the question, "If I could only accomplish *one thing*, what would it be?" Think about your Higher Purpose and definition of success. They will help guide your decisions. Now, assume you've accomplished the first thing on the list; then ask the question again: "If I could only accomplish one more thing, what would it be?" Keep going through this process until you feel like you have captured the three to five goals that will have the most impact on your definition of success.

Goals (in priority order)	Date
(If I could only accomplish one thing in life, it would be…) 1.	
(Assuming I will accomplish #1, if I could only accomplish one more thing in life, it would be…) 2.	
(Assuming I will accomplish #1 and #2, if I could only accomplish one more thing in life, it would be…) 3.	
(Assuming I will accomplish #1 through #3, if I could only accomplish one more thing in life, it would be…) 4.	
(Assuming I will accomplish #1 through #4, if I could only accomplish one more thing in life it would be…) 5.	

Re-read your top three to five goals and take the following actions:

1. Put an O by each milestone that you own. It is your goal and does not come from your parents or someone else's expectations. It is what you want to do, not what you think you should do.

2. Put an S by each milestone that is specific enough for you to understand exactly what you want to accomplish.

3. Put an M by each milestone that is measurable. You will be able to objectively know if you accomplished it.

Re-write any goals that don't have an O, S, or M next to them.

It is important to be excited about your goals. How do your goals align with your Higher Purpose? How do they make someone else's life better? Do they make you feel excited and a little scared? Are they difficult and challenging? Are they something you really want, or just something you think you should want? Do they fit your life today, or are they creating the life you want? Go back and edit your goals. Make them a little bigger and a little scarier so they get your blood pumping. Connect them to your Higher Purpose and definition of success. Delete any goals that you don't feel compelled to accomplish.

Once more, sit back and contemplate your list. It can be changed and updated, but only through a conscious choice and process. Make sure these are goals you are confident you will be happy pursuing and putting 100% effort into.

Share them with friends and family and get their input. But in the end, it is your decision, and they have be goals you believe in and are willing to commit your life to accomplishing.

Step 4: Activity – Board of Milestones

We started with a dream board that included everything we wanted or even dreamed we wanted. Now we will create a Board of Milestones. It will only contain pictures that represent our three to five top goals. Visually being able to see where we are going is more effective than just reading the words.

Follow the same process as the Dream Board. You can even re-use the same pictures.

Every day review the pictures of your milestones. Picture what you want to accomplish and then think of the steps you need to take to get there. Specifically think about what the next step is.

Board of Milestones – A visual representation of my top goals

Step 5: Activity – Build a list of supporting actions to accomplish your goals

You now have a list of the three to five goals that will have the most impact on living your definition of success. Next, we will take each goal or milestone and write a list of actions or next steps. For example, if your milestone was "By March 1st 2016, be part of an organization where I can donate at least 4 hours a week to help children have better lives," then what actions do you need to take? You may want to:

1. Make a list of charities and organizations you could contact

2. Research and learn about each organization

3. Contact and meet people who work at those organizations

4. Choose three and volunteer at each one to find a good fit

5. Choose your favorite and determine how they can best use your four-hour-per-week commitment

Also, for every action, you need to know a clear next step. For example, your first action is to make a list of charities and organizations you could contact. Your next step might be to do a search on Google, ask your friends, or talk to someone at your church.

Goal/Milestone #1 (From your list of prioritized goals in Step 3)		
Action	Date	Next Step
1.		
2.		
3.		
4.		
5.		

Goal #2 (From your list of prioritized goals in Step 3)		
Action	Date	Next Step
1.		
2.		
3.		
4.		
5.		

Goal #3 (From your list of prioritized goals in Step 3)		
Action	Date	Next Step
1.		
2.		
3.		
4.		
5.		

Goal #4 (From your list of prioritized goals in Step 3)		
Action	Date	Next Step
1.		
2.		
3.		
4.		
5.		

Goal #5 (From your list of prioritized goals in Step 3)		
Action	Date	Next Step
1.		
2.		
3.		
4.		
5.		

You should now have a list of three to five prioritized goals or milestones that will have the most impact on living your definition of success. For each of those goals/milestones you have five actions you can take to achieve them, a date by which you will complete those actions, and a next step so you know what to do to keep the process moving forward.

Mind Map

If you are struggling to compile all the different opportunities and the different directions they could take you, try drawing a mind map.

Mind Mapping is a visual representation of information and thoughts that include a central idea surrounded by connected "branches" of associated topics. It is a process of brain storming, where ideas are added to the "map" radially around the central node without implicit prioritization or hierarchy. Although it may sound complex, mind maps are very easy to create and usually come naturally, as they are more of a non-linear form of note taking.

Mind maps generally start as hand-written rough notes and begin with your main theme – in this instance, start with where you are today. Write your current job in the middle as the main idea and create "branches" to next level nodes that represent other jobs you might want to have. Each of those jobs might have an additional branch or topic. For example, if you are currently a mortgage analyst but you like teaching people, then write "Mortgage Analyst" in the middle. Your first branch might be Mortgage Trainer, another branch might be High School Teacher, and another branch might be College Professor. A branch from High School Teacher might be Math, History, or Science to represent the subjects you might want to teach. You could also have a branch for Principal to represent growth from teacher to high school administration. You can have as many branches as you want and can follow your thoughts out until you have considered every possibility. Your mind map will look a lot like a spider with many legs. (See Mind Map below)

Mind Map

Once you have all your thoughts down on paper, you can apply ratings to each bubble based on how much it fits with what you want to do. Choose your three highest ratings and evaluate which direction you want to pursue most. Save your mind map, so that if one direction doesn't work out you can try something else.

Mind maps are a great tool and can be used to generate, visualize and structure ideas to aid in problem solving and decision making. Another great aspect of creating a mind map is that you don't need anything more than a clean sheet of paper, a pencil and your imagination. You can add colored pencils or pens to add dimension and creativity to your mind map. Colors can help you differentiate topics or levels within your mind map.

Fundamental Steps for Creating a Mind Map

1. Get a clean sheet of paper (turn it sideways) and a pencil (colored, if possible).

2. Start by putting your main theme in the center of your page to give you the freedom to spread out in a number of directions.

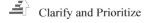

3. Connect major categories to your central node. Categories can represent words, ideas, tasks, or other items related to your central theme.

4. Add as many major categories as you can think of – remember, this is a brain-storming process.

5. Connect sub-categories to each category. Sub-categories are simply ideas/thoughts that are related to the next level up category.

6. Use curved lines to connect your nodes. This adds a level of creativity and enforces the "un-structured" format of your mind map.

I hope this helps you with your idea generation. Enjoy the process and let your ideas flow.

The Change Process

What if something changes? One of the most challenging aspects of pursuing goals is staying on track. There are so many things we want to do and accomplish, and we get more ideas every day. So how do we stay on track and reach the goals that really matter to us? The answer is in building and maintaining a rigorous process for making changes to our goals. If we are headed to New York, we don't want to get sidetracked to Georgia and never reach New York. If we find that Georgia is becoming more and more of an important goal, we will want to make a conscious decision to either switch our goal to Georgia or skip the Georgia opportunity and go to New York.

The change process:

1. Clarify your new goal, its measurement, and timeframe.

2. Evaluate the goal's fit with your Higher Purpose and definition of success.

3. Honestly and thoroughly evaluate its impact on your current list of other goals.

4. Make a conscious decision to pursue the new goal, postpone the new goal, or skip the new goal.

5. Adjust your current list and priorities to include the new goal with a reasonable date for accomplishment, or ignore the new goal and move forward with your current plan.

Let's imagine that your final list of goals includes starting your own business. At some point, a friend mentions the benefits of going back to school and getting a graduate degree. Rather than immediately adding "get a graduate degree" to your goals list, you would evaluate that goal's impact on any higher level goals. For example, will taking the time to get a graduate degree interfere with starting your own business? Your answers could be that:

A.   It will sidetrack the process of starting your own business.

B.   It will provide some benefit to starting your business.

C.   It is not related to starting a business; it is just something you want to do.

D.   It is a necessity to start the business.

E.   It is more important than starting a business.

If your answer is A, then getting a graduate degree should *not* be put on your goals list; or, at the very least, it should be added with a long-term date several years after you have started your business.

If your answer is B or C, then you have to weigh the costs and the benefits, and determine whether the value of getting a graduate degree is worth the time and effort you have to put in. Please be honest with yourself and ask others to help keep you honest. The biggest mistake we see in this step is underestimating how much time and work it will take to accomplish the new extra goal. The result is, you end up with a list of goals that is unwieldy, unclear, and lacks prioritization.

If your answer is D or E, then move starting a business down on your list and consider extending the date. Delete your #5 goal so you don't have more than five goals. Add getting a graduate degree to the top of your list. If you are not willing to move starting a business down on the list and to delete a goal, then don't add getting a graduate degree. Trying to do both at the same time is a sign that you are unable to prioritize and could easily lead to neither being accomplished.

What do we do if we miss a goal or a date?

Another way we get derailed from our goals or milestones is by missing deadlines, or going days or weeks without taking some action we were supposed to take, such as exercising or eating right. This is extremely common. Our lives get busy or we have mental blocks that prevent us from doing what we know we should do. The easy solution is to start again and keep starting again until you reach your goals. A more challenging solution is to truly evaluate the underlying mental block that is getting in our way. It could be a fear of failure, a fear of success, poor organization or prioritization, or a lack of belief in the goal. Work with your friends and family, or even seek professional help, to identify the challenge and make adjustments in your life to overcome it. Often just five minutes of raw honesty with yourself can get to the root of the problem. If you can't identify the mental block or challenge, then keep pushing and keep starting again. Don't let a lack of success derail your success. Each day find some way to accomplish something on your action plan.

I had a goal to finish this book in August and publish by December 31st. Unfortunately, the research and writing took me longer than I expected. I also had higher priorities of spending time with my family and making sure I gave 100% to my paying job. Given my two higher priorities, I set a new date for delivering my first draft to the editor. I didn't give up on the goal; I adjusted my expectations based on my other priorities.

Prioritization: $100 Rocks

Our list of things to do always seems to be getting longer rather than shorter. In order to reach our goals, we want to make sure that we are focused on accomplishing the tasks most related to achievement of our goals. One method of prioritization is the $100 Rocks. As an analogy, picture two rooms. One is filled with rocks and the other is empty. Every day, in order to reach our goals, we have to move as many rocks as we can from the first room to the second room. Every rock has a value on it, from $1 to $100, which corresponds to the impact that rock will have on achieving our goals. If we can only move five rocks a day, we want to make sure they are the rocks that most help us reach our goals. We can go into the first room and pick up two $5 rocks, two $25 rocks, and a $30 rock. Now at the end of the day we have moved five rocks and made $90 of progress toward our goals ($5 + $5 + $25 + $25 + $30 = $90). The other option is to pick out five $100 rocks. This time we have moved the same number of rocks and made $500 of progress toward our goals. The fastest way to reach our goals is to take a few extra minutes to pick out the $100 rocks. Once the $100 rocks are gone, we pick out the $99 rocks, and then the $98 rocks, etc.

So what are $5 rocks and what are $100 rocks? It is up to each person to define what will have the most impact on achieving his goals. But some of the lower-value rocks that often get in people's way include reading non-essential email; answering texts or instant messages; playing games on our phones; surfing iFunny, Facebook, or our digital distraction of choice; watching television; or handling projects that are urgent but not important to reaching our goals. We are not saying you shouldn't do these things; just keep their value in perspective and don't do them instead of moving your $100 rocks. We all need to take a break and relax, but we will feel better about ourselves if we make progress toward our goals first. If we move enough $100 rocks, then we can relax and spend some time on $20 rocks.

We often find ways to procrastinate by dealing with $5 rocks because we are not sure how to tackle the $100 rocks. We need and want to read through our emails, find out what is happening on Facebook, organize our desk, and track the progress of our favorite stock or sports team. Understanding those are lower-value rocks when measured against achieving our goals will help us allocate the appropriate amount of time to them on our schedule.

Activity: Prioritize Your List

1. Make a list of everything you have to do today. You can also do this for the week or the month.

2. Give everything a rock value based on how important it is to reaching your goals. For example, if your goal is to be healthier and that includes an exercise routine, then exercise would be a $90 rock while cleaning off your desk would be a $25 rock.

3. No rock values can be the same. You have to make a decision about each item relative to the other items on the list.

4. Start with the highest dollar rock and work your way down. You don't have to complete each task; you just have to make progress on it and know the next steps and timeframes before you start another task.

To Do	**Rock Value**
1. Example – 30 Minutes on the Treadmill	$85 Rock
2. Example – Organize Desk	$25 Rock

Prioritization: Urgent vs. Important

Another way to prioritize is to look at what is urgent vs. important. Important means they have a direct impact on accomplishing our goals. Urgent means they are in our face and are begging for our attention. When our phone pings because we received a text, email, or some other notification, that feels urgent. It makes us want to stop whatever we are doing and see what we are missing.

Covey describes the four quadrants as:

1. <u>Important but not Urgent</u> – includes long-term planning, taking care of our health, taking time to prioritize, and other investments in our happiness and success.

2. <u>Urgent and Important </u>– includes "fires," projects that we had put off but now the deadline is near, trips to the emergency room, and family or work crises.

3. <u>Urgent but not Important</u> – includes smartphone notifications, some email, many unscheduled phone calls, someone else's crisis.

4. <u>Not Important and Not Urgent</u> – includes checking sports scores or stock prices, the majority of email and texts, smartphone games, and watching videos.

The first two quadrants include items that are important to our reaching our goals, so we want to spend most of our time on those types of items. The challenge is that we often distract ourselves with items in quadrants three and four. We get caught up watching a series of funny videos or texting with our friends about our plans for Friday night.

It seems easier to sit down and watch television then it is to spend time exercising or working on that big project that is not due until next month. If we can classify our list of to-do items based on how important they are to reaching our goals and understand how to reduce the sense of urgency connected to the non-important actions, we can be more productive and accomplish our goals. We can also relax more when we eventually do allocate time for the not important and not urgent distractions in Quadrant 4, because we are confident we have completed everything that is important.

The lesson is not that you can only work on things that are important. It is not to get distracted by the urgent items and to do the important things first, so you will eventually have time and can fully relax doing what is fun.

Failure and Prioritization

> *"Success is not final; failure is not fatal: it is the courage to continue that counts." Winston Churchill*

Most of the people who ask me about success are really asking how not to fail. They want to know how they can do it all. One of the most common fears of failure is letting other people down. It is very common not to want to let anyone down. Unfortunately, that is an impossible task. Expectations come from friends, family, romantic relationships, peers, and bosses.

Of course these people want and expect the best from you, so the expectations are almost always overwhelmingly high. Also, they don't coordinate with each other. Your boss doesn't call your friend and change the due date of the project because you are going to the game that weekend. So the number of expectations is always growing. Just as time marches on, expectations eventually mount up to a level where it would be impossible to meet them all. Eventually expectations are missed, and we start feeling like failures trying to balance, explain, and excuse why we didn't fulfill those expectations. If, however, we have our own definition of success and action plan to meet our goals, and we can live daily according to that plan, then we can re-categorize those failures to meet expectations as choices to do what best meets our criteria for success.

We can start resetting expectations with all of our stakeholders and communicate with them about what will and what will not be accomplished. Most, but not all, will appreciate your clarity of direction. More importantly, you will feel good about your choices and your accomplishments, and you can enjoy your successes rather than worrying about your failures.

In Chapter One, we talked about Tina. Tina was poised and confident, the kind of person that her peers wanted to emulate and every manager wanted to hire. She showed great leadership and had tremendous success in her early career. Now five years, two promotions, and one baby later, she was sitting in a restaurant, tears streaming down her face from the stress of trying desperately to be successful in so many areas of her life, while wondering what happened to the promise of happiness.

Tina is a great example of how we get caught up trying to meet everyone's expectations, rather than prioritizing our goals and supporting actions. We are trying not to fail, rather than focusing on success. We have a list of goals and actions to accomplish those goals. If we prioritize those actions, we will meet many people's expectations; but more importantly, we will be living our definition of success. We will be taking steps to fulfill our Higher Purpose. Unfortunately, that process also inevitably includes not meeting some people's expectations. It includes experiencing failure in meeting those particular expectations.

Success Includes Failure

To successfully live the life we choose, we will have to prioritize our actions, and not meet the expectations of some people we love and respect. It is important to understand that it is impossible to meet all the expectations of everyone in our lives. We can try and struggle; but eventually we become overwhelmed, and it all comes crashing down. We have to choose to take actions that lead to our success and happiness, rather than choosing actions that prevent us from failing.

When we are presented with expectations that don't fit into our action plan, we can politely reset those expectations. We can let people know that what they expect is important, but it is not something we can commit to because it doesn't fit into our action plan for success. This is extremely difficult and one of the biggest challenges you will face. But it is critical to your ability to be successful and happy on a daily basis.

Many of the expectations sneak up on us. If your long-term goal is to be healthy, but your boss needs you to start a new project, do you skip your workout to get it done? The answer may be yes once, but how many other times will you say yes? Can you skip your workout for a week, for a month, for six months? We tend to believe that this is a one-time thing, and it won't happen again. But those expectations don't get smaller and fewer. They grow.

Even worse, by skipping your workout, you reduce your energy levels and your productivity, which affects your ability to complete the project. You can instead set expectations with your boss that exercise is an important part of your success and you will complete the project first thing the next morning when you will have more energy and can be more focused. You could also communicate that you will skip your workout this time, but you would prefer to fit workouts in as well as work projects. Ninety percent of the time, your boss will understand. They will have similar goals, or at least respect your sticking to your goals. Sometimes, however, they won't. You will have to decide whether it is worth sacrificing your long-term health for a boss that is not going to support your long-term success. Are you going to sacrifice success because you are avoiding failure? Hard work and long hours are part of career success. But they will be more productive and you will be more successful if you fit them into a well-rounded action plan that supports your happiness and success. If you feel like you are making the choices, you will be happier and more successful than if you are forced by expectations to do things that don't fit into your action plan.

Marriage and family are other examples. If your long term goal is a strong relationship with your kids or romantic partner, should you take on those extra projects or volunteer opportunities? Letting them pass you by feels like failure. Do they fit into your goals and action plan? Can you commit to them and still meet your goals related to your relationships? Can you still do what you need to do every day to be successful in your relationships? Success and happiness require that on a daily basis we choose actions consistent with our goals and action plans, and that we say no to opportunities and expectations that will interfere with our long-term success. We have to let go of the belief that everything is important and that we can always fit one more thing into our lives. These are difficult and emotionally charged decisions. They will require that we continuously find anchors in our Higher Purpose, definition of success, goals, and action plans. We have to believe that prioritizing our actions daily will lead to success and happiness. It is critical that we stop using our energy to avoid failure and start directing it toward daily success.

Don't run away from failure; run toward success. Prioritize the actions in your life so they represent success on a daily basis. Prioritize and stick to an action plan that leads you toward your milestones for success.

Go back and re-read your goals and action plan. In the next chapter, we will talk about how to implement them with discipline.

7th Concept

Implement with Discipline

Chapter 22
Implement with Discipline

"A man or woman becomes fully human only by his or her choices and his or her commitment to them. People attain worth and dignity by the multitude of decisions they make from day to day." Rollo May

Happiness is not found at the end of the rainbow. It is found in each moment of each day and in how those moments connect us to our future. The key to connecting happiness and success is to be disciplined in implementing actions daily that will make you happy and successful. Happiness and success are not a destination; happiness and success are a way of living daily. Only daily action directed toward your Higher Purpose and definition of success will provide you with contentment, fulfillment, and satisfaction.

Happiness and success are a choice. We can choose to be the victim of our circumstances, or we can choose to make our lives different. Though it may be hard to admit, our past is a result of the choices we have made daily up to this point in our lives. We can continue with the old patterns, or we can make new choices. We can accept all the excuses we have for not doing something, or we can take action and change our lives one day at a time.

By this point in the book, we have discussed a Higher Purpose and a definition of success, which both provide something to strive for. You have goals or milestones to help you measure your progress along the way and actions to move you towards those milestones. Now let's discuss how to implement those actions with discipline every day and how to overcome many of the obstacles that interfere with success.

Getting Started

We will start with small changes rather than big changes. Small wins lead to other small wins. A lot of small wins together create change that leads to big wins. Small wins don't all add up in a neat path to success. They are like planting a lot of seeds. A few seeds start to grow, so you nurture those seeds and learn how to help other seeds grow. Eventually the seeds you planted turn into an orchard that consistently and predictably bears fruit.

Baby Steps

The first step is to create a keystone habit—something you can do in only 15 minutes each day. It is important to note that we are only going to work on one thing each month. Let's make one small change and then build from there. This applies to any habit you want to create. Start with baby steps and grow from there. If you are running into difficulty accomplishing a goal, find the smallest increment of accomplishment possible, and begin there. If you can't run two miles, start by walking to the neighbor's house and back. Do that over and over again to build up your confidence in your ability to succeed. Prove to yourself that you do have the self-discipline to accomplish a goal on a regular basis, and then extend the goal. Walk to the second neighbor's house. Increase the distance whenever you feel confident but still a little anxious. Push yourself past your comfort zone, but not so far that you want to give up altogether.

Make Time Every Day

Set aside the first 15 minutes every morning. You may have to get up 15 minutes earlier or postpone one of your morning rituals. We want to start every morning on the right track and use the first 15 minutes to prepare for a successful day.

Research by Tom Corley showed that successful people were four times more likely to put their goals in writing and 80 times more likely to review their daily lists than were unsuccessful people. So you are going to put your

Higher Purpose, definition of success, and three to five milestones in writing and review them on a daily basis.

On an index card or piece of paper, write your Higher Purpose and definition of success on one side and your three to five goals or milestones on the other side. These are your own personalized Life Instructions for happiness and success. Keep them in a place where you can quickly pick them up and where you can't help but see them, even if you're not looking. That could be on your nightstand, with your socks or other clothes, in the corner of your mirror, in the kitchen with the dishes or silverware, or on the desk where you keep your computer. It is even a good idea to make more than one copy and put them in multiple places. If you travel a lot, you may want to make an extra copy for your luggage and backpack.

At the same time every morning, pick up your Life Instructions and read the Higher Purpose and definition of success. After a few weeks you will have them memorized. Even so, continue to read them and repeat them to yourself every day. We want them not just to become something you can remember when asked; we want them to become part of your subconscious—something your brain is aware of, even when you are not. Then turn your Life Instructions over and review your three to five goals or milestones. Pick one milestone and spend the next 12 minutes taking action to move it forward. If your milestone is related to health and exercise, then put on your workout clothes. If it is related to healthy eating, then plan your meals for the day. If it is related to your career, then plan what you will accomplish today on a special project. If it is about relationships, then write a note to someone special or plan what time today you will call and talk to them. No matter what it is, find some action that will move you closer to reaching at least one of your milestones.

That's it. Now you can go back to your normal routine for the rest of the day. Spend just 15 minutes, first thing in the morning for the 30 days. It is important to focus on the 15 minutes and make sure you build that into a habit. If you start out trying to commit to one or two hours, you will run into too many obstacles and possibly become overwhelmed by what you have to accomplish.

Stick to 15 minutes until not investing that 15 minutes makes you feel like you have missed something in your day. We are recommending 15 minutes for 30 days so it will become a habit. For many people, that may take less than 30 days; and for others it could take more. The key to forming the habit is to focus for 15 minutes at the same time every day and not miss any days until you feel uncomfortable if you don't do it.

Month 2 through 12

Once you have established a habit of spending at least 15 minutes every day focused on your happiness and success, you can add in another habit. This book has covered a lot of different opportunities to help you be happy and successful. It is important that you not try to implement them all at once. Willpower is a limited resource, and you will want to focus it on creating one habit at a time. Once one habit is created and becomes automatic, you can focus your willpower on the next habit.

The first habit is every morning spending 15 minutes with your Life Instructions and moving one milestone forward. In Month 2, you can extend the 15 minutes to one hour. Start the first 15 minutes reviewing your Life Instructions and then spend the next 45 minutes extending the work on one or several of your milestones.

For example, we discussed using the first 15 minutes to get your workout clothes on if you were focused on a milestone related to exercise or health. Now you can spend the next 45 minutes actually working out. If your milestone was related to health and diet, we talked about using the first 15 minutes to plan your meals for the day. In Month 2 you can spend the next 45 minutes actually preparing the meals. In many cases you may have already done some of this. Month 2 will be focused on creating the habit of spending the full hour on your happiness and success activities. You are creating the habit of a consistent exercise schedule, daily food preparation, or whatever will help you reach your milestones.

Continue to add new habits in Months 3 through 12, so at the end of a year you have made significant progress toward changing your life. Most new habits will only require five to ten minutes of additional time each day. So you don't have to worry about needing to add another hour into the day for each new habit. For example, in Month 3, you could focus on starting each day by thinking about three things you are grateful for, which should take less than a minute. In Month 4 you could end every day by thinking about three things that went great that day, another habit that would take less than a minute. See below for a list of what you might choose to accomplish in a year.

<u>Month</u>   <u>Habit</u>

1	15 minutes every morning with your Life Instructions
2	45 additional minutes moving one milestone activity forward
3	1 minute each morning reviewing what you are grateful for
4	1 minute each evening reviewing three positive things that happened that day
5	At 3 pm each day, spend 15 minutes moving your second milestone forward
6	Get to work 30 minutes early each day and spend that time planning and moving forward a milestone related to your career
7	At 1 pm each day, as you are finishing your lunch, call someone you love
8	At lunch each day, think about, plan, or talk about your next vacation.
9	At the end of each day, send an email to a friend or mentor telling them what action you took to reach your milestones
10	Do one random act of kindness each day
11	Write your dreams or other thoughts in a journal each day
12	Slow down and savor each meal. Take small bites and spend time appreciating the tastes, smells, and textures of your food

As you are looking at this today for the first time, it looks like a list. It seems like at the end of the year you have a long list of things to do. But that is not the case. We are building these into habits. If you practice them every

day at the same time, eventually they will happen without your even thinking about them.

On another note, don't worry if all 12 of the activities don't become habits. Six or eight habits that help you get closer to daily happiness and success will significantly impact your outlook on life in a very positive way.

This is just a sample list. You should make your own list. Every section of the book includes a list of activities you can choose from. Pick a concept you really want to focus on and do three or four activities from that section; or, most importantly, decide what activities you can do daily that will help you reach your milestones. Find anywhere from a few minutes to an hour each day to work on those activities.

As you begin to implement this process, you will run into a variety of obstacles. They might include:

1. Trouble getting started each day

2. Committing to a time or place

3. Missing days

4. Starting over after missing a week or more

5. Not having the discipline or willpower to follow through

In the rest of this chapter we will talk about how to overcome those obstacles so you can implement them with discipline on a daily basis.

Overcoming Obstacles

"The true test of a champion is not whether he can triumph, but whether he can overcome obstacles." Garth Stein

Obstacle: Getting Started Each Day

Solution: Activation Energy and the 20 Second Rule

In Shawn Achor's book, *The Happiness Advantage*, he talks about Activation Energy and the 20 Second Rule. Activation energy is the energy it takes to start something. The concept is that it takes more energy to get started then it does to keep moving. If you are studying for a test, it takes more energy to get your books out, get to the right chapter, determine what you are supposed to learn, and then sit down and actually start doing the work.

Once the studying has actually begun, it doesn't take as much effort to just keep studying. If you are going to work out, it takes extra energy to wake up early; put on your workout clothes, socks, and shoes; grab any other accessories or equipment you might need; and then get to the gym or workout location. Once you have started your workout, much less effort is needed to keep it moving.

Shawn recommends creating a 20 second rule. Plan ahead of time so that you can get started using the least amount of activation energy in under 20 seconds. If you are going to work out in the morning, go to sleep with your workout clothes on and your shoes next to your bed. If you are going to study, lay out your books, laptop, pens, highlighters, etc. ahead of time. You might even open your book or laptop to the exact section you plan on studying. Create a situation where you can sit down at your desk and start studying in under 20 seconds. Creating a 20-second rule helps you eliminate distractions. If you have to hunt for your shoes and socks, you may end up trying to get a load of laundry started or focusing on cleaning up a little bit before you go exercise. If you don't go straight to your study information, you could get sidetracked by your email or the morning news. The 20 Second Rule helps you go straight to the activities that help you reach your

milestones without being distracted by the multitude of other things in your life.

With your Life Instructions, you can use the 20 Second Rule to reduce the amount of activation energy required by keeping multiple copies in multiple places and by preparing the materials you will need ahead of time. Also, focusing on the 20 Second Rule will help you move straight into your 15 minutes after you wake up rather than stopping to make coffee, check text messages, or read email. Wake up, and in less than 20 seconds, get started on your 15 minutes of planning your life or moving your goals forward. After your 15 minutes is completed, go back to your daily routine.

After 30 days, or however long it takes to create the habit, you can increase your time investment to an hour and spend more time working on activities directly related to reaching your milestones. So for the first month, you will spend 15 minutes with your Life Instructions. In the second month, you will spend the first 15 minutes with your Life Instructions, and then another 45 minutes working on your chosen activity related directly to moving one of your milestones forward.

Activation energy and The 20 Second Rule can be applied to every positive habit we want to create. Getting started is difficult; and as humans, we always tend to follow the path of least resistance, even if that is not what is best for us or what will most help us in reaching our milestones. So we need to create an environment with the fewest possible distractions and the fewest possible decisions between us and the action we want to take. We can prepare by creating simple rules to follow.

Obstacle: Committing to a Time and Place

Solution: Decide When, Where, and for How Long

One set of rules we can follow is scheduling specific dates and timeframes for each action we want to take. Make an appointment with yourself and put it in your calendar every day for the next year. We often get caught up in the busyness of our days and don't get to working on our goals, when we could have found 15 extra minutes if it had been top of mind for us. This appointment is about creating your happiness and success so it should be a top priority.

Setting a specific time and location to review your Life Instructions will eliminate several decisions you have to make each morning. When you are tired and groggy, lying in a warm bed, trying to decide what you are going to do, how you are going to get started, and where you are going to do it, seems overwhelming. You will automatically lean toward the path of least resistance, where you don't have to make all these decisions, and you will stay in bed. But if you already know that you are going to wake up, go to your desk and spend 15 minutes reviewing and advancing your Life Instructions, then you have removed enough obstacles to create the momentum and get started.

Initially limiting yourself to a 15-minute timeframe also helps you mentally prepare and not be overwhelmed by what is in front of you. Knowing there is an end point makes it easier to get started. It makes the activity feel doable.

Obstacle: Missing Days

Solution: Create a Habit

"We are what we repeatedly do. Excellence, then, is not an act, but a habit." Aristotle

We start with the best intentions, but we miss days and forget to work on moving toward our milestones. One reason is the activities are on our to-do

lists, but we have not created habits that make getting them done part of our daily routine.

Research by Quinn and Wood showed that 45% of the actions people take each day fall into the category of habits because they are consistently performed in the same place almost every day. Think about the habits you currently engage in before you go to work. Do you take time to read the news or have a thoughtful breakfast? Do you have a consistent routine for getting ready and going through some form of exercise? What about when you get to work? Do you grab a cup of coffee and chat with a few co-workers? Do you start your day by checking your calendar or reading your email? What about when you get home from work? Do you set your keys down in a certain place? Do you check the mail? Do you sit down in front of the television or computer? We want taking actions that will make you happier and more successful to become one these habits you automatically do every day.

When we first start a task, we have to focus our energy on thinking through each step. For example, if you are cooking something for the first time using a recipe, you probably read and re-read the instructions several times and carefully move from step to step, checking the directions again each time. After you have cooked something for the hundredth time, you no longer need the directions and you can probably carry on a full conversation without even thinking about the ingredients and steps you are going through.

Doing something over and over again builds synaptic pathways in our brains. Our brain works by passing electrical impulses along a pathway to create our thoughts and actions. If we fire those same impulses over and over again, our brain gets used to them, and the impulses travel faster and faster as the pathway becomes burned into our brain. This process helps us think less so we can do more.

The more things the brain can do on automatic pilot, the more capacity it has to take in new information and make additional decisions to move us forward. We are able to dress quickly and think about our day because it has become a habit. We know automatically how to put on our pants and that our shoes go on after our socks. If we had to stop and think about each action every morning, it would take a lot longer to get dressed and we could not get nearly as much done.

"We first make our habits, and then our habits make us." John Dryden

Activity: Don't break the chain of days

Get a monthly calendar and cross through every day that you complete your chosen activity for that month. Try not to break your string. If you miss a day, start over and see if you can go 30 days without missing a day.

Activity: Use your password as a reminder to reinforce your habits

One of my favorite IT people gave me this tip. At my office, we have to change our password every 60 days. So every time I change it, I use passwords that support the habits I am trying to create. For example; Write1Everyday, Help2bHappy, Say3Thanks, 3GreatThings, Call1Love. Every time I have to login, which seems like a lot, I am reminded and can practice my chosen habit.

Obstacle: Missing Consecutive Days that Turn into Weeks or Months

Solution: Start Over

Plan to fail and embrace being imperfect. Many times our goals are derailed due to lack of discipline and diligence, and we miss a day, a week, or a month of doing what we committed to do. We face an imperfect record or an outright failure, and it confirms all of our negative thoughts and feelings about our capabilities. For example, we commit to run two miles on Monday, Wednesday, and Friday at 6 am. Then we wake up at 7 am on Monday and find we have missed our run time and feel like the week is ruined before it gets started. Or we have a week of travel and forget our running gear. Or we have an injury and miss a month of running.

This is where most of us, especially the perfectionists among us, give up on the goal. We rationalize that it is just too difficult or that there is no use in continuing if we have already failed at it or will have an imperfect record. This is the time to rally our determination and keep trying. This is when we need to get back up even though we have fallen multiple times. There is no reason we can't just start again. As a matter of fact, we will probably be starting again many times before we finally accomplish our goal. The key is to understand that starting again is proof that we can be successful and not an example of our failure. We are learning to be successful not perfect. If you miss a week, a day, or a month, just start over. Don't look back and judge your misses as failures; look forward and realize you always have the opportunity for new beginnings.

Rituals: Habits without the Intensity

We want to create positive habits that help us connect happiness and success, but that requires consistent daily discipline and a focus on one habit at a time. What about all those other great ideas we want to use to improve our lives that don't necessarily have to be done daily? For these we can create rituals. Rituals are more conscious than habits and should be something we look forward to. We also may not necessarily do them daily. They may be weekly or monthly. For example, hanging out with our friends on Friday night or calling our mom every Sunday morning are activities that bring happiness into our lives but they don't have to become daily habits. We can create rituals which may or may not become long-term habits.

Rituals follow the same process as habits. They will have a cue, a routine (the ritual), and a reward. One of my family's rituals is that we call our extended family on their birthdays. When aunts, uncles, nieces, nephews, and grandparents have birthdays, it is a race to see who will call first. My wife and kids gather around the phone and give happy birthday greetings or leave birthday messages on voicemail. The cue is a calendar reminder that announces a family birthday, the routine or ritual is the family call, and the reward is the excitement and fun of interacting with the family.

Another example is that most evenings, my wife and I walk the dog around the park together. It gives us time to spend together and talk. It has almost become a habit in that we want to go in all types of weather and all temperatures. The cue is the dog starts to get restless and excited, anticipating the walk; the ritual is walking around the park and talking; the reward is the enjoyment of spending time together.

Decide what kinds of rituals you already have or would like to start. They are like a gift you give yourself. Creating the ritual is giving yourself permission to focus on what you think is important and rewarding. Follow the ritual long enough and it can become a habit, so you won't have to think about it; you will just do it automatically.

A great time to create rituals is when something changes (for example, when you get a new job, move to a new apartment, or get a new boyfriend or girlfriend). Think about what fun things you want to make a part of your life and create a new ritual to make it happen. Getting Starbucks with a friend on Friday mornings, weekly meetings with your boss or team, or visiting your parents on a weekly or monthly basis can be rituals you look forward to. There is no pressure for achievement; they just seem like things you want to do.

Put an appointment on your calendar for your ritual. Talk with your friends and family about the rituals you would like to establish, so they can support you and provide reminders.

Obstacle: Not Having the Discipline and Willpower to Follow-Through

Solution: Build Your Willpower Muscle

In a 2013 study titled "Stress in America," 31% of Americans said lack of willpower was the number one barrier to change when asked about making changes related to improving their lives. Willpower is the ability to override your natural impulses and habits in order to choose actions that support your Higher Purpose and goals. It is the ability to delay short-term gratification in favor of long-term goals. Willpower also includes the ability to override unwanted thoughts and feelings so your decisions are more thoughtful than emotionally driven. Willpower is not a lack of feelings; it is an ability to regulate your behavior given those feelings, rather than letting them control your actions. Other terms used to indicate willpower are self-control and self-discipline.

Research has shown that the use of willpower can improve your grades, your spending and savings habits, your relationship skills, and your physical health, all of which lead to higher self-esteem. More willpower is also associated with less substance abuse, fewer criminal convictions, and less binge eating. Research has shown that if developed in children, willpower can remain a strong influence throughout their lives.

Martin Seligman and Angela Duckworth conducted research that showed willpower was a better predictor of success in school than IQ. Students with more willpower were more likely to get higher grades and get into top schools. They had fewer absences, spent less time watching TV, and spent more time on homework.

Willpower is like a muscle that can become fatigued from overuse. The more willpower we use, the less is available for a new task later in the day.

Willpower is also like a muscle because we can exercise it and make it stronger. You can increase your willpower through practice. Two researchers from Australia, Megan Oaten and Ken Cheng, conducted an experiment where participants made no significant changes for two months, then implemented an exercise routine for the next two months. Oaten and Cheng tested the participant's willpower at the beginning of the experiment and for the next four months, the last two of which included the exercise. Participants showed no changes in the first two months; but after the two months of implementing the exercise routine, not only did they increase their willpower based on laboratory tests, but they showed improvements in other aspects of their lives as well. They showed lower stress and less frequent smoking, as well as decreased alcohol and caffeine consumption. They also showed improvements in healthy eating, controlling their emotions, study habits, financial budgeting, and meeting other commitments. Find one area you want to improve and focus your willpower on changing that one area. It will make your willpower muscle stronger so it can be used to positively impact other areas of your life.

Reduce Stress

Willpower is compromised by stress. You use willpower to manage stress created by internal conflict. You know what you should do, and that conflicts with what you want to do. Your prefrontal cortex is the part of the brain that connects goals and actions in an attempt to override impulses that may have negative consequences. Using willpower draws down your energy reservoir to send extra energy to your prefrontal cortex to deal with the stress.

Stress is part of your fight or flight response and pushes your body to act instinctively for preservation. That conflicts with your willpower because your body places survival above goal achievement. The challenge is that in modern society, we are rarely in situations that are life-threatening, but our instincts kick in anyway. For example, when we are nervous about making a presentation, our instincts think we are in danger and should run away. We use our willpower to push down those instincts and focus on making the presentation. The more we can reduce those internal conflicts and the resulting stress, the more willpower we will have to achieve our goals. When you feel stressed, take a moment to revisit your Higher Purpose.

What is the big picture and how does the current situation affect the big picture. Pausing to gain perspective will help you become calmer and make choices that are in line with your goals. Getting enough sleep, sticking to a healthy diet, and meditating or having 15 minutes of quiet time, can also help reduce your levels of stress, which will help increase your willpower.

Sleep, Nutrition, Authenticity and Meditation

Sleep

Willpower is depleted by a lack of sleep. A lack of sleep impairs the ability of your prefrontal cortex to recall your goals, control your stress, and use willpower to make decisions that support your goals. Getting seven or more hours of sleep per night will strengthen your willpower and your ability to reach your goals. Create a ritual of going to bed at the same time every night. Reduce late night snacks and late night TV. Write journals or make lists to empty your brain of all your swirling thoughts.

Nutrition

Willpower is reduced by poor nutrition. As you run low on energy, less is directed to your prefrontal cortex where it can be used for willpower. Research has shown that glucose levels are a good proxy for the amount of willpower you have left. The lower your glucose levels, the lower your willpower. By eating and increasing your glucose levels, your levels of willpower get restored. Therefore, you can increase or enhance your willpower by regularly eating a healthy diet, and by recognizing when your glucose levels are low and eating a healthy snack to help replenish them.

Authenticity

Suppressing your feelings or thoughts also drains your willpower. Social interactions where you don't feel you can act naturally drain your willpower. Laughing and having fun can help you maintain your willpower. The

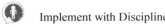

answer? Hang out with people where you feel like you can be yourself. Being authentic is more enjoyable and will help you reach your milestones faster.

Meditation or Quiet Time

Willpower can be strengthened through meditation, quiet time, and physical exercise. They positively impact the prefrontal cortex, and as a result increase your willpower. Meditation and prayer also help reduce stress and improve impulse control.

Start Early

Since willpower is a limited resource that is used throughout the day, it is best to start early. Accomplish your most important activities first, while your willpower is strongest. Plan the small steps you need to take to accomplish your milestones and attack them first. If your milestone is a promotion, start the day with one hour of uninterrupted time on a career-related project. Don't try to accomplish a lot of small, disconnected tasks that don't have a clear connection to your Higher Purpose, such as answering random emails and texts or reading the latest gossip on Facebook. Pick one major goal and tackle the first small step, then the second small step, and then another, until you create momentum and are making good progress toward your most important goals. You will feel happier and more relaxed the rest of the day, knowing you have already made progress toward your most important milestones.

Practice Autonomy

Every activity we tackle does not drain our willpower. Some activities build our willpower. For example, we all have friends and family that are energy suckers and ones that are energy givers. When we force ourselves to go see a family member because of guilt or some other obligation, we don't have autonomy. It takes a lot of willpower. But if we choose to see a friend or family member because we love being around them, then no willpower is expended. My wife loves to go out in the yard and pull weeds, plant flowers, and make the yard look nice. It gives her energy, and she enjoys the results of her hard work. It doesn't sap her willpower to go outside and get the yard work done; it actually energizes her. I, on the other hand, find it tedious and boring to pull weeds, cut grass, and spread the mulch. It takes willpower for me to schedule time, put on my work clothes and get started on the yard.

Activities that we believe in and really want to do don't use up our willpower. So the key is to find activities that align with our Higher Purpose. The more activities we do because we love them and believe in how they will benefit ourselves and others, the more willpower we have left to apply to the more challenging activities that we feel obligated to take on.

Another experiment by Deci and Ryan helped clarify desirable activities from obligations. They created conditions where the participants connected the completion of a task to how people would perceive them. When the participants were trying to look good for others, they didn't feel the same autonomy as when they were just trying to do the best they could.

Trying to impress others uses our willpower and produces the same results as not getting to choose how we implement a task. Don't choose activities because of what other people will think about you; choose them because you really believe they are the best thing for you or they will genuinely help someone else.

In many cases, autonomy may be a matter of perspective. If we focus on what we want to do instead of what we *don't* want to do, we can recognize and appreciate the autonomy in our lives. When we spend our time thinking and talking about not wanting to clean up, take out the trash, do our homework, go to work, etc., our mind fills up with negative thoughts about what we feel forced to do and our efforts rally around making sure we don't do those things. We have to use a lot of willpower to get them done. But if we connect those activities to our "Why," then we will want to do them. For example, we want to live in a clean place that smells good, so taking out the trash is part of what we want. We want to graduate from college and get a good job, so doing our homework is part of that milestone. We want to save enough money to buy a new house or go on vacation, so spending less is part of our choice. The first step in accomplishing any of our goals often includes activities we are not thrilled about doing. We want to live in a clean house, so we need to clean the house and take out the trash. If we are focused on the clean house rather than not wanting to clean, then we can quickly get it done and move on to other things we do want.

If every morning we get up and think about that vacation we are saving for, it will be easier and almost fun to go to work. Focus on what we do want to do. If we focus on what we want to accomplish, then the less appealing tasks that are a requirement will become more fun because they have a

positive purpose. We are doing them for a good reason, we believe in them, and they will require less willpower.

This all comes back to being clear on your goals and making sure they are self-chosen. Knowing and revisiting your Higher Purpose or your "Why" will help you feel like you are choosing your path and your actions and will provide more willpower throughout the day to take the actions that support your purpose.

Create Positive Habits

Activities that become habits or rituals take little to no willpower. Also, the practice it takes to create a habit builds your willpower muscle. So as you establish more and more positive habits and rituals, you are also creating a larger and larger reservoir of willpower to draw from. It is a virtuous circle that starts slowly and almost imperceptibly, but then builds momentum over time.

"If-Then" Plans

One of the most effective methods for managing your willpower is "If-Then" plans. "If-Then" plans, also called implementation intentions, help conserve willpower. It works like this: your plan is to exercise first thing in the morning. "If" you wake up late, "then" you will work out during your lunch break at the gym near your office, or immediately after work at the gym nearest your route home. The more details you can add to your "If-Then" plans, the easier they will be to implement. If you have a plan B of what you will do when faced with temptation or unexpected circumstances, you can move to plan B without using a lot of your limited willpower resource. You are creating a cue-response mechanism that primes your brain to automatically know how to react when you encounter an obstacle. Research has shown that having "If-Then" plans to support your goals is twice as effective as having goals alone. "If-Then" plans prepare your mind to quickly solve challenges you didn't foresee, because it is now primed to recognize opportunities that move you toward your goals rather than away from them.

Manage your willpower wisely by understanding what drains it and what you can do to use it efficiently and build it back up.

Drains Willpower	Solution
Stress	Focus on your Higher Purpose, get enough sleep, implement healthy eating habits, and have a daily meditation or quiet time
Lack of sleep	Sleep at least seven hours per night
Low glucose levels	Eat nutritious meals and healthy snacks when glucose levels are low
Low priority activities and decisions	Start early while willpower is strong, create positive habits
Doing things we don't want to do	Practice Autonomy
Daily obstacles	Use "If-Then" plans

To connect happiness and success, create positive habits, choose to be more self-disciplined, improve your willpower, and implement your chosen actions on a daily basis.

Many people believe life comes down to a few choices we make, what college we go to, our major, what job we choose, and who we marry. The truth is, those decisions are a result of decisions we make every day.

Every day we can choose actions that lead us toward our Higher Purpose and our definition of success, or we can choose decisions that lead us away from that path. When the big decisions come, we have already made a lot of daily decisions that have resulted in our opportunities and choices. If we worked hard and studied daily, then we probably got good grades; and as a result, we have many opportunities to attend a good college. If we've hung around the people that shared our values and beliefs, then we most likely have met someone we can marry who shares those values and beliefs. If we bring energy and enthusiasm to work every day, then we probably have several opportunities for promotions, special projects, and raises. If, on the

other hand, we have spent every day complaining and putting off the things we know we needed to do, then our big decisions will be less clear and we will have fewer options. Spend every day making good decisions, and the big lifetime decisions will be clear and will be filled with options.

Daily Happiness Tool

We have created an application that will provide you with daily happiness nudges. Go to MyHappiness.io on any device to login.

Success and happiness are born out of an ability to do small things on a daily basis that move you toward your long term goals. They result from doing the right things day in and day out because you are confident in your direction, even when your progress is slow and unclear. Your Higher Purpose and definition of success will provide the lighthouse for your direction. Your goals or milestones will help you measure progress along the way. Consistency and stamina are keys. Keep moving forward and keep re-directing when you get off track. Don't quit, and don't constantly change direction. Take daily, purposeful action. Follow through on your goals and commitments, and you will be able to connect happiness and success.

Start Today

You can be happy and successful. Don't wait. Start today.

Someday Isle (I'll)

There is an island fantasy
A "Someday I'll" we'll never see,

When recession stops, inflation ceases,
Our mortgage is paid, our pay increases.

That Someday Isle where problems end,
Where every piece of mail is from a friend,

Where the children are sweet, already grown,
Where all the nations can go it alone,

Where we all retire at forty-one,
Playing Football in the island sun.

Most unhappy people look to tomorrow,
To erase this day's hardship and sorrow.

They put happiness on lay-away,
And struggle through a blue today.

But happiness cannot be sought,
It can't be earned, it can't be bought.

Life's most important revelation,
It's the journey that means as much as the
destination.

Happiness is where you are right now,
Pushing a pencil or pushing a plow.

It's knocking on doors and making your calls,
It's getting back up after your falls.

It's going to school or standing in line,
Tasting defeat, tasting the wine.

If you live in the past you become senile,
If you live in the future you're on "Someday I'll."

The fear of results is procrastination,
The joy of today is a celebration.

You can save, you can slave, trudging mile after mile,
But you'll never set foot on your "Someday I'll."

When you've paid all your dues and put in your time,

Out of nowhere comes another Mt. Everest to climb.

**I have decided Today to make it my Vow,
To take "Someday I'll" and make it NOW.**

Shared/Recited by Ken Purcell, Written By Dennis Waitley

In their book *Habits Die Hard*, Mac Anderson and John Murphy tell a great quick story about starting now. Five frogs are on a log. One decides to jump off. How many are left? Five. Because deciding is not doing. We have to take action daily—not just think about the action we want to take.

Don't stop at having a list of goals or even a list of actions. Every day you have to take action and make progress. The difference between connecting happiness and success and in living the same unfulfilled life as millions of other people will be in the actions you take every day to move your life forward. You can start small with just 15 minutes each day. But do something every day.

Find a way each day to move closer to your goals and closer to being the person you want to be. It will be difficult at first; but over time you will build momentum, and 15 minutes will turn into an hour, which will eventually turn into a day. Those days will become a life where you will be happy and successful.

Happiness and success are intertwined in our lives, and they both need to be practiced and experienced every day. Don't believe that success is some distant accomplishment or that happiness can be sacrificed today because it will come later. Make them a part of your day, every day. Happiness and success are connected, and they are both within your reach. Start today. Write your Life Instructions and spend 15 minutes every day planning your happiness and success.

To connect Happiness and Success

1. Know the difference between pleasure and happiness.

2. Take control of your life.

3. Build positive relationships.

4. Find your Higher Purpose.

5. Define success.

6. Clarify and prioritize your actions.

7. Implement with discipline on a daily basis.

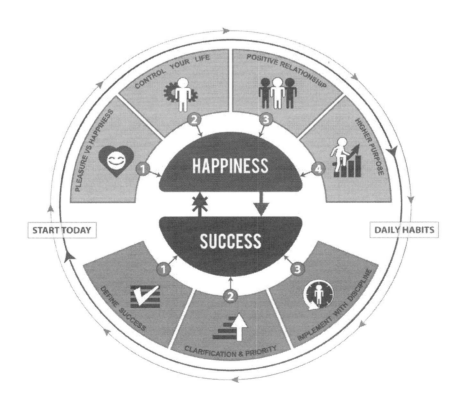

Start now. Finishing this book is a great accomplishment and a significant step toward being happier and more successful. Take a moment to savor that accomplishment. Do a little happy dance and celebrate your achievement. Think about two things you get to do tomorrow to be happier and more successful. End the day knowing that today you are happy and successful and tomorrow you will be as well.

NOTES

Notes from Overview and 1st Concept – Pleasure vs. Happiness:

1. Achor, Shawn. *The Happiness Advantage: The Seven Principles of Positive Psychology That Fuel Success and Performance at Work*. New York: Broadway Books, 2010.

2. Baumeister, Roy F., and Mark R. Leary. "The Need to Belong: Desire for Interpersonal Attachments as a Fundamental Human Motivation." *Psychological Bulletin* 117, no. 3 (1995): 497-529.

3. "Be Better Everyday." *Be Better Everyday* (web log), October 16, 2013. Accessed December 17, 2013. http://bebettereveryday.com/happiness-vs-pleasure/.

4. Cox, Jeff. "BofA Intern Dies after Reportedly Working 3 Straight Days." *CNBC.com*, August 20, 2013. Accessed December 17, 2013. http://www.cnbc.com/id/100974434.

5. Haneef, KPM. "HAPPINESS vs PLEASURE." *K.P.M. Haneef: HAPPINESS vs PLEASURE* (web log), November 27, 2011. Accessed December 17, 2013. http://kpmhaneefblog.blogspot.com/2011/11/happiness-vs-pleasure.html.

6. Haneef, KPM. "WHAT IS HAPPINESS?" K.P.M. Haneef: WHAT IS HAPPINESS? July 23, 2010. Accessed December 17, 2013. http://kpmhaneefblog.blogspot.com/2010/07/what-is-happiness_23.html.

7. Lyubomirsky, Sonja. *The How of Happiness: A Scientific Approach to Getting the Life You Want*. New York: Penguin Press, 2008.

8. Melendez, Eleazar David. "Bank of America Intern Death Sheds Light On Cutthroat World Of Aspiring Bankers." *The Huffington Post*, August 23, 2013. Accessed December 17, 2013. http://www.huffingtonpost.com/2013/08/23/bank-of-america-intern-death_n_3806918.html.

9. Seligman, Martin E. P. *Flourish: A Visionary New Understanding of Happiness and Well-being*. New York: Free Press, 2011.

Notes from 2nd Concept – Taking Control of Your Life

1. "7 Doors to Happiness: Door 2 Obstacles." Project Happiness: 7 Doors to Happiness. Accessed December 18, 2013. http://7doorstohappiness.com/site/door2.php.

2. Algoe, Sara, and Jonathan Haidt. "Witnessing Excellence in Action: The 'other-praising' Emotions of Elevation, Gratitude, and Admiration." *The Journal of Positive Psychology* 4, no. 2 (2009): 105-27. doi:10.1080/17439760802650519.

3. Ally. "Category: Joy - The Positive Psychology Foundation." *The Positive Psychology Foundation*, August 08, 2011. http://www.positivepsyc.com/1/category/joy/1.html.

4. Babyak, M., J. A. Blumenthal, S. Herman, M. Doraiswamy, P. Khatri, K. Moore, W. E. Craighead, T. T. Baldewicz, and K. R. Krishnan. "Exercise Treatment for Major Depression: Maintenance of Therapeutic Benefit at 10 Months." *Psychosomatic Medicine* 62 (2000): 633-38.

5. Biswas-Diener, Robert. "From the Equator to the North Pole: A Study of Character Strengths." *Journal of Happiness Studies* 7, no. 3 (2006): 293-310. doi:10.1007/s10902-005-3646-8.

6. Blake, Trevor. *Three Simple Steps: A Map to Success in Business and Life*. Dallas, TX: BenBella Books, 2012.

7. Blumenthal, J. A., M. A. Babyak, K. A. Moore, W. W. Craighead, S. Herman, P. Khatri, R. Waugh, M. A. Napolitano, L. M. Forman, M. Applebaum, and P. M. Doraiswamy. "Effects of Exercise Training on Older Patients with Major Depression." *Archives of Internal Medicine* 159, no. 19 (October 25, 1999): 2349-356.

8. Brissette, Ian, Michael F. Scheier, and Charles S. Carver. "The Role of Optimism in Social Network Development, Coping, and Psychological Adjustment during a Life Transition." *Journal of Personality and Social Psychology* 82, no. 1 (2002): 102-11. doi:10.1037//0022-3514.82.1.102.

9. Britton, Kathryn. "Positive Psychology News Daily » Positive Core and Strengths at Work." *Positive Psychology News Daily*, May 7, 2007. http://positivepsychologynews.com/news/kathryn-britton/20070507231.

10. Broom, D. R., R. L. Batterham, J. A. King, and D. J. Stensel. "Influence of Resistance and Aerobic Exercise on Hunger, Circulating Levels of Acylated Ghrelin, and Peptide YY in Healthy Males." *AJP: Regulatory, Integrative and Comparative Physiology* 296, no. 1 (2008): R29-35. doi:10.1152/ajpregu.90706.2008.

11. Brown, Kirk Warren, and Richard M. Ryan. "The Benefits of Being Present: Mindfulness and Its Role in Psychological Well-being." *Journal of Personality and Social Psychology* 84, no. 4 (2003): 822-48. doi:10.1037/0022-3514.84.4.822.

12. Brown, Kirk Warren, Tim Kasser, Richard M. Ryan, P. Alex Linley, and Kevin Orzech. "When What One Has Is Enough: Mindfulness, Financial Desire

Discrepancy, and Subjective Well-being." *Journal of Research in Personality* 43, no. 5 (2009): 727-36. doi:10.1016/j.jrp.2009.07.002.

13.   Carver, Charles S., Jessica M. Lehman, and Michael H. Antoni. "Dispositional Pessimism Predicts Illness-related Disruption of Social and Recreational Activities among Breast Cancer Patients." *Journal of Personality and Social Psychology* 84, no. 4 (April 2003): 813-21. doi:10.1037/0022-3514.84.4.813.

14.   Cawley, M., J. Martin, and J. Johnson. "A Virtues Approach to Personality1." *Personality and Individual Differences* 28, no. 5 (2000): 997-1013. doi:10.1016/S0191-8869(99)00207-X.

15.   Cohn, Michael A., Barbara L. Fredrickson, Stephanie L. Brown, Joseph A. Mikels, and Anne M. Conway. "Happiness Unpacked: Positive Emotions Increase Life Satisfaction by Building Resilience." *Emotion* 9, no. 3 (2009): 361-68. doi:10.1037/a0015952.

16.   Danner, Deborah D., David A. Snowdon, and Wallace V. Friesen. "Positive Emotions in Early Life and Longevity: Findings from the Nun Study." *Journal of Personality and Social Psychology* 80, no. 5 (2001): 804-13. doi:10.1037//0022-3514.80.5.804.

17.   Davidson, R. J. "Alterations in Brain and Immune Function Produced by Mindfulness Meditation." *Psychosomatic Medicine* 65, no. 4 (2003): 564-70. doi:10.1097/01.PSY.0000077505.67574.E3.

18.   Deci, Edward L., and Richard M. Ryan. "The "What" and "Why" of Goal Pursuits: Human Needs and the Self-Determination of Behavior." *Psychological Inquiry* 11, no. 4 (2000): 227-68. doi:10.1207/S15327965PLI1104_01.

19.   Diener, Robert, and Robert Biswas-Diener. *Happiness: Unlocking the Mysteries of Psychological Wealth*. Malden, MA: Blackwell Pub., 2008.

20.   Dinges, D. F., F. Pack, K. A. Gillen, J. W. Powell, G. E. Ott, C. Aptowicz, and A. I. Pack. "Cumulative Sleepiness, Mood Disturbance, and Psychomotor Vigilance Performance Decrements during a Week of Sleep Restricted to 4-5 Hours per Night." *Sleep* 20, no. 4 (April 1997): 267-77.

21.   Emmons, Dr. Robert. "Emmons Lab." *UC Davis Emmons Lab*, February 2, 2013. http://psychology.ucdavis.edu/Labs/emmons/PWT/index.cfm?Section=1.

22.   Emmons, Robert A., and Michael E. McCullough. "Counting Blessings Versus Burdens: An Experimental Investigation of Gratitude and Subjective Well-Being in Daily Life." *Journal of Personality and Social Psychology* 84, no. 2 (2003): 377-89. doi:.1037/0022-3514.84.2.377.

23.   Emmons, Robert A. *Thanks!: How the New Science of Gratitude Can Make You Happier*. Boston: Houghton Mifflin, 2007.

24.   Fowler, J. H., and N. A. Christakis. "Dynamic Spread of Happiness in a Large Social Network: Longitudinal Analysis over 20 Years in the Framingham Heart Study." *British Medical Journal* 337, no. Dec04 2 (December 2008): 337-46. doi:10.1136/bmj.a2338.

25. Fredrickson, Barbara L., and Marcial F. Losada. "Positive Affect and the Complex Dynamics of Human Flourishing." *American Psychologist* 60, no. 7 (2005): 678-86. doi:10.1037/0003-066X.60.7.678.

26. Fredrickson, Barbara L. "The Role of Positive Emotions in Positive Psychology: The Broaden-and-build Theory of Positive Emotions." *American Psychologist* 56, no. 3 (2001): 218-26. doi:10.1037//0003-066X.56.3.218.

27. Fredrickson, Barbara. *Positivity*. New York: Crown Publishers, 2009.

28. Fredrickson, Barbara. "The Value of Positive Emotions." *American Scientist* 91, no. 4 (2003): 330-35. doi:10.1511/2003.4.330.

29. Froh, J., W. Sefick, and R. Emmons. "Counting Blessings in Early Adolescents: An Experimental Study of Gratitude and Subjective Well-being☆." *Journal of School Psychology* 46, no. 2 (2008): 213-33. doi:10.1016/j.jsp.2007.03.005.

30. Froh, Jeffrey J., Charles Yurkewicz, and Todd B. Kashdan. "Gratitude and Subjective Well-being in Early Adolescence: Examining Gender Differences." *Journal of Adolescence* 32, no. 3 (2009): 633-50. doi:10.1016/j.adolescence.2008.06.006.

31. Gagne', Maryle'ne, and Edward L. Deci. "Self-determination Theory and Work Motivation." *Journal of Organizational Behavior* 26, no. 4 (2005): 331-62. doi:10.1002/job.322.

32. Garland, Eric L., Barbara Fredrickson, Ann Kring, David P. Johnson, Piper S. Meyer, and David L. Penn. "Upward Spirals of Positive Emotions Counter Downward Spirals of Negativity: Insights from the Broaden-and-Build Theory and Affective Neuroscience on The Treatment of Emotion Dysfunctions and Deficits in Psychopathology." *Clinical Psychology Review*, November 2010, 849-64. http://www.ncbi.nlm.nih.gov/pmc/articles/PMC2908186/.

33. Gillham, Jane E., Karen J. Reivich, Derek R. Freres, Tara M. Chaplin, Andrew J. Shatté, Barbra Samuels, Andrea G. L. Elkon, Samantha Litzinger, Marisa Lascher, Robert Gallop, and Martin E. P. Seligman. "School-based Prevention of Depressive Symptoms: A Randomized Controlled Study of the Effectiveness and Specificity of the Penn Resiliency Program." *Journal of Consulting and Clinical Psychology* 75, no. 1 (February 2007): 9-19. doi:10.1037/0022-006X.75.1.9.

34. Given, Charles W., Manfred Stommel, Barbara Given, Janet Osuch, and Et Al. "The Influence of Cancer Patients' Symptoms and Functional States on Patients' Depression and Family Caregivers' Reaction and Depression." *Health Psychology* 12, no. 4 (July 1993): 277-85. doi:10.1037//0278-6133.12.4.277.

35. Graham, C. "Happiness And Health: Lessons And Questions For Public Policy." *Health Affairs* 27, no. 1 (2008): 72-87. doi:10.1377/hlthaff.27.1.72.

36. Graham, Kathy. *Mindfulness in 10 Easy Steps*. WorldHappinessForum.org, 2013.

37. Guo, Teng, and Lingyi Hu. *Economic Determinants of Happiness: Evidence from the US General Social Survey*. Diss., Cornell University. Accessed December 20, 2013. http://arxiv.org/ftp/arxiv/papers/1112/1112.5802.pdf.

38. Ironson, Gail, Elizabeth Balbin, Rick Stuetzle, Mary Ann Fletcher, Conall O'Cleirigh, J. P. Laurenceau, Neil Schneiderman, and George Solomon. "Dispositional Optimism and the Mechanisms by Which It Predicts Slower Disease Progression in HIV: Proactive Behavior, Avoidant Coping, and Depression." *International Journal of Behavioral Medicine* 12, no. 2 (2005): 86-97. doi:10.1207/s15327558ijbm1202_6.

39. Kamen, Leslie P., and Martin E. P. Seligman. "Explanatory Style and Health." *Current Psychology* 6, no. 3 (1987): 207-18. doi:10.1007/BF02686648.

40. KONNIKOVA, Maria. "The Power of Concentration." *New York Times*, December 15, 2012, U.S. ed., Opinion sec.

41. Lambert, N. M., S. M. Graham, and F. D. Fincham. "A Prototype Analysis of Gratitude: Varieties of Gratitude Experiences." *Personality and Social Psychology Bulletin* 35, no. 9 (2009): 1193-207. doi:10.1177/0146167209338071.

42. Langer, Ellen J. *Counterclockwise: A Proven Way to Think Yourself Younger and Healthier.* London: Hodder, 2010.

43. Lyubomirsky, Sonja. *The How of Happiness: A Scientific Approach to Getting the Life You Want.* New York: Penguin Press, 2008.

44. Maruta, T., R. C. Colligan, M. Malinchoc, and K. P. Offord. "Optimists vs Pessimists: Survival Rate among Medical Patients over a 30-year Period." *Mayo Clinic Proceedings* 75, no. 2 (2000): 140-43. doi:10.4065/75.2.140.

45. Matthews, K. A. "Optimistic Attitudes Protect Against Progression of Carotid Atherosclerosis in Healthy Middle-Aged Women." *Psychosomatic Medicine* 66, no. 5 (September/October, 2004): 640-44. doi:10.1097/01.psy.0000139999.99756.a5.

46. McCullough, Michael E., Robert A. Emmons, and Jo-Ann Tsang. "The Grateful Disposition: A Conceptual and Empirical Topography." *Journal of Personality and Social Psychology* 82, no. 1 (2002): 112-27. doi:10.1037//0022-3514.82.1.112.

47. "Money Can't Buy Happiness: Individualism a Stronger Predictor of Well-Being Than Wealth, Says New Study." *ScienceDaily*, June 14, 2011. doi:10.1037/a0023663.

48. Park, Nansook, and Christopher Peterson. "Character Strengths and Happiness among Young Children: Content Analysis of Parental Descriptions." *Journal of Happiness Studies* 7, no. 3 (2006): 323-41. doi:10.1007/s10902-005-3648-6.

49. Park, Nansook, Christopher Peterson, and Martin E. P. Seligman. "Strengths of Character and Well-Being." *Journal of Social and Clinical Psychology* 23, no. 5 (2004): 603-19. doi:10.1521/jscp.23.5.603.50748.

50. Pelé, and Robert L. Fish. *My Life and the Beautiful Game: The Autobiography of Pelé.* Garden City, NY: Doubleday, 1977.

51. Peterson, Christopher, and Martin E. P. Seligman. *Character Strengths and Virtues: A Handbook and Classification.* Washington, DC: American Psychological Association, 2004.

52. Peterson, Christopher, and Martin E. P. Seligman. *Character Strengths and Virtues: A Handbook and Classification*. Washington, DC: American Psychological Association, 2004. 553-68.

53. Peterson, Christopher. *A Primer in Positive Psychology*. Oxford: Oxford University Press, 2006.

54. Pink, Daniel H. *Drive: The Surprising Truth about What Motivates Us*. New York, NY: Riverhead Books, 2009.

55. Pollay, David J. "Positive Psychology News Daily » Gratitude and Giving Will Lead to Your Success." *Positive Psychology News Daily*, June 2, 2007. http://positivepsychologynews.com/news/david-j-pollay/20070602268.

56. Ryan, Richard M., and Edward L. Deci. "Self-Regulation and the Problem of Human Autonomy: Does Psychology Need Choice, Self-Determination, and Will?" *Journal of Personality* 74, no. 6 (2006): 1557-586. doi:10.1111/j.1467-6494.2006.00420.x.

57. Salmonsohn, Karen. "Bouncing Back: The Art (and Science) of Resilience." Psychology Today. June 30, 2011. http://www.psychologytoday.com/blog/bouncing-back/201106/the-no-1-contributor-happiness.

58. Schou, I., Ø. Ekeberg, and C.M. Ruland. "The Mediating Role of Appraisal and Coping in the Relationship between Optimism-pessimism and Quality of Life." *Psycho-Oncology* 14, no. 9 (2005): 718-27. doi:10.1002/pon.896.

59. Schwartz, Tony. "Slow Down, You Move Too Fast | The Energy Project." *Slow Down, You Move Too Fast | The Energy Project* (web log), April 3, 2012. http://www.theenergyproject.com/blog/slow-down-you-move-too-fast.

60. Seligman, Martin E. P. *Authentic Happiness: Using the New Positive Psychology to Realize Your Potential for Lasting Fulfillment*. New York: Free Press, 2002.

61. Seligman, Martin E. P. "What Is Well Being?" In *Flourish: A Visionary New Understanding of Happiness and Well-being*. New York: Free Press, 2011.

62. Shapiro, Shauna L., Doug Oman, Carl E. Thoresen, Thomas G. Plante, and Tim Flinders. "Cultivating Mindfulness: Effects on Well-being." *Journal of Clinical Psychology* 64, no. 7 (2008): 840-62. doi:10.1002/jclp.20491.

63. Sharot, Tali. "Tali Sharot: The Optimism Bias." *TED: Ideas worth Spreading*, May 2012. http://www.ted.com/talks/tali_sharot_the_optimism_bias.html.

64. Sheldon, Kennon M., and Sonja Lyubomirsky. "How to Increase and Sustain Positive Emotion: The Effects of Expressing Gratitude and Visualizing Best Possible Selves." *The Journal of Positive Psychology* 1, no. 2 (2006): 73-82. doi:10.1080/17439760500510676.

65. Sohl, Stephanie J., Anne Moyer, Lukin Konstantin, and Sarah K. Knapp-Oliver. "Why Are Optimists Optimistic?" *Individ Differ Res* 9, no. 1 (2011): 1-11.

66. Taft, Michael W. "Concentration and Flow." Deconstructing Yourself. August 6, 2011. Accessed December 20, 2013. http://deconstructingyourself.com/concentration-and-flow.html.

67. Tough, Paul. "What If the Secret to Success Is Failure?" *New York Times*, September 14, 2011. http://www.nytimes.com/2011/09/18/magazine/what-if-the-secret-to-success-is-failure.html?pagewanted=all&_r=0.

68. Watkins, Philip C., Kathrane Woodward, Tamara Stone, and Russell L. Kolts. "Gratitude And Happiness: Development Of A Measure Of Gratitude, And Relationships With Subjective Well-Being." *Social Behavior and Personality: An International Journal* 31, no. 5 (2003): 431-51. doi:10.2224/sbp.2003.31.5.431.

69. Waugh, Christian E., and Barbara L. Fredrickson. "Nice to Know You: Positive Emotions, Self–other Overlap, and Complex Understanding in the Formation of a New Relationship." *The Journal of Positive Psychology* 1, no. 2 (2006): 93-106. doi:10.1080/17439760500510569.

70. Weinberg, Rabbi Noah. Comment on "The Secret of Happiness." *Aishcom* (web log), January 25, 2000. http://www.aish.com/sp/f/48968901.html.

71. Winston-Macauley, Marie. "Perfection vs. Good Enough." *Aishcom* (web log), December 25, 2010. http://www.aish.com/sp/pg/Perfection_vs_Good_Enough.html.

72. Wiseman, Richard. *The Luck Factor*. London: Arrow, 2004.

73. Wood, A., J. Maltby, N. Stewart, and S. Joseph. "Conceptualizing Gratitude and Appreciation as a Unitary Personality Trait." *Personality and Individual Differences* 44, no. 3 (2008): 621-32. doi:10.1016/j.paid.2007.09.028.

74. Wood, A., J. Maltby, R. Gillett, P. Linley, and S. Joseph. "The Role of Gratitude in the Development of Social Support, Stress, and Depression: Two Longitudinal Studies." *Journal of Research in Personality* 42, no. 4 (2008): 854-71. doi:10.1016/j.jrp.2007.11.003.

75. Wood, A., S. Joseph, and J. Maltby. "Gratitude Predicts Psychological Well-being above the Big Five Facets." *Personality and Individual Differences* 46, no. 4 (2009): 443-47. doi:10.1016/j.paid.2008.11.012.

76. Wood, A., S. Joseph, J. Lloyd, and S. Atkins. "Gratitude Influences Sleep through the Mechanism of Pre-sleep Cognitions." *Journal of Psychosomatic Research*, 2008. doi:10.1016/j.jpsychores.2008.09.002.

77. Wood, Alex M., John Maltby, Neil Stewart, P. Alex Linley, and Stephen Joseph. "A Social-cognitive Model of Trait and State Levels of Gratitude." *Emotion* 8, no. 2 (2008): 281-90. doi:10.1037/1528-3542.8.2.281.

78. Yeager, John. "Positive Psychology News Daily » Make Your Goals Come Alive through Imagery." *Positive Psychology News Daily*, April 12, 2010. http://positivepsychologynews.com/news/john-yeager/2010041210567.

Notes from 3rd Concept – Positive Relationships

1. Achor, Shawn. *The Happiness Advantage: The Seven Principles of Positive Psychology That Fuel Success and Performance at Work*. New York: Broadway Books, 2010.

2. "Action for Happiness." Action for Happiness. Accessed May 10, 2013. http://www.actionforhappiness.org/10-keys.

3. Algoe, Sara B., Jonathan Haidt, and Shelly L. Gable. "Beyond Reciprocity: Gratitude and Relationships in Everyday Life." *Emotion* 8, no. 3 (2008): 425-29. doi:10.1037/1528-3542.8.3.425.

4. Anik, Lalin, Elizabeth W. Dunn, Michael I. Norton, and Lara B. Aknin. "Feeling Good about Giving: The Benefits (and Costs) of Self-Interested Charitable Behavior." Digital image. Harvard Business School - Working Knowledge. September 9, 2009. http://hbswk.hbs.edu/item/6272.html.

5. Anik, Lalin, Lara Aknin, Michael Norton, and Elizabeth Dunn. "Feeling Good about Giving: The Benefits (and Costs) of Self-interested Charitable Behavior." *Harvard Business School Marketing Unit Working Paper* 10-012 (2009).

6. Ballas, D., and D. Dorling. "Measuring the Impact of Major Life Events upon Happiness." *International Journal of Epidemiology* 36, no. 6 (2007): 1244-252. doi:10.1093/ije/dym182.

7. Bates, Claire. "How Hugging Can Lower Your Blood Pressure and Boost Your Memory." *Daily Mail*, January 22, 2013. http://www.dailymail.co.uk/health/article-2266373/Hugging-lower-blood-pressure-boost-memory.html.

8. Baumeister, Roy F., and Mark R. Leary. "The Need to Belong: Desire for Interpersonal Attachments as a Fundamental Human Motivation." *Psychological Bulletin* 117, no. 3 (1995): 497-529. doi:10.1037//0033-2909.117.3.497.

9. "Belonging to Groups Makes You Physically Resilient - The Daily Stat." Harvard Business Review. April 29, 2013. http://web.hbr.org/email/archive/dailystat.php?date=042913.

10. Ben-Shahar, Tal. *Happier: Learn the Secrets to Daily Joy and Lasting Fulfillment*. New York: McGraw-Hill, 2007.

11. Berkman, L. F., and S. L. Syme. "Social Networks, Host Resistance, and Mortality: A Nine-year Follow-up of Alameda County Residents." *American Journal of Epidemiology* 109 (1979): 186-204.

12. Berkman, Lisa F., and Lester Breslow. *Health and Ways of Living: The Alameda County Study*. New York: Oxford University Press, 1983.

13. Berscheid, E. "Human Strengths." Lecture, The Human's Greatest Strength: Other Humans, University of Texas, Austin. Accessed August 12, 2013. https://webspace.utexas.edu/emc597/positivepsych5.html.

14. Brooks, David. "The Heart Grows Smarter." The New York Times. November 5, 2012. http://www.nytimes.com/2012/11/06/opinion/brooks-the-heart-grows-smarter.html.

15. Buettner, Dan. *Thrive: Finding Happiness the Blue Zones Way*. Washington, D.C.: National Geographic, 2010.

16. Campbell, Angus, Philip E. Converse, and Willard L. Rodgers. *The Quality of American Life: Perceptions, Evaluations, and Satisfactions*. New York: Russell Sage Foundation, 1976.

17. Campion, Michael A., Ellen M. Papper, and Gina J. Medsker. "Relations Between Work Team Characteristics And Effectiveness: A Replication And Extension." *Personnel Psychology* 49, no. 2 (1996): 429-52. doi:10.1111/j.1744-6570.1996.tb01806.x.

18. "Caring." Pursuit of Happiness. Accessed June 21, 2013. http://www.pursuit-of-happiness.org/science-of-happiness/caring/.

19. Carmeli, Abraham, Daphna Brueller, and Jane E. Dutton. "Learning Behaviours in the Workplace: The Role of High-quality Interpersonal Relationships and Psychological Safety." *Systems Research and Behavioral Science* 26, no. 1 (2009): 81-98. doi:10.1002/sres.932.

20. Christakis, Nicholas A., and James H. Fowler. *Connected: The Surprising Power of Our Social Networks and How They Shape Our Lives*. New York: Little, Brown and, 2009.

21. Cohen, Sheldon, and Thomas A. Wills. "Stress, Social Support, and the Buffering Hypothesis." *Psychological Bulletin* 98, no. 2 (1985): 310-57. doi:10.1037//0033-2909.98.2.310.

22. "Critical Positivity Ratio." *Wikipedia*, November 19, 2013. http://en.wikipedia.org/wiki/Critical_positivity_ratio.

23. Deci, Edward L., and Richard M. Ryan. "The "What" and "Why" of Goal Pursuits: Human Needs and the Self-Determination of Behavior." *Psychological Inquiry* 11, no. 4 (2000): 227-68. doi:10.1207/S15327965PLI1104_01.

24. Diener, Ed, and Martin E.P. Seligman. "Very Happy People." *Psychological Science* 13, no. 1 (2002): 81-84. doi:10.1111/1467-9280.00415.

25. Diener, Robert, and Robert Biswas-Diener. *Happiness: Unlocking the Mysteries of Psychological Wealth*. Malden, MA: Blackwell Pub., 2008.

26. Dutton, Jane E., and Belle R. Ragins. *Exploring Positive Relationships at Work: Building a Theoretical and Research Foundation*. 1st ed. Vol. 1. Organizational Management. Psychology Press, 2006.

27. Dutton, Jane. "Fostering High-Quality Connections How to Deal with Corrosive Relationships at Work." *Stanford Social Innovatin Review* Winter (2003): 54-57. http://www.ssireview.org/articles/entry/fostering_high_quality_connections.

28. Eisenberger, Robert, Florence Stinglhamber, Christian Vandenberghe, Ivan L. Sucharski, and Linda Rhoades. "Perceived Supervisor Support: Contributions to Perceived Organizational Support and Employee Retention." *Journal of Applied Psychology* 87, no. 3 (2002): 565-73. doi:10.1037//0021-9010.87.3.565.

29. Emmons, Robert A., and Michael E. McCullough. *The Psychology of Gratitude*. Oxford: Oxford University Press, 2004.

30. "Executive Summary: 2011 Deloitte Volunteer IMPACT Survey." *Deloitte*. Accessed October 18, 2013. http://www.deloitte.com/view/en_US/us/About/Community-Involvement/volunteerism/impact-day/f98eec97e6650310VgnVCM2000001b56f00aRCRD.htm.

31. Felicetti, Marcus J. "10 Reasons Why We Need at Least 8 Hugs a Day." MindBodyGreen. August 10, 2012. http://www.mindbodygreen.com/0-5756/10-Reasons-Why-We-Need-at-Least-8-Hugs-a-Day.html.

32. Gable, Shelly L., Harry T. Reis, Emily A. Impett, and Evan R. Asher. "What Do You Do When Things Go Right? The Intrapersonal and Interpersonal Benefits of Sharing Positive Events." *Journal of Personality and Social Psychology* 87, no. 2 (2004): 228-45. doi:10.1037/0022-3514.87.2.228.

33. Gielan, Michelle. "Lights, Camera... Happiness! Finding Clarity and Happiness in This Media-driven World." *Psychology Today* (web log), January 7, 2011. http://www.psychologytoday.com/blog/lights-camera-happiness/201101/5-ways-develop-meaning-work.

34. Gottman, John M., and Julie Gottman. "How To Keep Love Going Strong." YES! Magazine. January 3, 2011. http://www.yesmagazine.org/issues/what-happy-families-know/how-to-keep-love-going-strong.

35. Gottman, John Mordechai. *What Predicts Divorce?: The Relationship between Marital Processes and Marital Outcomes*. Hillsdale, NJ: Lawrence Erlbaum Associates, 1994.

36. Griffin, Ricky W. "Supervisory Behaviour as a Source of Perceived Task Scope." *Journal of Occupational Psychology* 54, no. 3 (1981): 175-82. doi:10.1111/j.2044-8325.1981.tb00057.x.

37. Gruber, June, Maya Tamir, and Iris B. Mauss. "A Dark Side of Happiness? How, When, and Why Happiness Is Not Always Good." *Perspectives on Psychological Science* 6, no. 22 (2011). doi:10.1177/1745691611406927.

38. Gutman, Ron. "Ron Gutman: The Hidden Power of Smiling." TED: Ideas worth Spreading. March 2011. http://www.ted.com/talks/ron_gutman_the_hidden_power_of_smiling.html.

39. Haden, Jeff. "Be Happier: 10 Things to Stop Doing Right Now BY Jeff Haden." *Inc.com*, October 1, 2012. http://www.inc.com/jeff-haden/how-to-be-happier-work-10-things-stop-doing.html?cid=sy01301.

40. "Happiness Has a Dark Side." *Science Daily*, May 17, 2011. http://www.sciencedaily.com/releases/2011/05/110516162219.htm.

41. Hawkley, Louise C., and John T. Cacioppo. "Loneliness Matters: A Theoretical and Empirical Review of Consequences and Mechanisms." *Annals of Behavioral Medicine* 40, no. 2 (2010): 218-27. doi:10.1007/s12160-010-9210-8.

42. Hawkley, Louise C., Ronald A. Thisted, Christopher M. Masi, and John T. Cacioppo. "Loneliness Predicts Increased Blood Pressure: 5-year Cross-lagged Analyses in Middle-aged and Older Adults." *Psychology and Aging* 25, no. 1 (2010): 132-41. doi:10.1037/a0017805.

43. Heaphy, Emily D., and Jane E. Dutton. "POSITIVE SOCIAL INTERACTIONS AND THE HUMAN BODY AT WORK: LINKING ORGANIZATIONS AND PHYSIOLOGY." *Academy of Management Review* 33, no. 1 (2008): 137-62.

44. Heaphy, Emily D., and Jane E. Dutton. "The Power of High-quality Connections." In *Positive Organizational Scholarship: Foundations of a New Discipline*, 263-78. Vol. 3. San Francisco, CA: Berrett-Koehler, 2003.

45. "Higher Levels of Social Activity Decrease the Risk of Cognitive Decline." *Science Daily*, April 26, 2011.

46. House, J., K. Landis, and D. Umberson. "Social Relationships and Health." *Science* 241, no. 4865 (1988): 540-45. doi:10.1126/science.3399889.

47. "How Can We Become Happier?" *Global Happiness Organization*. Accessed October 9, 2013. http://www.globalhappiness.com/en/about-happiness/how-can-we-become-happier.

48. James, Bryan D., Robert S. Wilson, Lisa L. Barnes, and David A. Bennett. "Late-Life Social Activity and Cognitive Decline in Old Age." *Journal of the International Neuropsychological Society* 17, no. 6 (November 2011): 998-1005. doi:10.1017/S1355617711000531.

49. Kogan, Aleksandr, Emily A. Impett, Christopher Oveis, Bryant Hui, Gordon M. Amie, and Dacher Keltner. "When Giving Feels Good: The Intrinsic Benefits of Sacrifice in Romantic Relationships for the Communally Motivated." *Association for Psychological Science* 21, no. 12 (2010): 1918-924. doi:10.1177/0956797610388815.

50. Lu, L., and M. Argyle. "Happiness and Cooperation." *Personality and Individual Differences* 12, no. 10 (1991): 1019-030. doi:10.1016/0191-8869(91)90032-7.

51. Luskin, Fred. *Forgive for Good: A Proven Prescription for Health and Happiness*. San Francisco: HarperSanFrancisco, 2002.

52. Lyubomirsky, Sonja. *The How of Happiness: A Scientific Approach to Getting the Life You Want*. New York: Penguin Press, 2008.

53. Lyubomirsky, Sonja, Laura King, and Ed Diener. "The Benefits of Frequent Positive Affect: Does Happiness Lead to Success?" *Psychological Bulletin* 131, no. 6 (2005): 803-55. doi:10.1037/0033-2909.131.6.803.

54. Myers, David G. "The Funds, Friends, and Faith of Happy People." *American Psychologist* 55, no. 1 (2000): 56-67. doi:10.1037//0003-066X.55.1.56.

55. Olsen, Kate. "3 Predictions: Employee Engagement in 2013 - The Network for Good."
     The Network for Good (web log), January 1, 2013.
     http://www.thenetworkforgood.org/t5/Companies-For-Good/3-Predictions-
     Employee-Engagement-in-2013/ba-p/10889.

56. Olsen, Kate, and Allison McGuire. "Put a Ring on It: Engaging Your Employees with
     Goo... - The Network for Good." The Network for Good. March 20, 2013. Accessed
     December 21, 2013. http://www.thenetworkforgood.org/t5/Companies-For-
     Good/Put-a-Ring-on-It-Engaging-Your-Employees-with-Good/ba-p/12169.

57. Opton, E. M. "A Psychology of Human Strengths: Fundamental Questions and
     Future Directions for a Positive Psychology." *American Journal of Psychiatry* 161, no. 8
     (2004): 1516. doi:10.1176/appi.ajp.161.8.1516.

58. Perkins, H. W. "Religious Commitment, Yuppie Values, and Well-Being in Post-
     Collegiate Life." *Review of Relogous Research* 32, no. 3 (March 1991): 244-51.

59. Pryor, John H., Linda DeAngelo, Laura Palucki Blake, Sylvia Hurtado, and Serge
     Tran. *The American Freshman: National Norms Fall 2011.* California: Higher Education
     Research Institute, 2011.

60. "Psych Your Mind: Making the Most of It When Your Partner Shares Good News."
     Psych Your Mind: Making the Most of It When Your Partner Shares Good News (web log),
     May 17, 2011. http://psych-your-mind.blogspot.com/2011/05/making-most-of-it-
     when-your-partner.html.

61. Rabin, Roni C. "Reading, Writing, 'Rithmetic and Relationships." *New York Times*,
     December 20, 2010. http://well.blogs.nytimes.com/2010/12/20/reading-writing-
     rithmetic-and-relationships/?hp.

62. Renner, Ronna, and Christine Carter. "Greater Good." Do You Have Enough Friends?
     November 2012.
     http://greatergood.berkeley.edu/gg_live/happiness_matters_podcast/podcast/ad
     ult_friendships.

63. Robison, Jennifer. "Wellbeing Is Contagious (for Better or Worse)." *Gallup Business
     Journal*, November 27, 2012.
     http://businessjournal.gallup.com/content/158732/wellbeing-contagious-better-
     worse.aspx.

64. Rosenbloom, Stephanie. "But Will It Make You Happy?" The New York Times.
     August 7, 2010.
     http://www.nytimes.com/2010/08/08/business/08consume.html?_r=0&adxnnl=1
     &pagewanted=1&adxnnlx=1387639085-b7KCKJwTzEej/l8lpJk99A.

65. Schwartz, Carolyn E., and Rabbi Meir Sendor. "Helping Others Helps Oneself:
     Response Shift Effects in Peer Support." *Social Science & Medicine* 48, no. 11 (1999):
     1563-575. doi:10.1016/S0277-9536(99)00049-0.

66. Seder, J. P., and Shigehiro Oishi. "Intensity of Smiling in Facebook Photos Predicts
     Future Life Satisfaction." *Social Psychological and Personality Science*, October 18, 2011.
     doi:10.1177/1948550611424968.

67. Silverblatt, Rob. "The Science of Workplace Happiness." *US News*, April 14, 2010. http://money.usnews.com/money/careers/articles/2010/04/14/the-science-of-workplace-happiness.

68. Stevens, L. E., and F. T. Fiske. "Motivation and Cognition in Social Life: A Social Survival Perspective." *Social Cognition* 13 (1995): 189-214.

69. Suedfeld, P. "R.S. Weiss, Editor, Loneliness: The Experience of Emotional and Social Isolation, MIT Press, Cambridge, MA (1975)." *Behavior Therapy* 8, no. 1 (1977): 120-21. doi:10.1016/S0005-7894(77)80143-3.

70. Thomas, Joe, and Ricky Griffin. "The Social Information Processing Model of Task Design: A Review of the Literature." *Academy of Management Review* 8, no. 4 (1983): 672-82.

71. Turner, Marlene E. "Jane E. Dutton and Belle Rose Ragins, Eds.: Exploring Positive Relationships at Work: Building a Theoretical and Research Foundation." *Administrative Science Quarterly* 53, no. 1 (2008): 192-93. doi:10.2189/asqu.53.1.192.

72. Uchino, Bert N., Darcy Uno, and Julianne Holt-Lunstad. "Social Support, Physiological Processes, and Health." *Current Directions in Psychological Science* 8, no. 5 (October 1999): 145-48. doi:10.1111/1467-8721.00034.

73. Warr, Peter B., and Guy Clapperton. *The Joy of Work?: Jobs, Happiness, and You*. London [u.a.: Routledge, 2010.

74. Wheeler, Ladd, Harry Reis, and John B. Nezlek. "Loneliness, Social Interaction, and Sex Roles." *Journal of Personality and Social Psychology* 45, no. 4 (1983): 943-53. doi:10.1037//0022-3514.45.4.943.

75. Whelan, Deanna C., and John M. Zelenski. "Experimental Evidence That Positive Moods Cause Sociability." *Social Psychological and Personality Science* 3, no. 4 (July 2012): 430-37. doi:10.1177/1948550611425194.

76. Williamson, Gail M., and Margaret S. Clark. "Providing Help and Desired Relationship Type as Determinants of Changes in Moods and Self-evaluations." *Journal of Personality and Social Psychology* 56, no. 5 (1989): 722-34. doi:10.1037/0022-3514.56.5.722.

77. Wiltshire-Bridle, Molly. "Giving Back to the Community: Charity in the Workplace." *Career FAQ's*. Accessed June 16, 2013. http://www.careerfaqs.com.au/news/news-and-views/giving-back-to-the-community-charity-in-the-workplace.

78. Wood, Wendy, Nancy Rhodes, and Melanie Whelan. "Sex Differences in Positive Well-being: A Consideration of Emotional Style and Marital Status." *Psychological Bulletin* 106, no. 2 (1989): 249-64. doi:10.1037/0033-2909.106.2.249.

Notes from 4ᵗʰ Concept – Higher Purpose

1. Adler, N., and K. Matthews. "Health Psychology: Why Do Some People Get Sick and Some Stay Well?" *Annual Review of Psychology* 45, no. 1 (1994): 229-59. doi:10.1146/annurev.ps.45.020194.001305.

2. Amabile, Teresa M., and Stephen J. Kramer. "May 2011." *The Power of Small Wins*, May 2011. http://hbr.org/2011/05/the-power-of-small-wins/.

3. Ardelt, Monika. "Effects of Religion and Purpose in Life on Elders' Subjective Well-Being and Attitudes Toward Death." *Journal of Religious Gerontology* 14, no. 4 (2003): 55-77. doi:10.1300/J078v14n04_04.

4. Arnold, Kara A., Nick Turner, Julian Barling, E. Kevin Kelloway, and Margaret C. McKee. "Transformational Leadership and Psychological Well-being: The Mediating Role of Meaningful Work." *Journal of Occupational Health Psychology* 12, no. 3 (2007): 193-203. doi:10.1037/1076-8998.12.3.193.

5. Baumeister, Roy F., and Brenda Wilson. "Life Stories and the Four Need for Meaning." *Psychological Inquiry* 7, no. 4 (1996): 322-25. doi:10.1207/s15327965pli0704_2.

6. Baumeister, Roy F., Ellen Bratslavsky, Catrin Finkenauer, and Kathleen D. Vohs. "Bad Is Stronger than Good." *Review of General Psychology* 5, no. 4 (2001): 323-70. doi:10.1037//1089-2680.5.4.323.

7. Baumeister, Roy F., Kathleen D. Vohs, Jennier L. Aaker, and Emily N. Garbinsky. "Some Key Differences between a Happy Life and a Meaningful Life." *The Journal of Positive Psychology* 8, no. 6 (July 2013): 505-16.

8. Baumeister, Roy F. *Meanings of Life*. New York: Guilford Press, 1991.

9. Berg, J. M., A. M. Grant, and V. Johnson. "When Callings Are Calling: Crafting Work and Leisure in Pursuit of Unanswered Occupational Callings." *Organization Science* 21, no. 5 (2010): 973-94. doi:10.1287/orsc.1090.0497.

10. Boyle, P. A., A. S. Buchman, L. L. Barnes, and D. A. Bennett. "Effect of a Purpose in Life on Risk of Incident Alzheimer Disease and Mild Cognitive Impairment in Community-Dwelling Older Persons." *Archives of General Psychiatry* 67, no. 3 (2010): 304-10. doi:10.1001/archgenpsychiatry.2009.208.

11. Boyle, P. A., L. L. Barnes, A. S. Buchman, and D. A. Bennett. "Purpose in Life Is Associated With Mortality Among Community-Dwelling Older Persons." *Psychosomatic Medicine* 71, no. 5 (2009): 574-79. doi:10.1097/PSY.0b013e3181a5a7c0.

12. Brassai, L., B. F. Piko, and M. F. Steger. "Meaning in Life: Is It a Protective Factor for Adolescents' Psychological Health?" *International Journal of Behavioral Medicine* 18, no. 1 (March 2011): 44-51. doi:10.1007/s12529-010-9089-6.

13. Brooks, Chad. "Workers Willing to Make Less to Work for Sustainable Companies." *Yahoo! News*, December 26, 2012. http://news.yahoo.com/workers-willing-less-sustainable-companies-150603104.html.

14. Cameron, Kim S., Jane E. Dutton, and Robert E. Quinn. *Positive Organizational Scholarship: Foundations of a New Discipline*. San Francisco, CA: Berrett-Koehler, 2003.

15. Campbell, Angus, Philip E. Converse, and Willard L. Rodgers. *The Quality of American Life: Perceptions, Evaluations, and Satisfactions*. New York: Russell Sage Foundation, 1976.

16. Chalofsky, Neal. *Meaningful Workplaces: Reframing How and Where We Work*. San Francisco, CA: Jossey-Bass, 2010.

17. Chopra, Deepak. "7 New Ways to Find Happiness." *The Huffington Post*, December 17, 2009. http://www.huffingtonpost.com/deepak-chopra/7-new-ways-to-find-happin_b_396363.html.

18. Clarke, Katherine M. "Change Processes in a Creation of Meaning Event." *Journal of Consulting and Clinical Psychology* 64, no. 3 (1996): 465-70. doi:10.1037//0022-006X.64.3.465.

19. Cohen, Karen, and David Cairns. "Is Searching for Meaning in Life Associated with Reduced Subjective and Psychological Well-being?" *International Journal of Existential Psychology and Psychotherapy* 3, no. 1 (2010).

20. Condor, Bob. "Purpose in Life = Happiness." *Chicagotribune.com*, December 6, 2009. http://www.chicagotribune.com/sns-health-life-purpose-happiness%2C0%2C660311.story.

21. Crabb, Shane. "The Use of Coaching Principles to Foster Employee Engagement." *The Coaching Psychologist* 7, no. 1 (June 2011): 27-34. http://www.instituteofcoaching.org/images/ARticles/CoachingPrinciples.pdf.

22. Davis, Christopher G., Susan Nolen-Hoeksema, and Judith Larson. "Making Sense of Loss and Benefiting from the Experience: Two Construals of Meaning." *Journal of Personality and Social Psychology* 75, no. 2 (1998): 561-74. doi:10.1037//0022-3514.75.2.561.

23. Deci, Edward L., and Richard M. Ryan. "Self-determination Theory: A Macrotheory of Human Motivation, Development, and Health." *Canadian Psychology/Psychologie Canadienne* 49, no. 3 (2008): 182-85. doi:10.1037/a0012801.

24. Diener, Robert, and Robert Biswas-Diener. *Happiness: Unlocking the Mysteries of Psychological Wealth*. Malden, MA: Blackwell Pub., 2008.

25. Fineman, Stephen. *Emotion in Organizations*. Los Angeles, Calif. [u.a.: SAGE Publ., 2007.

26. Frankl, Viktor E. *Man's Search for Meaning*. Boston: Beacon Press, 2006.

27. Fredrickson, Barbara L., Karen M. Grewen, Kimberly A. Coffey, Sara B. Algoe, Ann M. Firestine, Jususa M. Arevalo, Jeffrey Ma, and Steven W. Cole. "A Functional

Genomic Perspective on Human Well-being." *PROCEEDINGS OF THE NATIONAL ACADEMY OF SCIENCES* 110, no. 33, 13684-3689. Accessed 2013.

28.   Frost, Amy. "Biz Wiz: Stepping Up and Out on Your Purpose - Delivering Happiness." *Delivering Happiness*, September 9, 2012. http://www.deliveringhappiness.com/biz-wiz-stepping-up-and-out-on-your-purpose.

29.   Gallup, George, and Jim Castelli. *The People's Religion: American Faith in the 90's*. New York: Macmillan, 1989.

30.   Garnett, Laura. "The Big Secret to Happiness at Work That's Right Under Your Nose." *Delivering Happiness*, May 30, 2013. http://www.deliveringhappiness.com/the-big-secret-to-happiness-at-work-thats-right-under-your-nose.

31.   Gielan, Michelle. "Lights, Camera... Happiness! 5 Ways to Develop Meaning at Work." *Psychology Today*, January 7, 2011. http://www.psychologytoday.com/blog/lights-camera-happiness/201101/5-ways-develop-meaning-work.

32.   Gittell, Jody Hoffer. *The Southwest Airlines Way: Using the Power of Relationships to Achieve High Performance*. New York: McGraw-Hill, 2003.

33.   Graham, Kathy. "How to Find Fulfilling Work." Think and Be Happy. June 29, 2013. http://blogs.terrapinn.com/happiness/2013/06/29/find-fulfilling-work/?utm_source=Think+%26+Be+Happy&utm_campaign=cdcb5e1fb9-T_BH_9July_2013&utm_medium=email&utm_term=0_8d56b8eabc-cdcb5e1fb9-33123333&ct=t%28T_BH_15_January_20131_3_2013%29&mc_cid=cdcb5e1fb9&mc_eid=aac27c08e4.

34.   Grant, Adam M., and Justin M. Berg. "Prosocial Motivation at Work: When, Why, and How Making a Difference Makes a Difference." *The Wharton School*. Accessed September 14, 2013. http://justinmberg.com/grant__berg_poshandbook.pdf.

35.   Hansen, Morten, and Dacher Keltner. "HBR Blog Network." *Harvard Business Review*, December 20, 2012. http://blogs.hbr.org/cs/2012/12/finding_meaning_at_work_even_w.html.

36.   "Having Greater Purpose in Life Associated With a Reduced Risk of Alzheimer's Disease." *Science Daily*, March 2, 2010. Accessed September 16, 2013. http://www.sciencedaily.com/releases/2010/03/100301165619.htm.

37.   Hicks, Joshua, and Laura King. "Meaning in Life and Seeing the Big Picture: Positive Affect and Global Focus." *Cognition & Emotion* 21, no. 7 (2007): 1577-584. doi:10.1080/02699930701347304.

38.   Irvine, Derek. "Focusing on the Real Purpose of Employee Engagement." TLNT. July 8, 2013. http://www.tlnt.com/2013/07/10/focusing-on-the-real-purpose-of-employee-engagement/.

39. Jonathan. "How to Identify Your Passions." *Advanced Life Skills RSS*. Accessed October 11, 2013. http://advancedlifeskills.com/blog/how-to-identify-your-passions/.

40. Kashdan, Todd B., and Michael F. Steger. "Curiosity and Pathways to Well-being and Meaning in Life: Traits, States, and Everyday Behaviors." *Motivation and Emotion* 31, no. 3 (2007): 159-73. doi:10.1007/s11031-007-9068-7.

41. Kennedy, James E., and H. Kanthamani. "Empirical Support for a Model of Well-Being, Meaning in Life, Importance of Religion, and Transcendent Experiences." 1995. Accessed September 8, 2013. http://jeksite.org/research/path.pdf.

42. Kerns, Charles D., PhD, MBA. "Putting Performance and Happiness Together in the Workplace." *Graziado Business Review* 11, no. 1 (2008). http://gbr.pepperdine.edu/2010/08/putting-performance-and-happiness-together-in-the-workplace/.

43. King, Laura A., Joshua A. Hicks, Jennifer L. Krull, and Amber K. Del Gaiso. "Positive Affect and the Experience of Meaning in Life." *Journal of Personality and Social Psychology* 90, no. 1 (2006): 179-96. doi:10.1037/0022-3514.90.1.179.

44. Kleftaras, G., and E. Psarra. "Meaning in Life, Psychological Well-Being and Depressive Symptomatology: A Comparative Study." *Psychology* 3, no. 4 (March 2012): 337-45.

45. Kobau, Rosemarie, Joseph Sniezek, Matthew M. Zack, Richard E. Lucas, and Adam Burns. "Well-Being Assessment: An Evaluation of Well-Being Scales for Public Health and Population Estimates of Well-Being among US Adults." *Applied Psychology: Health and Well-Being* 2, no. 3 (2010): 272-97. doi:10.1111/j.1758-0854.2010.01035.x.

46. Legault, L., T. Al-Khindi, and M. Inzlicht. "Preserving Integrity in the Face of Performance Threat: Self-affirmation Enhances Neurophysiological Responsiveness to Errors." *Psychological Science* 23, no. 12 (December 2012): 1455-460. doi:10.1177/0956797612448483.

47. McGregor, Ian, and Brian R. Little. "Personal Projects, Happiness, and Meaning: On Doing Well and Being Yourself." *Journal of Personality and Social Psychology* 74, no. 2 (1998): 494-512. doi:10.1037//0022-3514.74.2.494.

48. Moeller, Philip. "Religion Makes People Happier-But Why?" *US News RSS*, April 12, 2012. http://money.usnews.com/money/personal-finance/articles/2012/04/12/religion-makes-people-happierbut-why.

49. Nadel, Laurie, Ph.D. "Dr. Wayne Dyer on His New DVD, The Shift & His Latest Book, Excuses Begone!" *Dr. Wayne Dyer on His New DVD, The Shift & His Latest Book, Excuses Begone!*, June 2009. http://www.drwaynedyer.com/articles/wayne_dyer_on_his_new_dvd_and_latest_book.

50. Newport, Frank, Dan Witters, and Sangeeta Agrawal. "Religious Americans Enjoy Higher Wellbeing." *Religious Americans Enjoy Higher Wellbeing*, February 16, 2012.

http://www.gallup.com/poll/152723/religious-americans-enjoy-higher-wellbeing.aspx.

51. Pavlina, Steve. "How to Discover Your Life Purpose in About 20 Minutes." *How to Discover Your Life Purpose in About 20 Minutes*, January 16, 2005. http://www.stevepavlina.com/blog/2005/01/how-to-discover-your-life-purpose-in-about-20-minutes/.

52. Pennebake, James W., and Cindy K. Chung. *Expressive Writing and Its Links to Mental and Physical Health*.

53. Perry, Susan. "MinnPost." *MinnPost*, April 13, 2012. http://www.minnpost.com/second-opinion/2012/04/are-religious-people-happier-atheists.

54. Peterson, Christopher, and Martin E. P. Seligman. *Character Strengths and Virtues: A Handbook and Classification*. Washington, DC: American Psychological Association, 2004.

55. Pink, Daniel H. *Drive: The Surprising Truth about What Motivates Us*. New York, NY: Riverhead Books, 2009.

56. Pinquart, Martin. "Creating and Maintaining Purpose in Life in Old Age: A Meta-analysis." *Ageing International* 27, no. 2 (2002): 90-114. doi:10.1007/s12126-002-1004-2.

57. Proulx, Elise. "Three Insights from the Frontiers of Positive Psychology." *The Greater Good Science Center*, August 7, 2013. http://greatergood.berkeley.edu/article/item/three_insights_from_the_frontiers_of_positive_psychology.

58. Qubein, Nido. *Seven Choices for Success and Significance: How to Live Life From The Inside Out*. Naperville: Simple Truths, 2011.

59. Reker, G. T., E. J. Peacock, and P. T. Wong. "Meaning and Purpose in Life and Well-being: A Life-span Perspective." *Journals of Gerontology* 42, no. 1 (January 1987): 44-49.

60. Rosso, Brent D., Kathryn H. Dekas, and Amy Wrzesniewski. "On the Meaning of Work: A Theoretical Integration and Review." *Research in Organizational Behavior*, 2010. doi:10.1016/j.riob.2010.09.001.

61. Routledge, Clay, Ph.D. "Are Religious People Happier Than Non-religious People?" *Psychology Today*, December 5, 2012. http://www.psychologytoday.com/blog/death-love-sex-magic/201212/are-religious-people-happier-non-religious-people.

62. Ryff, Carol D., and Corey Lee M. Keyes. "The Structure of Psychological Well-being Revisited." *Journal of Personality and Social Psychology* 69, no. 4 (1995): 719-27. doi:10.1037//0022-3514.69.4.719.

63. Ryff, Carol D. "Happiness Is Everything, or Is It? Explorations on the Meaning of Psychological Well-being." *Journal of Personality and Social Psychology* 57, no. 6 (1989): 1069-081. doi:10.1037/0022-3514.57.6.1069.

64. Seligman, Martin E. P. *Flourish: A Visionary New Understanding of Happiness and Well-being*. New York: Free Press, 2011.

65. Smith, Emily E. "There's More to Life Than Being Happy." *The Atlantic*, January 9, 2013. http://www.dailygood.org/more.php?n=5366.

66. Snyder, Charles R., and Shane L. Lopez. "Meaningfulness in Life." In *Handbook of Positive Psychology*, 607-18. New York, NY: Oxford Univ. Press, 2002.

67. Steger, Michael F., and J. Y. Shin. "The Relevance of the Meaning in Life Questionnaire to Therapeutic Practice." *International Forum on Logotherapy* 33 (2010): 95-104.

68. Steger, Michael F., Todd B. Kashdan, Brandon A. Sullivan, and Danielle Lorentz. "Understanding the Search for Meaning in Life: Personality, Cognitive Style, and the Dynamic Between Seeking and Experiencing Meaning." *Journal of Personality* 76, no. 2 (2008): 199-228. doi:10.1111/j.1467-6494.2007.00484.x.

69. Tackett, Mike. "Obama's Task: That Elusive Sentence." *Bloomberg.com*, January 21, 2013. http://go.bloomberg.com/political-capital/2013-01-21/obamas-task-that-elusive-sentence/.

70. Vaillant, George. "Positive Psychology News Daily » A Fresh Take on Meaning." *Positive Psychology News Daily*, August 13, 2008. http://positivepsychologynews.com/news/george-vaillant/20080813939.

71. Vallacher, R. R., and D. M. Wegner. "The Trouble with Action." *Social Cognition* 5 (1987): 179-90.

72. Vallacher, Robin R., and Daniel M. Wegner. *A Theory of Action Identification*. Hillsdale, NJ: L. Erlbaum, 1985.

73. Vallacher, Robin R., and Daniel M. Wegner. "What Do People Think They're Doing? Action Identification and Human Behavior." *Psychological Review* 94, no. 1 (1987): 3-15. doi:10.1037//0033-295X.94.1.3.

74. Waitley, Dennis. "A Compelling "Why"" *Denis Waitley International*, November 3, 2009. http://deniswaitley.com/ezines/2009/ezineissue142.html.

75. "Well-being Concepts." *Centers for Disease Control and Prevention*, March 06, 2013. http://www.cdc.gov/hrqol/wellbeing.htm.

76. Wrzesniewski, A., J. Dutton, and G. Debebe. "Interpersonal Sensemaking And The Meaning Of Work." *Research in Organizational Behavior* 25 (2003): 93-135. doi:10.1016/S0191-3085(03)25003-6.

77. Wrzesniewski, Amy, Clark McCauley, Paul Rozin, and Barry Schwartz. "Jobs, Careers, and Callings: People's Relations to Their Work." *JOURNAL OF RESEARCH IN PERSONALITY* 31 (1997): 21-33.

78. Wrzesniewski, Amy, Justin M. Berg, and Jane E. Dutton. "Managing Yourself: Turn the Job You Have into the Job You Want." *Harvard Business Review*, June 2010. http://hbr.org/2010/06/managing-yourself-turn-the-job-you-have-into-the-job-you-want/ar/1.

79. Zika, S., and K. Chamberlain. "On the Relation between Meaning in Life and Psychological Well-being." *British Journal of Psychology* 83 (February 1992): 133-45. doi:10.1111/j.2044-8295.1992.tb02429.x.

Notes for 5th Concept – Defining Success

1. "Accenture: Defining Success: 2013 Global Research Results." *Accenture*, 2013, 1-44. http://www.accenture.com/SiteCollectionDocuments/PDF/Accenture-IWD-2013-Research-Deck-022013.pdf.

2. Bounds, Gwendolyn. "How Handwriting Trains the Brain." *The Wall Street Journal*, October 5, 2010. http://online.wsj.com/news/articles/SB10001424052748704631504575531932754922518.

3. Brunstein, Joachim C., and Peter M. Gollwitzer. "Effects of Failure on Subsequent Performance: The Importance of Self-defining Goals." *Journal of Personality and Social Psychology* 70, no. 2 (1996): 395-407. doi:10.1037/0022-3514.70.2.395.

4. Dingfelder, S. "Writing Exercises All Aspects of Working Memory." *Monitor on Psychology* 37, no. 7 (July/August 2006): 19. http://www.apa.org/monitor/julaug06/memory.aspx.

5. Farnoosh. "Define Success in Your Words with 10 Clarity Questions." *Prolific Living RSS* (web log), October 24, 2012. http://www.prolificliving.com/blog/2012/10/24/define-success-10-questions.

6. Foskett, Allison. "How Your Reticular Activating System Helps You Achieve Your Goals." *Goal Setting Motivation* (web log), June 2, 2012. http://www.goal-setting-motivation.com/how-your-reticular-activating-system-helps-you-achieve-your-goals/.

7. Henry, Todd. "Re-defining Failure (And Success!)." Accidental Creative. Accessed June 23, 2013. http://www.accidentalcreative.com/growth/re-defining-failure-and-success/.

8. Hudson, Paul. "In Order To Succeed You Must Define Success | Elite Daily." Elite Daily. June 12, 2013. http://elitedaily.com/money/entrepreneurship/in-order-to-succeed-you-must-define-success/.

9. Jonathan. "Clarity Goes Beyond Just Knowing What You Want." Advanced Life Skills RSS. June 27, 2013. http://advancedlifeskills.com/blog/clarity-beyond-knowing-what-you-want/.

10. Mahdavi, Iraj. "Comparing Men's and Women's Definition of Success." *Journal of Behavioral Studies in Business* 2 (May 2010). http://www.aabri.com/manuscripts/09255.pdf.

11. "Study Backs up Strategies for Achieving Goals." Dominican University of California. Accessed June 24, 2013. http://www.dominican.edu/dominicannews/study-backs-up-strategies-for-achieving-goals.

12. Wax, Dustin. "Writing and Remembering: Why We Remember What We Write." Lifehack. September 28, 2013. http://www.lifehack.org/articles/productivity/writing-and-remembering-why-we-remember-what-we-write.html.

13. Wooden, John, and Jay Carty. *Coach Wooden's Pyramid of Success*. Ventura, CA: Regal, 2005.

14. Wooden, John, and Steve Jamison. *Wooden: A Lifetime of Observations and Reflections on and off the Court*. Lincolnwood, IL: Contemporary Books, 1997.

15. "Your Definition of Success." *Career Success for Newbies* (web log). Accessed June 12, 2013. http://www.career-success-for-newbies.com/definition-of-success.html.

Notes from 6ᵗʰ Concept – Clarify and Prioritize

1.   Bounds, Gwendolyn. "How Handwriting Trains the Brain." *The Wall Street Journal*, October 5, 2010. http://online.wsj.com/news/articles/SB10001424052748704631504575531932754922 518.

2.   Carver, Charles S., and Michael Scheier. *Attention and Self-regulation: A Control-theory Approach to Human Behavior.* New York: Springer-Verlag, 1981.

3.   "Clarity Goes Beyond Just Knowing What You Want." *Advanced Life Skills RSS* (web log), June 27, 2013. http://advancedlifeskills.com/blog/clarity-beyond-knowing-what-you-want/.

4.   Covey, Stephen R. *The Seven Habits of Highly Effective People: Restoring the Character Ethic.* New York: Simon and Schuster, 1989.

5.   Dingfelder, S. "Writing Exercises All Aspects of Working Memory." *Monitor on Psychology* 37, no. 7 (2006): 19. http://www.apa.org/monitor/julaug06/memory.aspx.

6.   Emmons, R., and E. Diener. "A Goal-affect Analysis of Everyday Situational Choices*1." *Journal of Research in Personality* 20, no. 3 (1986): 309-26. doi:10.1016/0092-6566(86)90137-6.

7.   Freeman, Oliver. "What Is Consciousness? A Scientist's Perspective." *The Brain Bank* (web log), March 4, 2013. http://thebrainbank.scienceblog.com/2013/03/04/what-is-consciousness-a-scientists-perspective/.

8.   Gollwitzer, P. M., and G. Oettingen. "Implementation Intentions." In *Encyclopedia of Behavioral Medicine*, by Marc D. Gellman, 1043-048. New York: Springer, 2013.

9.   Gollwitzer, Peter M., and Veronika Brandstätter. "Implementation Intentions and Effective Goal Pursuit." *Journal of Personality and Social Psychology* 73, no. 1 (1997): 186-99. doi:10.1037//0022-3514.73.1.186.

10. Grant Halvorson, Heidi. "Nine Things Successful People Do Differently." *Harvard Business Review*, February 25, 2011. http://blogs.hbr.org/2011/02/nine-things-successful-people/.

11. Hall, Peter A. "Chapter 2 Neurophysiological Correlates of the Self-Regulation of Goal Pursuit." In *Social Neuroscience and Public Health: Foundations for the Science of Chronic Disease Prevention*, 19-33. New York, NY: Springer, 2013.

12. Halvorson, Heidi Grant-. *Succeed: How We Can Reach Our Goals.* New York, NY: Hudson Street Press, 2011.

13. LeVan, Angie. "Seeing Is Believing: The Power of Visualization." *Psychology Today*, December 2, 2009. http://www.psychologytoday.com/blog/flourish/200912/seeing-is-believing-the-power-visualization.

14. Locke, Edwin A., and Gary P. Latham. "Building a Practically Useful Theory of Goal Setting and Task Motivation: A 35-year Odyssey." *American Psychologist* 57, no. 9 (2002): 705-17. doi:10.1037//0003-066X.57.9.705.

15. Locke, Edwin A., and Gary P. Latham. "New Directions in Goal-Setting Theory." *Current Directions in Psychological Science* 15, no. 5 (2006): 265-68. doi:10.1111/j.1467-8721.2006.00449.x.

16. "Locke's Goal Setting Theory." *Mind Tools*. Accessed November 14, 2013. http://www.mindtools.com/pages/article/newHTE_87.htm.

17. Mathews, G. "Study Backs up Strategies for Achieving Goals." *Dominican University of California*. Accessed June 24, 2013. http://www.dominican.edu/dominicannews/study-backs-up-strategies-for-achieving-goals.

18. Ranganathan, V. "From Mental Power to Muscle Power—gaining Strength by Using the Mind." *Neuropsychologia* 42, no. 7 (2004): 944-56. doi:10.1016/j.neuropsychologia.2003.11.018.

19. Tkach, Chris, and Sonja Lyubomirsky. "How Do People Pursue Happiness?: Relating Personality, Happiness-Increasing Strategies, and Well-Being." *Journal of Happiness Studies* 7, no. 2 (2006): 183-225. doi:10.1007/s10902-005-4754-1.

20. VanSonnenberg, Emily. "Ready, Set, Goals!" *Positive Psychology News Daily*, January 3, 2011. http://positivepsychologynews.com/news/emily-vansonnenberg/2011010315821.

21. Wax, Dustin. "The Science of Setting Goals." *Http://www.lifehack.org*, July 7, 2013. http://www.lifehack.orhttp://www.lifehack.org/articles/productivity/the-science-of-setting-goals.htmlg/articles/productivity/the-science-of-setting-goals.html.

22. Wax, Dustin. "Writing and Remembering: Why We Remember What We Write." *Lifehack RSS* (web log), September 28, 2013. http://www.lifehack.org/articles/productivity/writing-and-remembering-why-we-remember-what-we-write.html.

23. Wiliams, Ray B. "Why Goal Setting Doesn't Work." *Psychology Today*, April 11, 2011. http://www.psychologytoday.com/blog/wired-success/201104/why-goal-setting-doesnt-work.

Notes for 7th Concept – Implement with Discipline

1.   Achor, Shawn. *The Happiness Advantage: The Seven Principles of Positive Psychology That Fuel Success and Performance at Work*. New York: Broadway Books, 2010.

2.   Anderson, Mac, and John Murphy. *Habits Die Hard; 10 Steps to Building Successful Habits*. Naperville: Simple Truths, 2011.

3.   Carter, Christine. "A New Theory of Elite Performance." *The Greater Good Science Center*, August 26, 2013. http://greatergood.berkeley.edu/raising_happiness/post/a_new_theory_of_elite_performance.

4.   Carter, Christine. "Passion + Adversity = Success?" *The Greater Good Science Center*, September 9, 2013. http://greatergood.berkeley.edu/raising_happiness/post/passion_adversity_success.

5.   Carter, Christine. "The Quiet Secret to Success." *The Greater Good Science Center*, September 2, 2013. http://greatergood.berkeley.edu/raising_happiness/post/the_quiet_secret_to_success.

6.   Colvin, Geoffrey. "Secrets of Greatness: Practice and Hard Work Bring Success." *CNNMoney*, October 19, 2006. http://money.cnn.com/magazines/fortune/fortune_archive/2006/10/30/8391794/.

7.   Corley, Thomas C. *Rich Habits: The Daily Success Habits of Wealthy Individuals*. Itasca Books, 2010.

8.   Duckworth, Angela L., Christopher Peterson, Michael D. Matthews, and Dennis R. Kelly. "Grit: Perseverance and Passion for Long-term Goals." *Journal of Personality and Social Psychology* 92, no. 6 (2007): 1087-101. doi:10.1037/0022-3514.92.6.1087.

9.   Duhigg, Charles. *The Power of Habit: Why We Do What We Do in Life and Business*. New York: Random House, 2012.

10.   Ericsson, K. Anders, Ralf T. Krampe, and Clemens Tesch-Römer. "The Role of Deliberate Practice in the Acquisition of Expert Performance." *Psychological Review* 100, no. 3 (1993): 363-406. doi:10.1037//0033-295X.100.3.363.

11.   Glei, Jocelyn K. "Hacking Habits: How To Make New Behaviors Last For Good." *99U: Insights on Making Ideas Happen* (web log). Accessed November 24, 2013. http://99u.com/articles/7230/hacking-habits-how-to-make-new-behaviors-last-for-good.

12. Gollwitzer, Peter M., and Veronika Brandstätter. "Implementation Intentions and Effective Goal Pursuit." *Journal of Personality and Social Psychology* 73, no. 1 (1997): 186-99. doi:10.1037//0022-3514.73.1.186.

13. Grant Halvorson, Heidi. "Nine Things Successful People Do Differently." *Harvard Business Review*, February 25, 2011. http://blogs.hbr.org/2011/02/nine-things-successful-people/.

14. Hall, Peter A. "Chapter 2 Neurophysiological Correlates of the Self-Regulation of Goal Pursuit." In *Social Neuroscience and Public Health: Foundations for the Science of Chronic Disease Prevention*, 19-33. New York, NY: Springer, 2013.

15. Halvorson, Heidi Grant-. *Succeed: How We Can Reach Our Goals*. New York, NY: Hudson Street Press, 2011.

16. James, William. *Talks to Teachers on Psychology and to Students on Some of Life's Ideals*. Cambridge, MA: Harvard University Press, 1983.

17. Layton, Julia. "Is It True That If You Do Anything for Three Weeks It Will Become a Habit?" *HowStuffWorks*. Accessed November 21, 2013. http://science.howstuffworks.com/life/form-a-habit.htm.

18. Lickerman, Alex, M.D. "Discipline." *Psychology Today*, July 19, 2010. http://www.psychologytoday.com/blog/happiness-in-world/201007/discipline.

19. Manseau, Claude, and Roger J. Broughton. "Bilaterally Synchronous Ultradian EEG Rhythms In Awake Adult Humans." *Psychophysiology* 21, no. 3 (1984): 265-73. doi:10.1111/j.1469-8986.1984.tb02933.x.

20. Maymin, Senia. "Taking Steps toward Goals: What Does Research Tell Us?" *Positive Psychology News Daily*, September 23, 2013. http://positivepsychologynews.com/news/senia-maymin/2013092327025.

21. Moller, A. C. "Choice and Ego-Depletion: The Moderating Role of Autonomy." *Personality and Social Psychology Bulletin* 32, no. 8 (2006): 1024-036. doi:10.1177/0146167206288008.

22. Muraven, Mark, Marylène Gagné, and Heather Rosman. "Helpful Self-control: Autonomy Support, Vitality, and Depletion." *Journal of Experimental Social Psychology* 44, no. 3 (2008): 573-85. doi:10.1016/j.jesp.2007.10.008.

23. Neal, David T., and Wendy Wood. "Automaticity in Situ and in the Lab: The Nature of Habit in Daily Life." *Oxford Handbook of Human Action*, 2009, 442-57.

24. Newport, Cal. "The Science of Procrastination Revisted: Researchers Rethink Willpower." *Study Hacks Blog*, April 23, 2008. http://calnewport.com/blog/2008/04/23/the-science-of-procrastination-revisted-researchers-rethink-willpower/.

25. Oaten, Megan, and Ken Cheng. "Longitudinal Gains in Self-regulation from Regular Physical Exercise." *British Journal of Health Psychology* 11, no. 4 (2006): 717-33. doi:10.1348/135910706X96481.

26. Schwartz, Tony, Jean Gomes, and Catherine McCarthy. *The Way We're Working Isn't Working: The Four Forgotten Needs That Energize Great Performance*. New York: Free Press, 2010.

27. Seifert, Colleen M., and Andrea L. Patalano. "Opportunism in Memory: Preparing for Chance Encounters." *Current Directions in Psychological Science* 10, no. 6 (2001): 198-201. doi:10.1111/1467-8721.00148.

28. Steakley, Lisa. "The Science of Willpower." *Scope*, December 29, 2011. http://scopeblog.stanford.edu/2011/12/29/a-conversation-about-the-science-of-willpower.

29. "Stress in America; The Missing Health Care Connection." *American Psychological Association*, February 7, 2013. http://www.apa.org/news/press/releases/stress/2012/full-report.pdf.

30. "What You Need to Know about Willpower: The Psychological Science of Self-Control." *American Psychological Association*, 2012. http://www.apa.org/helpcenter/willpower-limited-resource.pdf.

31. Wood, Wendy, and David T. Neal. "A New Look at Habits and the Habit-goal Interface." *Psychological Review* 114, no. 4 (2007): 843-63. doi:10.1037/0033-295X.114.4.843.

34373714R10161

Made in the USA
Lexington, KY
03 August 2014